HOW TO BUILD A LIE DETECTOR, BRAIN WAVE MONITOR & OTHER SECRET PARAPSYCHOLOGICAL ELECTRONICS PROJECTS

Other TAB books by the author:

No.   915   *The Build-It Book of Learning Playthings*
No. 1210   *How to Convert Ordinary Garages into Exciting
            Family Rooms*

Since everything is but an apparition
Perfect in being what it is,
Having nothing to do with good or bad,
Acceptance or rejection,
One may well burst out in laughter.

Longchenpa (A 14th - century Tibetan Buddhist)

To Russell Nees, first and best of my many parapsychology
teachers.

With Love.

HOW TO BUILD A LIE DETECTOR, BRAIN WAVE MONITOR & OTHER SECRET PARAPSYCHOLOGICAL ELECTRONICS PROJECTS

BY MIKE & RUTH WOLVERTON

681.7

12/82

TAB BOOKS Inc.

BLUE RIDGE SUMMIT, PA. 17214

FIRST EDITION

SECOND PRINTING

Printed in the United States of America

Library of Congress Cataloging in Publication Data

Wolverton, Mike.
    How to build a lie detector, brain wave monitor & other
secret parapsychological electronics projects.

    Includes index.
    1. Psychical research. 2. Electric apparatus and
appliances. I. Wolverton, Ruth. II. Title.
BF104.W7   681'.7   81-9173
ISBN 0-8306-0027-2   AACR2
ISBN 0-8306-1349-8 (pbk.)

Contents

Introduction

As an experimenter in radio, electronics and electrical circuits I was never too interested in the basic science on which such experiments were based. Electronic experimentation was my hobby and I just wanted to build new and interesting projects and experiment with them without "sweating out" the physics. But when, several years ago, as a professional journalist, I began to investigate and report on the scientific research going on in the field of parapsychology, I searched for some sort of firm scientific footing like a desperate man going down in a bottomless pit of quicksand! I was being told and shown things that would send any self-respecting electronics experimenter to the nearest Funny Farm. Such things as a so-called *Hieronymus machines* that didn't need to be built—one just used the schematic diagram as the operating device! Or, the *Radionics* gadget that is literally an *empty* black box with knobs on the outside that connect to nothing, but which gives its *operator* information from far distant places! There were pyramids that preserved food without refrigeration units and sharpened razor blades without grinding wheels. I saw *psychotronic* machines that would seemingly run (sometimes) on nothing more substantial than imagination—or, if you believed the Russians, on *bioplasmic* energy, whatever that might be.

Of course I could have chalked it all up to cheap magic and let the Amazing Randi explain it all away for me on television, except that it was not just the kooks who were into this paranormal, paraphysics-parapsychology trip. As I learned to separate the silly from the serious I began to home in on such respectable institutions as the Menninger Foundation and the Stanford Research Institute, Princeton University and the Newark College of Engineering, to mention only a few. I found subjects of serious scientific investigation who were getting information accurately and under controlled conditions without even using dial adorned empty boxes! They were doing it with a cigar, a cup of coffee, and a really relaxed attitude!

I guess it was when one of the most casual of psychic subjects, Ingo Swann, drove a magnetometer at the Stanford Research Institute crazy under the watchful eyes of physicists Dr. Harold Puthoff and Russel Targ, that I finally ran screaming for "just a little basic theory please!" Swann (of the cigar, coffee and relax school) was taken to a large laboratory which contained, in the center of one room, a giant magnetometer. The magnetometer was one noted for its stability and resistance to outside interference. It was anchored to the concrete foundation of the building and shielded with the best magnetic shielding known—those made with *mu* metals. It was being used to monitor a radioactive source deep within a well. The device had been recording a continuous wave on a moving chart, running smoothly, for three nights and days. To illustrate its stability the physicists dollied in an enormous magnet big enough to drive an unshielded magnetometer to screaming fits. This one was completely unaffected.

Ingo Swann was allowed to study blueprints of the inner workings of the magnetometer and asked to see if he could, by thought alone, alter in some detectable way the subatomic emissions at the radioactive core of the device.

When Swann told the experimenters that he was concentrating his mental efforts on the core, the graph recorder abruptly changed its drawings from the three-day rhythmic pattern to high frequency spikes of an abrupt nature. As long as Swann directed his thoughts to the core the high frequency output continued. When he was distracted by the physicists, who intentionally broke his concentration from time to time, the graph recorded the smooth-wave output expected of it. But when his concentration switched back to the core deep in the well the high frequency spikes returned.

It would, of course, be absurd to claim that the Stanford Research Institute and their staff of respected scientists and administrators would risk their reputations and millions in grant money on any kind of cheap magic trick. The interaction of mind and matter was real enough, that had been demonstrated many times in many places. The Stanford Magnetometer reacting to the incredibly talented Ingo Swann simply underscored the fact that science has a long, long way to go before the true nature of reality is unraveled. Mother Nature has still got some secrets worthy of investigation. While it is the duty and responsibility of science to investigate nature impartially and without dogmatic notions, the investigation of such things as Extra Sensory Perception and other paranormal effects has challenged this basic dictum for over a hundred years now. Although parapsychological phenomena have been under serious investigation by proper and respected scientists ever since Sir William Crookes study of the psychic C.D. Home in the 1860's, the investigations have been plagued by controversy and much of our accepted scientific methodology has proved unreliable when applied to the efforts to detect remote stimuli and information not under the mediation of the usual sensory processes.

Despite all the controversy and difficulties of investigation however, a 1973 survey conducted by the publication *New Scientists* tells us that of almost 1500 readers responding to a parapsychology questionaire 67 percent (all working scientists and technologists) considered ESP to be an established fact or a likely possibility, and 88 percent said they believed ESP to be a legitimate area for undertaking scientific investigations.

Despite a hundred years of reputable research giving quite affirmative results, the study of parapsychology has not been taken as seriously as other scientific studies because of the lack of any truely satisfactory theoretical base from which to correlate data and to make predictions about new experimental outcomes. In fact, the current publications in the field of parapsychology remind one of the catalogs of interesting events published about that elusive and mysterious force called electrodynamics before Maxwell, Faraday, Ampere, and others got our heads together on the subject of electricity and magnetism.

In my own search for some unification of the dynamics of mind and the mechanics of consciousness I have discovered that the recent work in quantum theory, information theory, and neurophysiological theory relating to the hologramic concept of mind, has led many physicists bioligists and anatomists to the view that parapsychological phenomena is quite consistent with the framework of modern physics—the quantum science that has brought you all those marvelous solid state devices.

The present foothold of basic science on which parapsychological phenomena is supported, begins with a thought experiment invented by Albert Einstein, Boris Podolsky, and Nathan Rosen more than forty years ago. In the past few years several versions of this experiment, intended for the imagination only, have been carried out with real apparatus. Most of them support the idea that is implicit in Quantum theory: human consciousness is not separate from the objects that make up the world—and there is an innate *connectedness* between distant objects and events (seemingly separated in both space and time) that makes information about the whole instantly available to any part of the world. A model for this kind of universe would be the hologram, which contains enough information in each tiny of its interference pattern to reproduce an image of the whole. In other words, the EPR (Einstein-Podolsky-Rosen) effect seems to be telling us that our world is put together in such a way that an event going on in a distant galaxy or in the mind of our friend across town is also going on in some sort of analogous way in our own mind simultaneously! The EPR effect would also tell us that by simply making changes in our own mind-body system we can make changes in the objects and events that constitute our world! While this idea upsets our almost self-evident doctrine of local, or naive reality, and seems to fly in the face of common sense, it does give us a rallying point around which to correlate data and to predict new experimental outcomes. It also lets us know in no uncertain terms that we ourselves become apparatus along with our ICs and other solid state devices that makes new experimental approaches to the paranormal possible. Keep in mind always that in every parapsychology project you do, you yourself—your mind-body system—cannot be considered as separate from either the equipment or the events of your experiments.

This strange connectedness evidenced by the EPR effect has a mathematical proof known as Bell's theorem, which was published in 1964 by J.S. Bell, a physicist at the European Organization for Nuclear Research (CERN) in Switzerland. Bell's theorem was reworked and refined for more than 10 years after its initial publication and in its present form implies that at some deep and fundamental level the seemingly "separate parts" of the universe are connected in an intimate and immediate way. As a mathematical construct Bell's theorem is indecipherable to the nonmathematician, but there is an experiment designed by David Bohm, a physicist at the University of London, that shows this inexplicable connectedness very clearly.

The experiment involves what physicists call a two-particle system of zero spin. What that means is that you have two particles, such as two electrons, one spinning one way and the other spinning in exactly the opposite way so that the spin of each of the electrons cancels the other. What is required by the experiment is to separate the two particles electrically so that their spin is not affected. One spins right while the other spins left or one spins up while the other spins down.

Now the spin of a subatomic particle such as an electron can be reversed by a magnetic field. If a single electron is sent through a particular type of magnetic field created by an electromagnet called a Stern-Gerlach device it will come out with either a spin left or right, or up or down, depending on the orientation of the magnetic device. The odds are 50-50 on which way the spin will go. Now comes the moment of truth in this experiment, when the pair of electrons with opposite spin is sent off in opposite directions (illustration I-1) but only one of the pair will pass through a Stearn-Gerlach device. The results of countless experiments has shown that if the spin of the particle in area Y is reversed by the magnetic field *the particle in area X knows instantaneously that this has happened and reverses its own spin to maintain the zero spin equilibrium of the system*!

Looking at the results of these experiments, physicists of course have to ask themselves, "How can two things communicate so quickly as to seem instantaneous?"

The usual ideas of physics tells us that information gets about by some sort of signal. Without some sort of carrier wave there is no signal. If you and I are talking face-to-face for example, the information we exchange is carried by air in the form of sound waves. Sound waves travel about 700 miles per hour and so the length of time needed to get our information back and forth will depend on how far apart we are. The fastest carrier known is an electromagnetic wave which travels at about 186,282 miles per second. Nearly all of physics rests on the assumption that nothing can travel faster than that. We seem to see a flash of lightning the instant it occurs although we expect the clap of thunder to be delayed. But we know that even so, communication by light signal or radio signal is not really instantaneous. How long it takes for information to travel via light signal is still dependent on the distance between entities exchanging the information.

In Fig. I-1, just suppose that area X and area Y are very far apart. It will take a certain amount of time for a light signal to travel from area Y to area X with the news that one electron twin has had its spin reversed by the experimenter who operated the Stern-Gerlach device. If the two areas, X and Y, are so far apart that there is not enough time for a light signal to travel between the two, they have what physicists call "space-like" separation. According to our usual notions about physics, then, communications between objects or events with space-like separation is not possible. Yet this is what the particle-spin experiments seem to be telling us: that even though X and Y are space-like separated, the state of the particle in area X depends upon what the experimenter in area Y decides to observe (which way he orients the magnetic field of his Stern-Gerlach device)!

In other words, the EPR effect informs us that either information can be communicated at faster-than-light (*superluminal*) speeds or that the universe is constructed in some way like a hologram and information concerning the whole is always any everywhere present in each and every particle of the universe. In order to stay out of the quicksands of quasi-science I have opted for the latter assumption since the experiments give no indication what the speed might be of a superluminal signal traveling between the two areas and since the whole idea of superluminal signals flys in the face of most of our accepted ideas of physics. The simplest assumption we can make is that, in fact, no signal is sent or received between areas X and Y, but that the information is already present where it needs to be and simply has to be stored and retrieved as if the universe was one hologramic-type computer where everything is present in the same space and time with everything else. In fact, several physicists are now of the opinion that this concept is not at all inconsistent with the framework of physics in these latter decades of the twentieth century. All who have investigated parapsychological phenomena seriously, appear to agree that the popular science view that their observations are incompatible with known laws of physics is quite erroneous. This popular concept is based on the naive realism of nineteenth century science in vogue before the development of quantum theory.

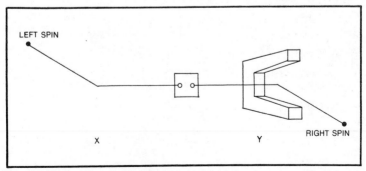

Fig. I-1. Schematic of EPR effect.

At any rate, the development of solid state technology, also made possible by quantum theory, and the underlying implications of Bell's theorem as proof of the validity of the EPR effect, now makes it possible for us project oriented experimenters to uncover patterns of cause-effect relationships in forms with which we are familiar.

Chapter 1
Telepathy

Communications by *extra sensory perception* (ESP) has been established as a fact for many years. Over those years a few experimental methods have been developed to find a noise-free channel over which reliable results can be attained at a reasonable transmission rate.

In the U.S. methods have been developed by physicists H.E. Puthoff and R. Targ first reported in the journal of *The Institute of Electrical and Electronic Engineers* in March, 1976 titled, "A Perceptual Channel for Information Transfer Over Kilometer Distances . . . ."

Soviet engineer Vladimir Fidelman, working in the late 1960s at the Bio-Information Section of Moscow's PoPov Institute, developed a simple electronic device to help reduce noise and enhance signal strength in our extra sensory perceptual channel. One of the parameters discovered early on by serious experimenters in telepathy was the necessity for single minded concentration on the part of the sender of telepathic messages. To help senders concentrate and clearly shape thought pulses, engineer Fidelman used what he called a teleflasher to enable his senders to successfully transmit 100 out of 134 numbers to receivers more than a mile distant.

I have been able to duplicate both Fidelman's teleflasher and his results and recommend that as a beginning aid to concentration and visualization in telepathic communications, the teleflasher is outstanding.

HOW TO MAKE A TELEFLASHER

The ideal teleflasher is a light box with a light inside flashing at the speed of the sender's pulse. Since most of us have a resting pulse of about 70 and since flasher buttons are commonly available that will flash at approximately this speed, the simplest Fidelman Teleflasher can be made as follows.

Materials:

1 polyethylene food-saver or food-crisper box
1 winker plug
1 flasher button
1 light socket
1 6- to 9-foot electrical cord
1 15-watt frosted light bulb

All of these items can be picked up at your friendly neighborhood hardware store, as can the tools if you don't already have them.

Tools:

Wire stripper
Pocket knife
Screwdriver

Construction

The top of your plastic box becomes the screen of your teleflasher so make sure to get one that is smooth and opaque. It can be rectangular, square or round, whatever suits you best. Cut a hole to accommodate the light socket in one wall of the box. Air holes should be punched in the bottom and in all four sides for ventilating and heat. Now secure the light socket to one wall of your box and attach the electrical cord to the light socket (see Fig. 1-1).

Use your wire stripper to cut off the insulation at a slight angle, rather than square. Remove only about ¼-inch of the insulation. Wrap the bare part of the wire around the screw shank on the light socket in a clockwise direction. This insures that the wire will tighten as the screw is tightened. Install the light bulb in the socket with the flasher button between the socket contact and the bottom contact on the light bulb. Plug in and test. Check your imprinter's resting pulse and see if it is close to the flasher rate. If your imprinters are all athletic specimens, or long-distance runners with low resting pulse rates—or if you want to optimize the signal to noise ratio on your ESP perceptual channel—you might want to build a solid-state flasher that will be actuated by the imprinter's pulse.

THE WOLVERTON PULSE-ACTUATED TELEFLASHER

Study the schematic for the teleflasher in Fig. 1-2, and I think you will agree it is the ultimate in teleflashers, surpassing anything the Russians have done! Figure 1-3 shows the

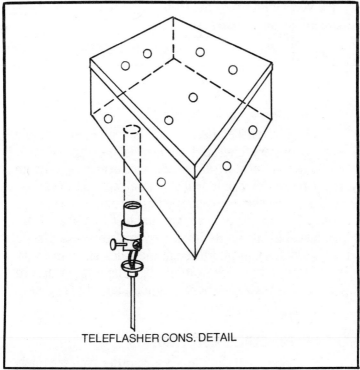

TELEFLASHER CONS. DETAIL

Fig. 1-1. Teleflasher construction detail.

finger-actuated transducer that senses the pulse beat and passes the signal along through a dc amplifier to actuate relay RY1, which switches the flasher light bulb on and off.

This project lends itself to breadboard construction with point to point wiring. Construction details for the finger pulse sensing transducer are shown in Fig. 1-4.

Parts

B1   1.5 volt battery
B2   22.5 volt battery
B3   6 volt battery
CL   photocell #903L
D1   diode type IN914
IC1   IC type 7404
L2   110-volt, 15- watt bulb
R1   5.6K resistor ¼-watt
L1   1.5 volt Grain of Wheat bulb
breadboard & misc. hardware
R2 & R3 10K
R4   47K

RY1 6-v 500 ohm relay
SW1 & SW2 combine into DPST
SW3 & SW4 combine into DPST off-on switch

BATTERY-OPERATED TELEFLASHER

The Wolverton Teleflasher can, of course, go portable by using a battery operated lantern as the light source; however, the simplest we have seen have been adapted from an auto safety-flasher unit available at all auto parts stores. The red cover is removed and the flasher unit placed inside an opaque plastic box as was our simplest Fidelman Teleflasher just described. Be sure to ventilate these plastic boxes with holes punched through the sides since the heat build up from even a low-wattage light bulb is enough to soften and distort the plastic if it is not allowed to escape.

PREPARING FOR EXPERIMENT PROJECTS

With a good teleflasher in working order, you are ready to do some serious "communicating" via ESP. The fun part of

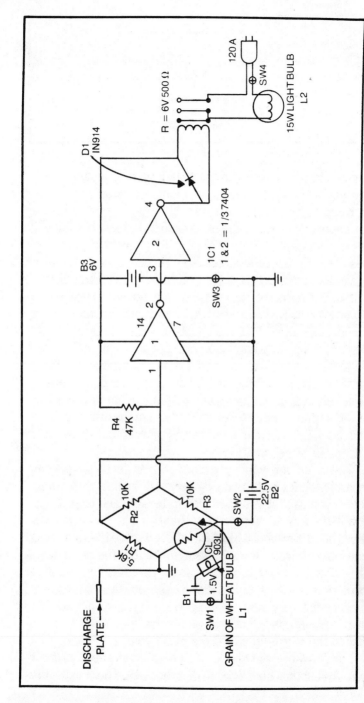

Fig. 1-2. Pulse actuated teleflasher.

19

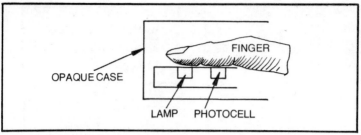

Fig. 1-3. Pulse sensing transducer.

communicating by telepathy is that it always works better when you are not at all serious about what you are doing.

Keep in mind that your own body-brain system is the most important piece of apparatus you have to work with and that experience has shown that our ESP channel is open at all times. Due to the EPR effect (see introduction) any knowledge present in one part of the system is known immediately in all other parts of the system and so our brain has a mammoth task of *inhibiting* all this information from entering our conscious mind lest we go crazy with confusion. So in order to consciously know something coming in on ESP we have to cue our brain *not to inhibit* or block out that which we wish to receive. An uninhibited, happy mood is called for and that is why relaxation and game playing are the most effective ways to succeed at telepathy, or any of the other projects in this book that make use of the ESP perceptual channel for the transfer of information over distance.

Warm up for your experimental projects by playing telepathic games with one or two good friends with whom you feel you can let your hair down, be silly and laugh a lot. Alcohol is okay in very small quantities to help you get relaxed but it can have a blocking effect if more than a trace is used (ditto for other drugs). Remember that the brain deals with current phases and chemical waves when handling information and that drugs distort the phase relationships that store the very information you are trying to get at. The best atmosphere is one of joking and good humor.

For the warm-up exercises place your teleflasher on a small table where the sender will be able to see it without strain. Adjust the room light so that the flasher dominates the light in the room. Place your receiver in a location where the flashing light or the messages illuminated by the flashing light cannot be detected by any of the five ordinary senses. Remember that distance does not have any effect on the information transfer since amplitude and propogation have no effect on the integrity of the information transfered.

HOW TO IMPRINT A MESSAGE FOR TELEPATHIC TRANSFER

Imprinting is the easy part. Once you can get away from the idea that telepathy is like radio and you have to "send" a message and realize that you are simply impressing or imprinting the information on your own neural circuits and your own brain chemistry. The "message" never leaves your head. The information becomes encoded in interference patterns created by certain phase relationships taking place in your own mind which, as we have shown in the "Introduction," becomes immediately available to be read out from

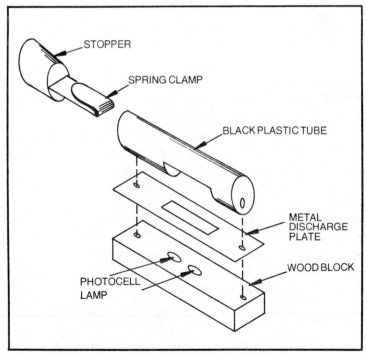

Fig. 1-4. Exploded view of how transducer is assembled.

another's mind due to the principle of non-separatability shown by the EPR effect.

For high-resolution encoding here are some techniques culled from my own and many other experimenters experience. Telepathic imprinting is a simple skill anyone can learn.

Relax physically and mentally into the most joyful mood you can manage. Try to feel quite certain that you will succeed in making an impression that can be picked up on by anyone anywhere in the universe—even alien life forms if they would care to try for a readout.

Concentrate and make yourself one with the subject matter. If it is a picture of a skier slaloming down hill, *become* the skier in your imagination. *Feel* the wind in your face. If the subject matter involves a mountain or a building or a piece of machinery become that object and try to imagine what it is like to be one. This is where the flashing light illuminating your subject matter helps you to keep your thoughts focused on the subject. Flashing images set up standing waves along your neural circuits much more quickly than still images.

Chant any verbal information you wish to imprint to yourself but feel that you are shouting it to the ends of the universe. Pick up the rhythm of the teleflasher and do your chanting in sync with the flashing light.

Visualize those you wish to readout the information retrieving it in whatever mode they will be using. If your reader is drawing what you are imprinting and you are imprinting the skier, visualize the reader drawing a picture of your skier. If your reader is selecting photographs to match what you are imprinting imagine him or her picking out the correct photograph.

The visualization step is very important in that it is the method by which the ESP channel can be addressed. If you write a letter, for example, that letter can theoretically be read by anyone in the world who reads the language in which it is written. But if the letter is *addressed* to be read by someone specific at a specific place then it will *likely* be read only by that person. So always address your telepathic imprints by visualizing the readout taking place just the way you desire it to be. Keep in mind during this visualization that you are not sending bits of information like a data transmission system, but that you are impressing *whole images* to be picked up or readout all in one piece. See your reader getting the message this way.

Release the images once you have gone through each of the above steps and know that they have been impressed in such a way that they will never be lost to the universal memory banks.

HOW TO READ AN IMPRINTED MESSAGE

Relaxation of body and mind are essential modes of being for successful readout of telepathic imprints. Ones mind has to be cleared of "noise" through some sort of meditative type activity. The relaxed-meditative mode engaged by Autogenic exercises is one that I have found to be the most effective for all types of parapsychology experimentation projects. It is also quick and easy to learn. And its effectiveness appears to increase with practice over time. It has great practical value for the experimenter because it does not require a mountain top or a water bed or any exotic setting. You may use the mode in a straight chair or any other type of sitting support. Sit with your spine straight and feet resting flat on the floor or ground. Be sure that the edges of your seat do not put pressure on your thighs.

What one is aiming at is the lowest possible level of nervous activity—to put the mind in idle—so that it can accept and handle some new information. Most telepathic projects fail because of the readers failure to reduce the nervous activity being processed by the mind. Under those circumstances the brain continues its watchdog job of not letting the desired data through. This blocking effect can be avoided by training oneself and one's subjects into a relaxed-meditative mode. *Autogenic* training exercises follow:

☐ Use a straight chair or any type of sitting support.

☐ Be certain both feet rest firmly on the floor and that the edge of the seat does not exert any pressure on your thighs.

☐ Straighten up completely while both arms are hanging down. Then *suddenly* relax by letting the trunk, shoulders, and neck collapse.

☐ Swing your arms forward and rest them comfortably on your thighs. Your hands and fingers should hang loosely between your knees without touching each other.

☐ Be certain that your trunk has collapsed *vertically* so that you are not bending forward. Your body should now be hanging and resting on its bones and ligaments. Your muscles should appear to be doing nothing.

☐ Close your eyes and say to yourself, "I am at peace with myself and completely relaxed."

☐ Next say to yourself, "My right arm is heavy," and concentrate on feeling that heaviness in your right arm. Proceed to the left arm, then right leg, left leg, neck, and shoulders. Concentrate on the part of the body to which the phrase is directed, just as you did with the right arm.

☐ Repeat the previous step, except that this time the phrase "*My_____is warm,*" concentrating on a feeling of warmth in those body parts.

☐ Repeat the following phrases several times. "My breathing is calm and regular." "My forehead is cool." "I am refreshed and alert." Take a deep breath and stretch.

There is a short cut method that works well to trigger in a low state of nervous activity condusive to clean signal readout and that is to do the following once you are seated comfortably:

☐ Close your eyelids and roll your eyes upward as if you were trying to look out of your head over the tops of your eyebrows. Be aware of the strain on your eyes.

☐ All at the same time relax your eyes and every other part of your body so that you "collapse" in your chair with your trunk, shoulders, and neck all sagging. Your back is arched, your head drops forward, and your arms hang down. You are hanging and resting on your bones and ligaments, your muscles are doing nothing.

☐ Swing your arms forward and drop them on your thighs so that your hands and fingers hang loosely between your knees without touching each other. Your forearms should rest balanced on the central portion of each thigh. Be sure that your trunk has collapsed vertically without bending forward. This keeps pressure off your abdomen. At the same time you swing your arms forward try to feel as if you are floating free of gravity as if you were drifting on a pool of clear water with a light blue sky overhead. It is in the sky where your readout will appear.

You don't have to see any sky as in a vision—it's fine if you do—but you *imagine* all this, and you *imagine* that the readout appears in the sky.

Request the information you want just as soon as the relaxation-meditation mode is established in your mind. Be as specific in this request as you would be if you were typing in the request on a computer keyboard. Let your mind know exactly what you want so that your brain will let it through into your consciousness.

Visualize an image forming in the sky. Don't let yourself make guesses—this is a game but it is not a guessing game—wait for an image to form just as you wait for an image to form on a cathode-ray tube when you have requested information when playing a computer game. Sometimes the image will pop on immediately. At other times it may take up to two minutes for the right images to take clear shape, or become clear in your imagination. If images want to flicker and fade don't try to hold on to them—these kinds of images usually just represent "noise."

Translate the images you readout as to function and name or other verbal labeling. Correct readouts will be nonanalytic in nature pertaining to color, form, shape and material only. You will need to make translations from your own individual language of imagery to verbal or mathematical language others will understand. For example, a rectangular building might appear in your mind in somber colors with solemn feelings about it. To you, does that mean a library or a church? Mistakes in translation are most often made when trying to process too little information. If in doubt try to get more. The readout is very much like looking at a *hologram*. You can shift your point of view if you instruct yourself to do so and see more of the image, or see it from another angle. You will seldom be aware of movement except by combining images and mentally moving past them (again, as in viewing "moving" hologramic images).

A little practice at translating your imagery will reveal to you a great deal about how you retrieve intuitive information. Keep in mind that everyone has their own style of response when reading out telepathically imprinted information and that the style is as individual as their signature or their fingerprint. No two of us read out in exactly the same symbolism, so lists of general symbols and "meanings" such as contained in dream interpretation books are useless. We all have to write our own translation program.

HOW TO MAKE THE BASIC TELE-GAME SETS

For warm-up exercises and training projects in telepathic communications with your teleflasher it is best to start with some simple tele-game sets made up of sets of five letters, numbers, symbols, colors, and simple pictures. The elements we suggest here are those we have found to eliminate confusion due to similarity between shapes. For numbers, use 0, 1, 4, 6, and 8. For letters, use B, R, A, Z, and M. For symbols, use isometric drawings of a diamond, cube, pyramid, tear drop, and heart. (See Fig. 1-5, from which you can trace these symbols.) And for colors, use construction paper—red, orange, yellow, green, and blue.

Draw each of these images on a separate sheet of paper and use a felt marker to outline them. This dark outline placed on your teleflasher screen will have light pulsing around it. You can also cut out the letters, numbers, and symbols and imprint them as images of light.

To put color on your flasher cut squares, circles, or triangles from opaque construction paper. These colors will seem "dark" to the imprinter—especially the red and blue—but they seem to encode better than "bright" colors.

To keep score in your telegames you will need to imprint and readout these images in random sets of one each—number, letter, symbol, and color. To generate these random sets you can assign numbers to each image within a set and roll a die to make your pick. Assign the sixth number on the die to "control" and imprint nothing when it turns up. You can also convert a spinner from an old kids game by refacing it with the pattern shown in Fig. 1-6.

Your tele-game set of images and random set generator along with some type of tele-flasher make up your basic game equipment.

Feedback Loop

Be sure to provide instant feedback between reader and imprinter during game sessions. Hits and misses comprise your score, of course, and the skill of the imprinter and reader will increase over time if information is immediately available on the hit or miss. This feedback loop can be any kind of communications device. I have found walkie-talkie sets and CB radios to be ideal. Over a kilometer, a friend's amateur radio rig can get a good workout as a communications feedback loop.

Choose one of your tele-sets and make sure your reader knows what images are included in the set. Cast a die or spin a spinner to make a selection. Put it on the teleflasher and imprint. When the reader calls out his readout inform both imprinter and reader *immediately* if it is a hit or miss. This will enable the imprinter to sharpen his concentration and the reader to learn to recognize and translate the images he is after.

If the reader gets two images he should mention both. If no readout appears, the reader should mention that. If imprinter is on "control" that, of course, would be a hit. Don't stay with any one image too long. Imprint and release. Readout, score, and go on to another image in the set.

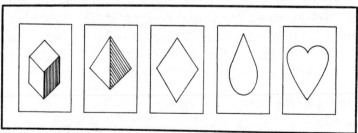

Fig. 1-5. Telesymbol set.

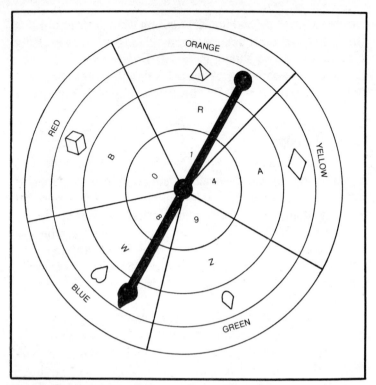

Fig. 1-6. Teleflashing spinner.

You may want to give the reader two chances at a readout because often the second image to appear in his "sky" will be the one he is after. You will also want to keep score in such a way as to match "before" and "after" calls since many experimenters have found that telepathic readout can actually *anticipate* the next random selection to come up. Also some readers will lag one or more imprints *behind* the imprinter. The advanced and retarded potentials as they are called by physicists are found to be a part of the individuality of the style of readout of certain individuals. Anytime a reader is scoring exactly as the law of probability allows these potentials should be looked for.

Scoring By the Laws of Probability

According to the law of probabilities one image out of the set of five can be guessed correctly in every five imprints. Any results above or below one-in-five indicate some kind of extra sensory perception is taking place and should be rewarded in the scoring. While it is more rewarding to the development of telepathic abilities to ignore proper scientific testing and just get with the fun and the skill of it, you should be aware of what constitutes what are called "statistically significant" results. For proper testing you will need to run through your 25 images at least four times (100 trials). Twenty-one or more or 19 or less hits out of 100 would be significant. The more trials you run the more nearly chance will give you the one-in-five result and therefore the larger the deviation in long runs the more significant the results.

HOW TO MAKE TELE-CLOCKS

For some reason we have never figured out one of the easiest pieces of information to imprint and readout is the face of a clock with its hands pointing to some specific time. Sending time by tele-clock will often get you such astounding results you will find it hard not to believe somone is cheating in the game. Make up a clock face on a sheet of white construction paper and put in the hour markings with a felt pen in Roman numerals. Cut one short and one long hand out of black construction paper. Fasten the hands to the clock face as shown in Fig. 1-7, with a paper brad.

Put the clockface on the teleflasher and position the hands at whatever time pops into your mind. Don't try to generate times at random. Get away from any idea of testing of statistical results and just have fun imprinting and reading out different times of day. See how many times in succession you or your reader can read out the correct time as set on the tele-clock. When imprinting pay close attention to the *angle* formed by the hands, and when reading out the time, look for the image of an angle and imagine that superimposed on the clock face.

HOW TO CONSTRUCT A TELEPATHIC MORSE CODE SENDER

For reasons that no one has been able to explain up to this writing, there is a paranormal connection between a person and his/her photograph. Voodoo Priests have made a fetish out of not having their pictures taken, believing that a photograph in some way damages the soul. There is a great deal of anecdotal evidence in the literature of parapsychology that supports this psi connection between people and their image frozen in a photographic emulsion. There are reports of a group of English investigators who have monitored physiological changes in a subject at the same time a light was being flashed on his photograph several thousand miles distant. And at least one serious scientific paper has been published on this and similar effects. Dr. E.D. Dean of the former Newark College of Engineering published the paper on this astounding effect in the September, 1966 issue of the *International Journal of Neuropsychiatry* (Vol. 2) under the title, "Plethysmograph Recordings as ESP Responses."

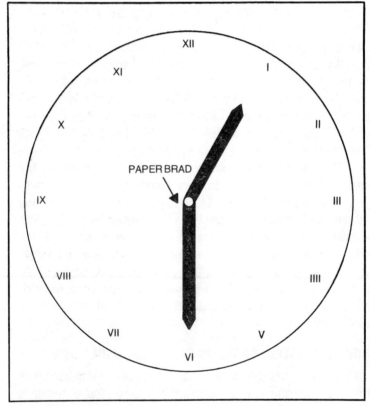

Fig. 1-7. Tele-Clock.

While the physiological responses are not usually felt on the conscious level, one can bring these responses into ones consciousness just as biofeedback techniques can make any so called "unconscious" activity of the body accessible to consciousness. Thus the experimenter can become a kind of Morse code receiver by sensing when his or her photograph is being scrutinized by others. By breaking this scrutiny up into dots and dashes on the teleflasher messages can be "sent" at a slow rate. Keep in mind, however, that messages are not sent in the sense that a wire or wireless message is sent via electromagnetic waves. The message is imprinted and read out much like storing and retrieving information in a computer.

To impress the message a telegraph key is connected in the teleflasher circuit as shown in Fig. 1-8. The readers photograph on the flasher screen and use the telegraph key to break up the flashes into short and long bursts, corresponding to the International Morse code listed in Table 1-1. Until the reader has trained himself/herself to become aware of this attention focused on his/her photograph at a distance, use simple patterns of single letters. Have the reader sit quietly in a relaxed-meditative mode and to try to become aware of the subtle currents of feeling running through his/her consciousness. At random times throughout a 10-minute interval key in a single letter of the alphabet slowly nine times in sets of threes. If possible have two or more persons concentrate on the photograph as the letter is being flashed. The reader should be furnished with pencil and paper and write down the letter he/she becomes aware of each time he/she thinks the flasher is operating. Some readers can train themselves to translate their growing awareness into imagined or actual flashes of light seen against closed eyelids, making a literal readout of the Morse code being sent on the telegraph key. If this kind of talent does not surface spontaneously after several hours of practice a simple plethysmograph can be built for direct readout of the ESP responses. The instrument can then be used as a biofeedback device to "teach" the awareness of when others are viewing ones photograph, or being otherwise nosey.

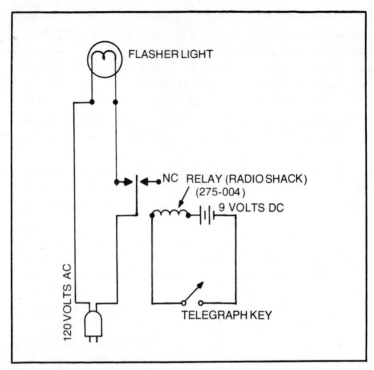

Fig. 1-8. Telegraph key in series with teleflasher.

HOW TO BUILD A SIMPLE TELEPATHIC MESSAGE RECEIVER

The *plethysmograph* is actually a medical instrument used in physiology to study variations in size of an organ or part of the body, as produced by the quantity and circulation of blood in that part. In 1962, Dr. E.D. Dean reported that the Plethysmograph could be used as an indicator of ESP in telepathy experiments (*Journal of the American Society of Psychical Research,* 41, No. 4 (1962): pages 351-353). Later Dr. Dean reported in the prestigious *International Journal of Neuropsychiatry* (Vol. 2, Sept, 1966, E.D. Dean, "Plethysmograph Recordings as ESP Responses") on further experiments that confirmed ESP responses as changes in blood flow through the fingers of experimental subjects in response to emotions triggered through the mind of a "sender," or imprinter, of telepathic messages. The imprinter looked at randomly arranged target cards consisting of names known to the reader, and other names picked at random from a telephone directory. Significant changes in finger blood volume occurred in the reader while the imprinter was looking at names known to the reader but there was no response when the unknown names were being looked at by the imprinter.

Our own contribution to this research has been to group the names according to a code and to send messages using the plethysmograph as a simple telepathic message receiver.

The Best Little Photoplethysmograph In Texas

This gadget was dubbed this by a medical engineer who checked it out for me. It is also inexpensive and easy to build. Parts will set you back less than $12 and only a few hours of construction time are involved.

Plethysmograph is derived from the Greek word "plethore," meaning filled and it works by measuring how "full" the blood volume flow is to the finger. For medical

Table 1-1. International Morse Code.

A	.-		S	...
B	-...		T	-
C	-.-.		U	..-
D	-..		V	...-
E	.		W	.--
F	..-.		X	-..-
G	--.		Y	-.--
H	....		Z	--..
I	..		1	.----
J	.---		2	..---
K	-.-		3	...--
L	.-..		4	....-
M	--		5	.....
N	-.		6	-....
O	---		7	--...
P	.--.		8	---..
Q	--.-		9	----.
R	.-.		0	-----

people this gives an excellent indication of how efficiently the heart is working.

Our photoplethymograph (okay PPG, for short) makes use of the fact that most tissues of the human body are transparent to the red part of the light spectrum; i.e., near the infrared band from 7000 to 8000 Angstroms, while blood is not.

The transducer consists of a reddish light source and a photocell. When a finger is placed between the two, flesh will provide a path for the light but blood will block the light. And so the resistance of the photocell will change with each heart beat as the amount of blood momentarily increases with each pulse.

When you have finished construction you will have three cable-connected devices: the transducer assembly, the bridge and the FET preamp. The circuit for all three is shown in Fig. 1-8.

The photocell is a part of a bridge circuit balanced so that each time the photocell changes resistance a signal is generated at the mid-point pickoff (Fig. 1-9). The output is a low-level low-frequency signal and so needs an FET preamplifier. The preamp will increase the signal level to an output usable by any small oscilloscope, chart recorder, or other recording or display device.

Parts List

2-22.5 volt batteries
1-1.5 volt battery
1-pilot bulb #222
1-photocell CL903L
1-dpst switch
1-spst switch
1-N-channel FET (MPF 103, *Motorola*)
All following are ½-watt resistors:
2-2 megohm
2-10K
1-7.5K
1-5.6K
1-470 ohm

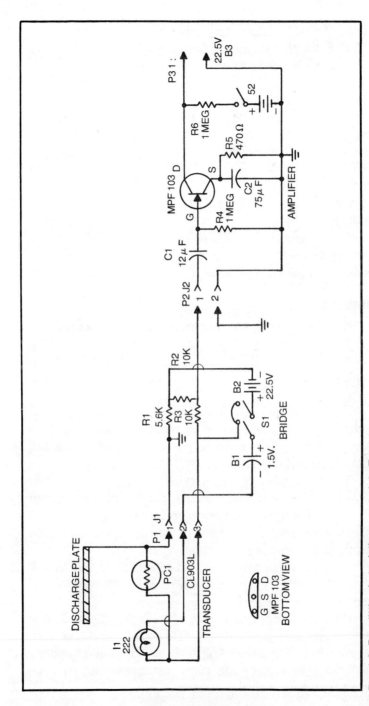

Fig. 1-9. Best little photoplethysmograph in Texas!

1-12μF 20 volt tantatum capacitor
1-75μF 6 volt electrolytic capacitor
1-3 contact polorized socket
1-2 contact polorized socket
1-3 contact polorized plug
1-2 contact polorized plug
1 piece wood 2½″ × 1½″ × ½″
1 thin metal discharge plate
1⅞″ black plastic tube
1 cork
1 spring clip
1 transistor socket
1 metal case approx. 4 × 4 × 2 in.
3-battery holders
1-length of shielded flexible cable

Construction

Begin by making the transducer. The piece of wood is drilled for the photocell and lamp as shown in Fig. 1-10. The lamp and the photocell are recessed so that the light from the lamp can be "seen" by the photocell only as it reflects off the finger.

The top of the block of wood is covered with the metal discharge plate to prevent false signals from the discharge of static electricity. It is connected to the ground lead of the cable connecting the transducer with the bridge.

The black plastic tube serves as a light shield. The stopper (rubber works better than cork) and clamp-spring will insure that the finger always bridges the light-photocell gap properly. The clamp should be inserted so that it forces the finger down to bridge the gap.

Wire the lamp, photocell, and ground plate to 3 feet or so of two-conductor shielded cable and terminate with a polarized three-prong plug.

Build the bridge in a small box, preferably metal. Mount the three-pin polarized connector (to accept the output from the transducer) on one end of the box. Wire point to point. The bridge elements—the three resistors—can be supported on a pair of three-terminal strip assemblies. Use a

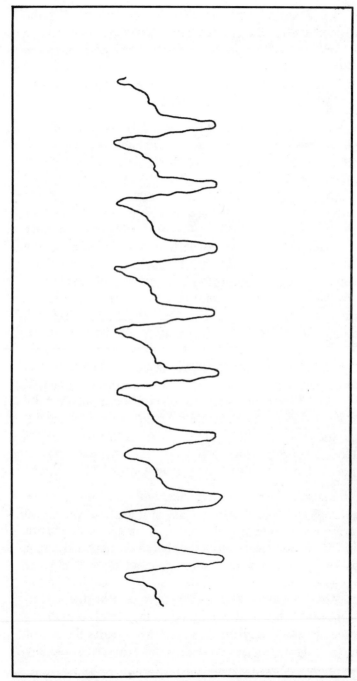

Fig. 1-10. Typical waveform displayed on scope connected to PPG.

length of phone cable to carry the bridge output, with the braid connected to the ground. Terminate the phone cable in a two-pin polarized plug for convenient connection to the FET preamp. Mount the off-on switch on top of the box where it can be reached conveniently, and put the two battery holders on the sides of the box.

Although you now have the best little photoplethymograph in Texas (and possibly one of the simplest) the output direct from the bridge is only about 0.05 volts, and the frequency we are interested in is very, very low. To read out the signal on an inexpensive oscilloscope or other not too sensitive readout or recording device, a special kind of FET amplifier needs to be built as the third component in your PPG assembly. The special part of this amplifier is the tantalum capacitor at the input which is really a cross between a capacitor and a diode. Because of the extremely low-frequency response requirements of the amplifier, it was necessary to have a device that would offer very high resistance in one direction and very low resistance in the other. The R4C1 circuit takes care of this requirement very nicely but be forewarned that the charging time for C1 is measured in seconds, not fractions of seconds. In fact, it takes about 15 seconds for ours to start operating after the transducer, bridge, and amplifier circuits are all turned on. Impatient types might want to put a momentary contact switch across R4, which will goose the amplifier into an instant start by charging C1 the instant it is pushed.

Be sure to build your amplifier in a metal box and use short leads and a good quality transistor socket. The signal we are interested in is in the millivolt range, so the circuit should be shielded and capacitance between input and output leads kept to a minimum. As in rf circuits any and all stray 60-Hz ac should be kept out. Take care to match the two-pin input connector to the plug coming from your bridge circuit, with hot lead to hot lead and a good solid ground connection. Use a length of shielded microphone cable to carry the output of the preamp to a plug or connector that will connect solidly to your scope or other readout or recording device.

There is one mistake easy to make when wiring this amplifier: getting capacitor C1 in reverse. If you get no output from the amplifier with an input signal coming from the bridge, reverse C1 end for end or reverse the battery powering the bridge. Be careful, however, and do *not* reverse the battery powering the FET.

To use your PPG for reading out ESP or telepathic messages connect transducer to bridge and amplifier and output of amplifier to the vertical input of your scope. When you have turned on the scope adjust it to a very slow horizontal sweep rate—one every 2 seconds for starters, or as slow a rate as your scope will deliver. Vertical gain should be set high and the trace centered on the screen. The wave form you are looking for is illustrated in Fig. 1-10. The trace may be downward if you have reversed the battery in the bridge circuit. But upward or downward, the trace is caused by an increase in blood volume due to a momentary dilation of the blood vessels in your finger. Don't wiggle your finger while doing your experiments because this will cause false signals.

What you are looking at on your scope is the amplitude, frequency, and waveform of pulsations of blood in the vascular system, originating in the action of the heart. It is interesting to note that the heart, true to folk wisdom, is very sensitive to emotions, especially through the ESP channel. E.D. Dean, Charles Tart, and other researchers have discovered that the finger pulse volume of an experimental subject will undergo significant and quite detectable changes at a time when another person at a distance is looking at names known to the subject which have some emotional significance attached to them. What one looks for is a significant change in the pulse pressure (either up or down), which is the midpoint between the systolic and diastolic pressure. The *systolic* is the pressure exerted by the heart when it is contracting; the *diastolic* pressure is when the heart is expanding. Systolic is the pressure high point, and diastolic the pressure low point. The pulse pressure is the mean, or midpoint, between the two. Changes in this midpoint will give you your ESP signal.

Biomedical engineer Itzhak Bentov, in his ground-breaking book on the mechanics of consciousness, *Stalking The Wild Pendulum,* suggests that the pulse pressure traveling from the heart to the bifurcation of the aorta (where the aorta forks to go into the legs) rebounds at the fork, and that these two pressure fronts produce an interference pattern. It is our own speculation that this interference pattern, as part of the whole series of interference patterns that form the hologram of the brain-body system, interacts through the phenomenon of resonance to produce the ESP response. Again, this is not like an electromagnetic signal traveling through space but the mysterious quantum mechanical effect of universal connectedness where every part of a system is the whole system in microcosm. The heart, therefore, can produce a waveform traced out through the photoplethysmograph, which discloses information presented to another person's senses at a distance. Telepathy, then, becomes no more impossible than tides on earth being caused by the moon in the sky, once the force of gravity has been discovered.

The ESP response detected by the PPG does, however, escape the consciousness of the experimental subject, or reader, and so to make use of it as a way of sending messages a code must be worked out. We have had considerable success using a variation of the communications theory concept of the use of redundancy as a means of coding a message to combat the effects of a noisy channel.

HOW TO MAKE DEVICES TO ENHANCE TELEPATHIC COMMUNICATIONS

Dr. Milan Ryzl, a chemist with the Institute of Biology of the Czechoslovakian Academy of Science, was the first serious researcher in telepathy to base his pioneering work on communications theory and, with his famous subject, Pavel Stepanek*, actually "transmit" five groups of three-digit numbers with complete accuracy. The 15 digits were encoded in binary form using green and white cards (green

---

*J. Pratt, "A Decade of Research With a Selected ESP Subject: An Overview and Reappraisal of the Work With Paul Stepanek," Proc. American Society for Psychical Research, Vol. 30, 1973.

cards = 1, white cards = 0) selected at random, and sealed in envelopes. Stepanek was able to tell with 60 percent accuracy, whether a hidden card was green side up or white side up. Making use of the redundancy principle, Ryzl was able, after 19,350 calls by Stepanek, to correctly identify all 15 numbers.

A similar procedure was used by another researcher, J.C. Carpenter, to transmit without error the word "peace" in International Morse code (presented at the annual meeting of the American Association for the Advancement of Science in New York, NY on Jan. 27, 1975).

Finally, Stanford Research Institute Physicists, H.E. Puthoff and R. Targ (1976), after duplicating the experiments of Ryzl and designing and executing many of their own concluded, "Independent of the mechanisms that may be involved in remote sensing, observation of the phenomenon implies the existence of an information channel in the information-theoretic sense." The two physicists were able to show that this channel, although extremely noisy and with very low bit-rate transmission capability, could nevertheless be used for error free transmission of information if sufficient redundancy coding is used. Their procedure for successful signal enhancement is slightly complicated for one not well versed in communications theory and statistical mechanics, but it is simple enough when stripped of the jargon and symbols of the physicist's trade. What it boils down to is this. If no message is being "sent," or no imprinter is operating, and a receiver or reader is just plain guessing one of two possible symbols such as 0 or 1, dot or dash, green or white, there is a 50-50 chance of guessing correctly or incorrectly. In other words, the probability factor is 0.5. If, however, an imprinter is concentrating on one of the two possible symbols, the "knowing-at-a-distance" principle of quantum mechanics appears to start operating. The probability factor for the reader will therefore increase or decrease by a factor of 0.1. The chance that the reader will "guess" which symbol the imprinter is concentrating on will now be 60-40 for "guessing" a certain way. If only a few trials are made, this slight change in the probability factor will not tell you anything. But introduce redundancy by making many, many trials, and the change in probability will actually tell you which of the two symbols is being concentrated upon by the imprinter.

As to the amount of redundancy necessary, this can be determined by a sequential sampling procedure of the type used in production-line quality control. This is outlined in all its technical glory by R. Taetzsch in an article titled, "Design of a Psi Communications System." in the *International Journal of Parapsychology,* Vol. 4, No. 1, p. 35, Winter 1962. However, I have found that if you simply make 100 trials for each symbol being imprinted, with a 5-bit code for each alphanumeric character, the character being imprinted can be retrieved with great accuracy (retrieval being a "head count" of the symbols written down as "guesses" by the reader). For example, using a binary number code where either a 1 or a 0 is being imprinted, if there are about 60 ones and 40 zeros, you can be almost certain that a 1 is being imprinted. There are some readers who will display a psi missing, or negative psi phenomenom, where the above count would indicate just the opposite; for instance, an 0 would have been imprinted. This is like a personality trait, however, and once discovered it will be consistent, requiring a simple transposition of all bits of information. I, myself, am a psi-misser—it's a little like being left-handed in a right-handed world.

What is needed, then, to enhance telepathic communications through redundancy coding is a table, such as Table 1-2, a bright-bulb stroboscope, a large card, (green on one side and white on the other) or two pieces of construction paper (one green and the other white), and a score pad as shown in Fig. 1-11. Table 1-1 gives the International Morse code for alphanumeric characters, which can be used in place of the 5-bit binary code. It does not have as much redundancy built into it as the binary code, but it has nonetheless been used successfully by me and other experimenters. Finally, to enhance imprinting and readout, a bright-bulb stroboscope capable of flashing in the 3- to 14-flash per second range is needed. We will explain the flashing range later, but for now flashing range later, but for now let's just say that if certain natural frequencies of the brain-body system are entrained and synchronized between the imprinter and reader, the resulting resonance reduces substantially the energy needed for both imprinting and readout. The bright-bulb stroboscope is used to entrain and synchronize both brain waves and the waves generated by the heart beat and movement of blood through the aorta.

Building the Bright Bulb Stroboscope

The schematic diagram of Fig. 1-12 shows a 555 IC timer controlling a relay that switches current to two timed outlets on and off at a frequency determined by timing capacitor C1 and the variable timing resistor R1. The time, in seconds, that the current flows through the timed outlets is equal to 1.1 times the resistance of R1, in megohms, multiplied by C1, in microfarads. The trimpot, R6, will also affect the timing because it varies the timing control voltage at pin 5 of the IC, accounting for tolerances of capacitor C1. It gives a kind of fine tuning to the timing current flowing through the relay, K1, from IC output at pin 3. The IC is provided with both on-off loads, R8 taking the load on the off side of the cycle. The IC thus draws a fixed load from the power supply, which R9 sets at about 13 volts. The power-supply voltage is

Table 1-2. Five-bit Alphanumeric Code.

E	00000	C,K,Q	11010	1	01011
T	11111	F	00110	2	10100
N	00001	P	11001	3	01100
R	11110	U	00111	4	10011
I	00010	M	11000	5	01101
O	11101	Y	01000	6	10010
A	00011	G,J	10111	7	01110
S,X,Z	11100	W	01001	8	10001
D	00100	V	10110	9	01111
H	11011	B	01010	Ø	10101
L	00101			•	10000

Five-bit code for alphanumeric characters chosen with uneven distribution of letter frequencies so that 0 and 1 have equal probability. The alphabet is listed in decreasing order of frequency. The same code is used for the very low frequency letters X, Z, K, Q, and J, grouped with the higher frequency S, C, and G. This is done to provide space for numbers.

TRANS-MISSION	ACCEPT ZERO	ACCEPT ONE	CONT. IMPRINT

Fig. 1-11. Score card for sequential sampling.

limited to a safe level, even in the face of increases in supply voltage by zener diode D2, which functions as a voltage clamp. D1 gives further protection to maintain accurate timing pulses by eliminating any possible voltage spikes in the relay, K1. The neon lamp, I1, connected across the timing relay, K1, gives a visual check on the frequency of timing pulses at the timed outlets and can be used to calibrate the stroboscope according to the settings of R1 by synchronizing the neon light flashes with another strobe light that is already accurately calibrated. Construction of the bright-bulb strobe is simple, and all parts are quite inexpensive. If you are an active electronics experimenter you will probably already have most of the necessary parts.

Parts List

C1 - 4.7μF mini-electrolytic capacitor (at least 35 WVDC).

C2 - .05μF capacitor (100 WVDC min.)

C3 - 1,000μF mini-electrolytic capacitor of at least 35 WVDC.

D1 - 1 amp 50 volt silicon rectifier (HEP 154).

D2 - 1 watt 15 volt zener diode (HEP 607).

D3 - L amp 50 volt bridge rectifier (HEP 176).

I1 - neon lamp with dropping resistor.

IC1 - integrated circuit timer type 555 (Radio Shack 276-1723)

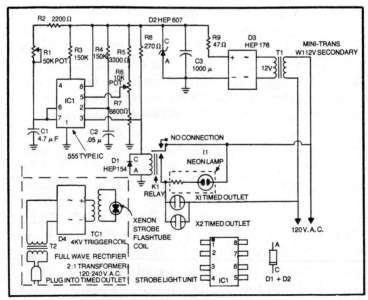

Fig. 1-12. Schematic for strobe light unit.

K1 - dpdt relay 12 volt D.C. 3 amp contacts (coil resistance 350 ohms, coil current 50mA—Radio Shack 275-206).

R1 - ½ watt 50K potentiometer.

R2 - ½ watt 2200-ohm resistor.

R3 - ½ watt 150K-ohm resistor.

R4 - ½ watt 150K-ohm resistor.

R5 - ½ watt 3300-ohm resistor.

R6 - 10K-ohm trimpot.

R7 - ½ watt 6800-ohm resistor.

R8 - 1 watt 270-ohm resistor.

R9 - 1 watt 47-ohm resistor.

S1 - spst toggle switch (on-off).

T1 - mini-transformer 117 VAC pri., 12 VAC sec., 300mA.

X1 & X2 - timed outlet ac receptacles for chassis mounting.

Misc. - panel knob or dial for pot perf. board case (8½×4½×3-in. We used Vector W30-86-46), IC 8-pin socket, line cord, wire, solder, etc.

Construction

Build the bright-bulb spectroscope in a metal container and begin by drilling suitable holes to mount the potentiometer, R1, and the off-on switch, S1.

Next, using 1/16-in. aluminum, make the compartment partition which supports the mini-transformer, T1, and timer relay, K1. Secure the partition with two spacer bolts (see Fig. 1-13 for suggested layout of major parts). You can make a simple bracket and fasten it to the partition to take the socket for K1. Mount and wire the timed outlet sockets, the neon lamp, and off-on switch before installing T1 and K1. Don't forget the dropping resistor in series with the neon lamp if it is supplied externally. Wire the open poles of the relay in parallel; this will effectively double the current rating of K1. Mount a socket for IC1 and complete the wiring. Be sure to observe the polarities of D1, D2, and C3. Figure 1-14 will help you here if you are in doubt. Figure 1-14 also shows the socket layout of the IC. Double check to be sure you are wiring in to the proper numbered pin.

Checkout on your bright-bulb strobe is simple. With a VOM verify the potential across C1 at approximately 13

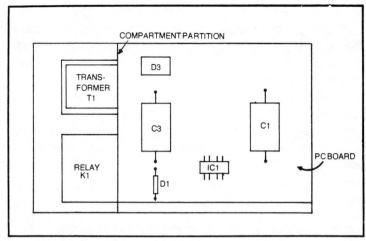

Fig. 1-13. Parts layout for strobe light unit.

volts dc and about 50 milliamperes of current in R9. If you have used a different transformer for T1 than the one specified, you will need to adjust the resistance of R9 t come up with the voltage and current specified above.

PLUG-IN STROBE UNITS

Two plug-in strobe flashtube units are needed. These units are identical and consist of a 2:1 ratio step up transformer to supply the necessary 200- to 300-volt primary source of the 4kV trigger coil that activates the xenon strobe flashtube. A full-wave bridge rectifier is interposed. The rectifier should be rated at 400 volts, because it is in the secondary circuit of the step-up transformer.

Parts List

D4 - 400 volt full-wave bridge rectifier (Radio Shack 276-1173 or equivilent).
FT1 - strobe flashtube (Xenon)
T2 - step-up transformer 1:2 ratio, 120 to 240 volts
TC1 - 4kV trigger coil

Construction

Build the plywood cube as shown in Fig. 1-15 and mount the parts as shown. Wire point to point according to the schematic of Fig. 1-12. Be careful to observe all polarities. Also, give yourself enough extension cord on one of the units (the one used by the reader) to get good separation between imprinter and reader. The two units will be automatically synchronized when plugged into timed outlets, X1 and X2.

For most experimental work, you will want to use a flash rate of 7 fps (flashes per second). This will entrain and synchronize the natural 7-Hz frequency that appears to "tune" the body-brain system in on the intuitive/psi information channel. This is also the low end of the Alpha brain wave band. These Alpha waves are also found to be associated with good psi functioning.

HOW TO MAKE AN INEXPENSIVE BRAIN WAVE MONITOR

In Chapter 3 on biofeedback devices, we will show how to build a monitor that detects and displays brain waves directly. There is a way, however, to learn to produce more of the Alpha waves in your mental activity by measuring not the waves themselves, but an effect that always accompanies an increase in Alpha wave production. That effect is an increase in the *temperature of the hands*. When one is in a relaxed Alpha state, the blood flow through the hands and fingers is more generous and nearer to the skin. One can measure this effect with a thermistor connected in series with a battery and an analog meter (0-1 mA dc), such as the Micronta® panel meter. This simple electronic thermometer, measuring the temperature of your index finger (preferably on your nondominant hand) is a more accurate indication of Alpha brain wave production (in my experience, anyway) than many of the electronic gadgets on the market costing up to several hundred dollars. I have found that cheap brain wave monitors are nearly worthless as alpha state indicators, but the simple measurement of finger skin temperature never fails to disclose when one is producing more Alpha waves than Beta or Theta waves.

The Alpha state is characterized by a *rise* in skin temperature. Individuals differ, of course, but, "warm hands, Alpha state," appears to be a rule that applies to all of us. By measuring your finger skin temperature when you are busy talking to business associates, solving problems in math, and doing logical, everyday thinking, you will have a good base line from which to work. This temperature range will be your Beta range. (In Chapter 3, we will talk about the meaning of the various bands of brain wave frequencies and what the experts have to say about them. For now we just want to be able to calibrate our simple Alpha monitor.) You will probably find that your finger skin temperature will be in the 65°F to 80°F range. As your temperature climbs into the 80°F to 98°F range, you are into a good Alpha state and much more receptive to information arriving via ESP.

Parts List

B1 - 9-volt battery
M1 - 1mA meter
R2 - 10,000-ohm potentiometer
S1 - spst switch (off-on)
TDR1 - thermistor (Fenwall GB41P2)
Misc.- small box for meter, pot and battery holder, two conductor-cable to run to finger thermistor, hardware, etc.

Construction

A chassis box (4×2¼×2¼ in.) is ideal for mounting the meter—my Micronta® takes a 1-⅞-in. mounting hole. Drill

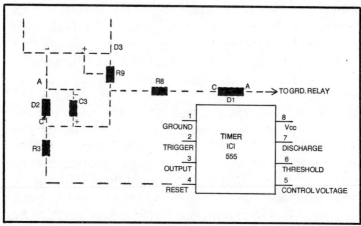

Fig. 1-14. Socket layout for IC1 (555 timer).

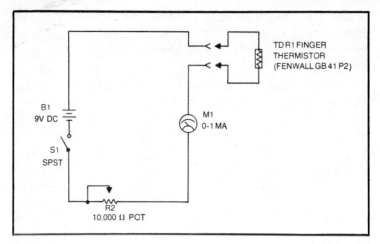

Fig. 1-15. Simple brain wave indicator.

and mount the potentiometer and battery holder. Drill a small hole for the thermistor cable (be generous with this cable). Wire point to point (The schematic is shown in Fig. 1-15). Mount S1 on or close to the battery holder. Make sure that the leads coming off the thermistor are firmly soldered to the two-wire cable. The thermistor should be taped to the finger when the device is in use.

Checkout and Calibration

Once all components are wired in series, turn on the unit and hold the thermistor between your thumb and forefinger. Adjust the potentiometer so that the meter reads about midscale. Heat a pot of water to a fairly high temperature and immerse the thermistor in it along with a good mercury thermometer. Adjust the potentiometer to read full scale when the water temperature has cooled to exactly 100°F. Next add ice to the water and calibrate the meter down the scale to about 50°F. The range you are interested in lies between about 65°F and 95°F. The correlation between skin temperature and brain wave production is an inverse one where the higher the temperature is the lower the frequency of produced brain waves is. A chart should be made for each individual who will be using this inexpensive brain wave monitor. The chart should show the base line skin temperature for the active waking state, when logical mental activity and problem solving are taking place; another for the kind of mental activity associated with meditation, day dreaming, and a very relaxed physical state; and still another for the zone between waking and sleep and during light sleep stages. Measurements of skin temperature during sleep or rapid-eye movement (REM) sleep does not seem to correlate with brain wave production at all. At all other times, however, the relationship appears to hold up well. The busy, waking, problem-solving activity is characterized by the production of much beta wave activity in the 13- to 26-Hz range and higher. The day dreaming, meditative, problem solving by intuition state is characterized by much brain wave production in the 8- to 13-Hz Alpha range. The drowsy zone and very light sleep range is referred to as Theta waves being produced in the 4- to 8-Hz band. Below 4 Hz, the brain is almost always in a deep sleep or Delta brain wave production state. Once you have a chart of your own or another's individual finger skin temperature in these various mental states, you can get a very good indication of their average brain wave production. Once you have a base line on yourself and a number of other individuals, you can even calibrate the potentiometer so that it can be reset for the individual and one can then read the meter scale directly in Beta, Alpha, and Theta brain wave patterns.

Whichever telepathy project you build, your results will be much better and more consistent if all concerned with your experiments are in a relaxed but alert Alpha state of awareness. Remember that you and your experimental subjects are key "pieces" of equipment in imprinting and reading out or sending and receiving telepathic messages. Keep yourselves functioning at optimum levels. Fatique, emotional upsets, and illnesses usually interfere with results, especially on the readout. I have also found that other factors, such as weather conditions and phases of the moon, seem to have an inexplicable affect on telepathic functioning.

Chapter 2
Paranormal Projects
for Plant Communications

Communicating with other human beings by telepathy, fascinating though that may be, can't really hold a candle to the weird and wonderful world of human to plant, or plant to human communications. This world is fraught with all the excitement of a science fiction thriller. Familiar as plants are to all of us they still must be considered "alien" life forms when we consider communicating with them.

Although we tend to feel that we are a superior life form to plants we should never forget that plants are the basic life link on this small planet and that without them we could not exist here. They have been around much longer than we have and just might be able to tell us a whole lot about the basics of life if we take the time and trouble to learn their language.

"Staggering as it may be to contemplate, a life signal may connect all creation," Cleve Backster is quoted as having said. Backster is an internationally known authority on lie-detector systems, but one evening in 1966 he had one of those classic experiences that catapulted him into fame as an international authority on communications between plant life and human life.

In the course of a routine and simple test to see how long it would take for water to rise from roots to leaves Backster wired a handy polygraph (so-called "lie detector") to a philodendron in his office. He had expected that there would be a simple change of electrical resistance when the water reached the leaf. What he saw, however, was a complex tracing that reminded him of human tracings when subjects were under stress. Fascinated by this seemingly emotional component in the electrical activity of his plant, and knowing that people react most strongly on the polygraph tracings when they were under threat of inflicted pain, Backster wondered what would happen if he hurt the plant. He reached for his cigarette lighter to burn a spot on the plant leaf and as he did so the pen recorder jumped wildly as if in response to his thoughts or intention. Again the tracings looked to Backster's experienced eye exactly like the tracings one gets from humans under similar threat.

Many years and thousands of experiments later, and after his results had been duplicated by researchers around the world (the Russian and Indian governments and good old AT&T in the U.S. set up research projects to explore communications in and with the plant kingdom, and who knows what the CIA is doing with plants as transducers of information?), Baxter made his statement about the inter-connectedness of all creation which seems to echo Bell's theorem and other quantum ideas about the nature of nature. I must warn you, however, that in my own experience, plants seem to shut up and turn off if one gets too serious and intellectual about experimenting with them. They seem to love to play and respond best to laughter and good humor. But those are my plants. Yours may very well be different. At any rate I would not think of depriving you of the experience of discovering this adventuresome world for yourself, beginning where all started, with polygraphs and philoden-drons.

CONSTRUCTING A LIE DETECTOR FOR YOUR PHILODENDRON

What you are about to build is not a lie detector (or polygraph) in the true sense, because such professional devices measure blood pressure, depth and rate of brea-thing, pulse rate, and skin resistance, and this doesn't. Of these parameters, however, the only one that applies to plants is skin resistance. The plant leaf sandwiched between two electrodes forms a resistor, just as human skin does, and when that resistance is used as one element of a Wheatstone bridge and balanced electrically, an output voltage from the bridge will be generated that will be an analogue of the electrical activity of the plant. Figure 2-1 shows this arrangement schematically, along with an operational amplifier to build up the weak dc signal coming from the plant. The output of this op-amp is sufficient to drive a voltmeter that has a 1000-ohm-per-volt movement with a 0-to-3-volt scale. I use a 0-1 mA meter with a 3000 ohm series resistor to measure 3 volts. And, of course, a conventional VOM or VTVM set in its 2.5 or 3 volt range can also be used as an output device. However, for serious (but playful) communications with plants and for establishing base lines and all those good things one needs to assign some significants to the electrical activity coming from your plants you will want to feed the output to a chart recorder. I'll share my home-built Shackleford chart recorder with you a bit later on in this chapter, but first things first.

Parts

B1,B2,B3 - 9 volt battery
C1 - .05μF capacitor
C2 - .005μF capacitor
C3 - 200pF capacitor
C4 - .01μF capacitor
D1,D2 - IN4004 silicon diode
IC1 - intregrated circuit μA741C (Radio Shack 276-007)
J1,J2 - contact polorized sockets
M1 - 0-1 mA meter
P1,P2,P3 - contact polorized plugs
R1 - 75K ½ watt resistor
R2 - 10K potentiometer
R3 - 100K potentiometer
R4,R5 - 1K ½ watt resistors
R6 - 1 meg-ohm potentiometer
R7 - 240K ½ watt resistor
R8 - 1.8K ½ watt resistor
R9 - 82 ohm ½ watt resistor
R10 - 10K ½ watt resistor

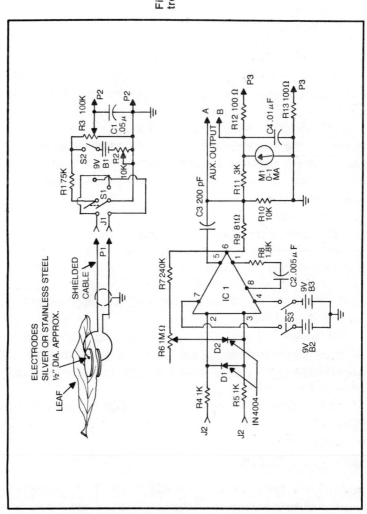

Fig. 2-1. Schematic of plant electrodes, bridge, and op amp.

55

R11 - 3K ½ watt resistor
R12, R13 - 100 ohm ½ watt resistors
S1 - dpdt switch
S2 - spst switch
S3 - dpst switch
Misc: eight-pin IC socket, 2 silver dimes or stainless steel
discs for electrodes, length of 2-wire shielded cable,
battery clips, suitable case if desired, mounting
hardware, etc.

Construction

Although this project lends itself to breadboard construction if that is your preference, we recommend that you use an etched circuit board to avoid inadvertent wiring errors. Figure 2-2 will give you the actual size printed board foil layout. If you wish you can create this circuit on perf board. Install the components as shown in Fig. 2-3. Fit the 8-pin IC socket into the hole drilled into the circuit board. Note that the socket locating projection is at pin 8. You'll want to notch out a small indentation for this. Solder the leads of the IC to the adjoining solder pads of foil. Remember that the diodes can be damaged by too much heat so go easy on the btu when soldering.

Be sure to trim down the leads of the IC to ¼-inch lengths before installing the little jewel in its socket. I suggest you use common wire strippers for this gentle cutting job rather than side-cutting wire cutters to protect the IC from damage. The tab on the IC is located at pin 8. Insert it in its socket.

Whatever type of case you use mount the meter, switches and potentiometers so they can all be controlled from the front panel. The sockets and cables with plugs can be tucked away at the rear panel.

Mount the batteries along one wall of the chassis held in place with strips of aluminum. Mount the PC board on standoffs.

Hooking Up to the Plant

Contact with the plant is made through one of its leaves onto a highly conductive metal disc. Any metal that has good conductivity can be used including stainless steel, but old-fashioned silver dimes are light and work wonderfully well. If you use silver be sure to keep it free of oxide by frequent light sanding. Use the same metal for both electrodes on the top and bottom of the leaf to avoid electrolysis. Be very careful not to bruise the plant's leaf when making contact with your electrodes. Conductance is greatly enhanced by using an electrode jelly of the type physicians use when making electronic medical tests. ECG Kontax is good and is available from Birtcher Corp., Los Angeles, CA 90032. Its catalog number is 391. It should be wiped off the leaf after each use. It is water soluable so just give the leaf a good rinse.

Use a stable support system to support the electrodes, don't expect the plant to support them. We use a metal laboratory stand with C-clamps and plastic discs to insulate the electrodes from the metal clamps and stand. The leaf should be compressed very gently between the electrodes. The connection between the electrodes and the bridge must be via shielded pair cable.

The resistance between the electrodes should never exceed 200,000 ohms. You will find that most plants generate small currents of their own and some are regular little mini-dynamos. The polarizing switch (S1) can be used

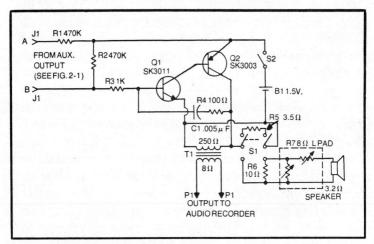

Fig. 2-2. Plant actuated audio oscillator.

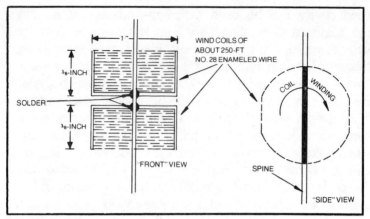

Fig. 2-3. Reels for coil made of brass tubing.

to superimpose these currents on the excitation current flowing in the circuit or to cancel some part of it, depending on which way the switch is thrown.

Testing: One, Two, Three, Four

With the plant of your choice plugged in to the bridge circuit and the bridge circuit plugged in to the op amp, turn on S2 to supply power to the bridge circuit. Power level is determined by R2. Now turn on S3 to activate the amplifier. Adjust R3 for a meter null reaction. Your plant will probably be all excited over all the attention it has been getting and so you will in all likelihood need to reset the null position when the plant is in a less stimulated condition. Actual use will have to determine the amount of excitation you allow through R2, the sensitive through R6, and the state of the polarization switch S1. This reversal of the current applied to the plant is necessary because plant tissue, like all living cells are tiny electric batteries and tend to become saturated and, over time, tend to cease functioning as an electrical resistor.

Don't get too carried away by stimulating your plant by burns, cuts, water deprivation and other mistreatments. Plants, like humans, will lapse into shock and die when subject to too much trauma. Discoloration and wilting are the symptoms of shock and usually mean that death is about to occur. A dead plant, of course, will give you no responses at all since it then becomes a simple carbon-type conductor. Don't wear your plant out. Give it plenty of TLC (Tender Love and Care) and allow plenty of time for it to recuperate in a quiet, sunny and damp area.

Don't be surprised if the responses of your plants are delayed. I have experienced this often. There are more than 300,000 species of plants known to science and they all seem to have minds of their own! You simply have to get to know them and love them and tolerate them as you do all your other friends. You will find, too, that plants develop definite preferences for certain people; in fact, Cleve Backster has reported that one plant that had developed some sort of emotional attachment to him responded to his feeling patterns when he was more than a thousand miles away from the plant. I have had plants respond to my amplified voice via telephone when I have been hundreds of miles away from the plant.

While you will find many interesting responses to your thinking, feelings and conversation from your plants with only a meter to wave back, the addition of a voice to the communications capability of your plants opens up a whole new area. Responses you may very well miss because you weren't looking at the meter can be had by allowing your plants to activate an audio signal.

Figure 2-2 gives you the schematic for a "plant voice" device. It ties in with your op amp at the auxiliary output A and B on the schematic in Fig. 2-1. I recommend the circuit be assembled on perf board, otherwise follow the instructions for the assembly of the bridge and op-amp circuits.

Parts

B1 - 1.5 volt battery
C1 - .005μF capacitor
J1 - contact polarized socket
P1 - contact polarized plug
Q1 - transistor (RCA SK3011)
Q2 - transistor (RCA SK3003)
R1,R2 - 470K resistor
R3 - 1K resistor

R4 - 100 ohm resistor
R5 - 3.5 ohm, 1 watt resistor
R6 - 10 ohm resistor
R7 - 8 ohm potentiometer L pad
S1 - dpdt switch
T1 - audio transformer; 250/8 ohm, 200-mW
Misc: - 3.2 ohm speaker, case, hardware, etc.

This plant voice is basically an audio oscillator with its frequency controlled by the dc input signal which in turn is a function of the amplitude of electrical activity in the plant. The audio tone thus produced is coupled to a speaker and a tape recorder output through audio transformer T1. S1 will serve to mute the speaker when that is desirable, and R7 serves as the volume control.

This circuit will respond to just a few microamperes of input current and the pitch of the oscillator changes as a function of the bias on Q1. C1 and R4, the capacitor-resistor team linking Q2 back to Q1 provide feedback to create the tone.

A two-way conversation can be recorded by feeding the audio output to one channel of a stereo recorder and recording your verbal stimulus to the plant on the other channel. Or by recording the time signals from WWV on the other channel you can have a record of plant responses over time.

A HOME BUILT CHART RECORDER TO RECORD YOUR PLANTS EAVESDROPPING ON YOUR THOUGHTS

The only way to really keep up with all the data you will begin to accumulate from your plant experiment projects and to truly keep an eye as well as an ear on your plants reactions to your thoughts and feelings is with a chart recorder. For a long time I pined away in vain for one of these dandy recording devices because of the four-figure price tag on the professional models. I looked into the idea of making one myself but soon learned that I would need the skill of an experienced watchmaker to make one that would respond to frequencies of more than a few hertz. Then I heard about the ingenious J. Barry Shackleford, who, at the time, was a simulation analyst with the Computer Sciences Corp. in

Huntsville, Alabama. He had built an inexpensive chart recorder at home in his spare time that has a feedback circuit with transistor amplifiers that compensate very nicely for the maveric bucking of an unrefined pen motor. It has some other neat features that, while not in the class with your $6000 telemetering electroencephalographs, make it ideal for recording private lives in the plant kingdom.

The heart of the Shackleford chart recorder is the easy-to-make motor, which is actually a galvanometer of the type in use since the 1800s. It is quite similar to the motors you find in all voltmeters and ammeters even today. A coil of fine copper wire rotates around its vertical axis between the poles of a permanent magnet. The shaft on the vertical axis operates the pen that makes the tracing. The shaft also turns a potentiometer that develops a reference voltage that is fed back to the input of a differential amplifier. The difference between the feedback voltage and a reference voltage is applied through a summing amplifier to the power amplifier. This causes the pen motor to rotate in a direction that reduces the difference between the feedback voltage and the reference voltage to zero, and that stops the motor. Thus the pen always returns to its zero position without overshooting. Setting the reference voltage sets the zero position of the pen. To construct this clever servomotor you will need the following

Parts

6-inches 1/16-inch brass tubing

8-inches 1/8-inch brass tubing

2-inches 3/32-inch brass tubing (available in hobby shops where model airplanes are sold)

2,000 gauss permanent magnet with 1¼-inch gap between poles (available from Edmund Scientific Co., Barrington, NJ 08007. Cat. # 70,571)

10K potentiometer of the low friction, ball bearing type. Helipot 6502 (available from American Design Components, 39 Laspenard St. New York, NY 10013)

250-ft. 28-gauge enameled copper magnet wire

Misc: length of 24-gauge wire for leads, silk thread, set screws, etc.

Construction

Make the form on which the coil is wound by making a pair of U-shaped brackets and solder them onto a 2-inch length of 1/16-inch tubing so that they face in opposite directions (Fig. 2-3). The 2-inch length of brass tubing forms the spine of the servomotor. The brackets are both made from the 1/16-inch tubing. These brackets are one-inch wide and ⅜-inch deep.

Cut the tubing carefully with a very sharp knife. Roll the tubing under the knife and groove it deeper and deeper all the way around until you have cut through. Use gentle pressure so as not to collapse the thin-walled tubing. Join all parts with solder and coat frame with Duco cement.

Wind the coil over the framework with 250 feet of 28 gauge copper enameled magnet wire in a random fashion. Layers need not be uniform. Terminate the ends of the coil in flexible leads of 24 gauge wire by soldering the inner flexible lead to the end of the magnet wire and tieing it to the spine with silk thread before winding the coil. After winding the coil do the same for the outer end of the coil and then tie both leads with the thread to the spine about ⅛-inch from the winding. Dab joints with Duco cement to insulate.

The arm that supports the pen is soldered to the spine parallel to the axis of the coil. Use the ⅛-inch tubing and use a little piece to brace the joint. Figure 2-4 shows the detail of the pen holder. To keep the frequency response of the pen within the range of bioelectric activity do not extend the pen holder more than three inches from the spine. The longer the arm is the lower the maximum frequency response is. A hinge about half way down the pen holder shaft is made of two diameters of brass tubing: ⅛-inch and 3/32-inch (Fig. 2-4). The bearing of the hinge is a ¼-inch length of ⅛-inch tubing soldered at right angles to the end of the pen holder shaft. The 3/32-inch shaft is a ⅝-inch length of the tubing slipped through the bearing and centered. Two 3/16-inch long collars, cut from the ⅛-inch tubing slide over the protruding end of the shaft. To hold the pen, a yoke is bent from 1/16-inch tubing and pressed to fit into the 3/32-inch sockets.

The sensitivity of the recorder is increased as the inertia of the system is reduced, so the lighter the pen the better. I have found that a No. 0 Rapidograph capillary pen, available from your local drafting supply shop, works quite well.

These pen tips do have a weight that needs to be eliminated and replaced by brass tubing to further reduce the inertia of the writing system. Cut off and throw away the weight and slip the wire that regulates the ink flow into the end of a little length of 1/16-inch tubing. Secure it in place by crimping the brass tubing. Two turns of the brass tubing at the end of the yoke around the ink reservoir will support the pen very nicely.

Pen tips of felt (hard) or porous plastic work well in this chart recorder, also. If you use one of these, however, be sure to cut away most of the body right down to the tip and the ink reservoir.

The magnet can be clamped to a block of wood attached to the base of the servomotor portion of the chart recorder as shown in Fig. 2-5. Mount the potentiometer shaft end up on

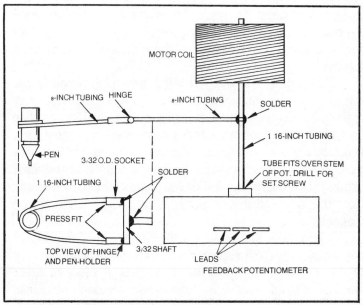

Fig. 2-4. Detail of pen holder.

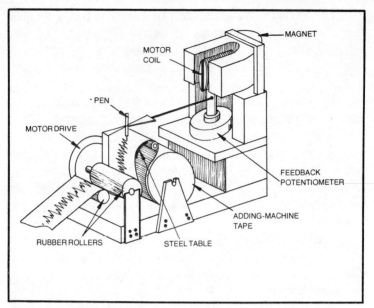

Fig. 2-5. Mechanical portion of Shackleford chart recorder.

the base so the shaft is centered directly below the area of the most intense magnetic field between the poles of the magnet. You can find this area by placing a piece of cardboard over the magnet and sprinkling iron filings on it. The filings will show you the area where the magnetic field is most intense.

To align the coil and pen holder assembly properly you will now need to connect a voltmeter between the wiper arm of the pot and one terminal of a source of about 15 volts of dc current. Connect the other end of the power source to the pot and rotate the shaft to a position where the meter indicates exactly one-half the voltage at the source. Hold the shaft firmly in that position and slide the spine of the coil assembly over the shaft so that the axis is at a right angle to the magnetic field.

Figure 2-5 shows how to complete the mechanical portion of your chart recorder with a simple adding-machine tape transport mechanism under the pen. A piece of sheet steel bent to an acute angle serves as a writing table. It is soldered at one edge to an upright plate attached to the base.

A rubber roller made of heavy-wall rubber tubing is slipped over a shaft to pull the paper across the writing table. Another piece of the rubber tubing makes a spring-loaded roller to increase friction between the driving roller and the paper. Although a nonsynchronous motor can be used to drive the transport mechanism very successfully, I recommend a synchronous motor drive so that timing of the recorded data can be done accurately.

Three interconnected amplifiers form the electronic portion of the chart recorder. A summing amplifier, a differential amplifier, and a power amplifier work in a closed loop system. The signal from the plant is fed into the input of the summing amplifier, which can accept two signals and multiply their algebraic sum. The output of the summing amplifier feeds into the power amplifier that drives the pen motor. It also drives the potentiometer (R4), which develops a voltage whose amplitude varies with the position of the pen. That voltage is fed back into a differential amplifier that multiplies the algebraic difference between that signal and the signal from the plant. The output of the differential amplifier is then fed back to the summing amplifier as its second signal, closing the loop. A potentiometer connected to the power supply (R1) supplies an adjustable reference voltage to the differential amplifier. If there is no signal coming in from the plant, the amplified difference between the reference voltage and the feedback voltage goes through the summing amplifier to the power amplifier. This will cause the pen motor to rotate in the direction that reduces the difference between the reference voltage and the feedback voltage to zero, which of course stops the motor. This allows the pen of the recorder to be positioned anywhere on the chart by adjusting the reference voltage. For if the reference is altered, the resulting difference voltage again causes the motor to seek a zero-voltage position.

The system will also compensate for variations of friction between pen and paper in much the same way. A signal fed into the summing amplifier energizes the power amplifier and causes the motor to seek a position where the sum of the signal voltage and the difference voltage falls to zero. Any voltages in the feedback loop are amplified, causing the system to apply more or less power exactly as required by the amount of friction present at any given moment.

These "Rube Goldberg" electronics work wonderfully smoothly—if you will pardon the grammar—so why not get started with the construction? With four 741 ICs, it is really very simple to build (Fig. 2-6).

Parts

C1 - 1μF capacitor
C2 - .1μF capacitor
C3, C4 - 500μF 50-volt capacitor
C5 - .1μF capacitor
C6, C7 - 500μF 50-volt capacitor
C8, C9, C10, C11 - .1μF capacitor
D1, D2, D3, D4, D5, D6, D7, D8 - 1 amp 50-PIV diodes
F1, F2, F3, F4 - 2 amp fuses
IC1, IC2, IC3, IC4 - integrated Circuits 741C
L1 - servo-motor coil, 15 ohm (see text)
M1 - 2500 gauss permanent magnet (see text)
Q1, Q2 - transistors, HEP 245
Q3 - transistor, HEP 246
Q4 - transistor, HEP 245
R1 - 10K potentiometer
R2 - 100K resistor
R3 - 15K potentiometer
R4 - 10K pot, ball bearing type (see text)
R5, R6 - 100K resistor
R7 - 1.2K resistor
R8 - 1 megohm potentiometer
R9 - 1K resistor
R10 - 1 megohm potentiometer
R11 - 1K resistor
R12 - 500 ohm resistor
R13 - 500 ohm resistor
R14 - 1.2K resistor
R15 - 100K resistor

R16 - 1 megohm resistor
R17, R18 - 5K potentiometer
R19, R20, R21, R22, R23, R24 - 100K resistors
S1 - spst off-on power switch
T1, T2 - power transformers 120V/25V 1 amp
ZD1, ZD2 - zener diodes, 15 volt, 1 watt
Misc. - heat sinks with cooling fins for all transistors, perf
    board and case to suit, hardware as needed etc.

Construction

Make and test each of the electronics sections one at a time, beginning with the voltage regulated power supply (Fig. 2-7 shows the schematic). And don't skip the fuses; they are quite necessary. Consider the power supply a big success when the voltage output does not vary more than 2 percent with a 30-ohm load across the output. All resistors in the power supply (R7, R9, R12, R13, and R14) need to have a capacity for dissipating at least 30 watts. R12 and R13 are in series and can share the load at 15W each.

After your power supply is built and working properly, build the power amplifier section. Figure 2-8 shows a schematic of just the power amplifier. Breadboard it, perf board it, or etch it—suit yourself—but double check your completed wiring against this diagram. Make certain you use adequate heat sinks with large cooling fins on the transistors in this amplifier, as well as in the power supply. The best operational test of this power amplifier is to connect its output to one of those cheap little hobby motors rated to run on about 30 volts (or several of the lower voltage motors hooked up in series). Connect both ends of a 5K ohm potentiometer across the output of the power supply and plug the rotor arm of the pot into the input of the amplifier. Your op amp is operating just like it should if you can control the speed and direction of rotation of the motor by turning the pot through its full range.

With all that experience under your soldering iron, don't get overconfident and miswire your summing and differential amplifier circuits. I did and blew several; ICs. So again double check your wiring before applying power to this section of

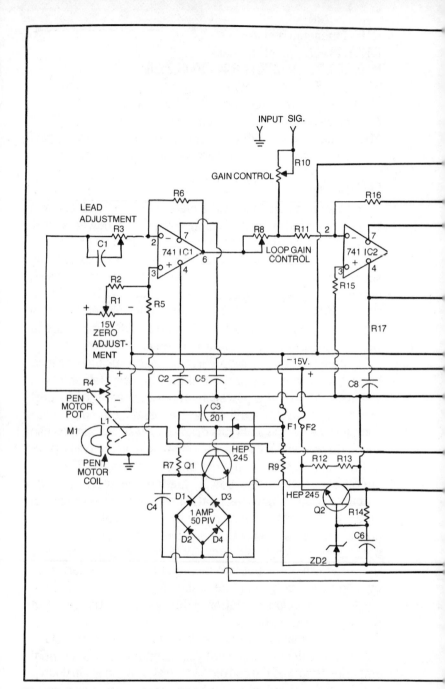

Fig. 2-6. Schematic for electronic portion of Shackelford chart recorder.

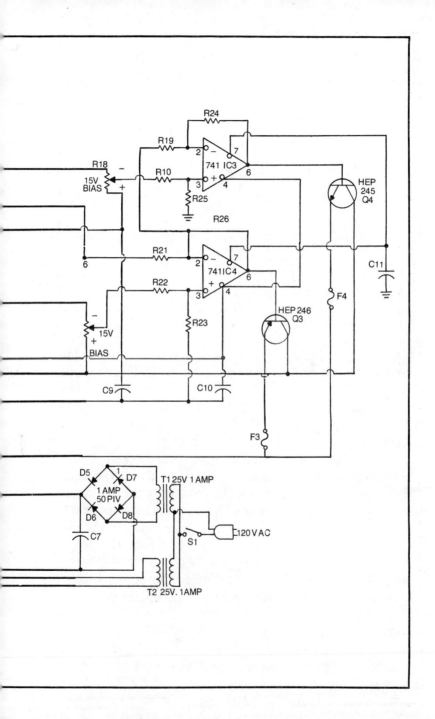

69

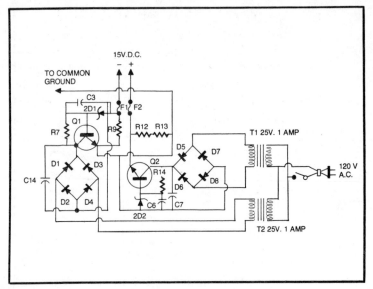

Fig. 2-7. Power supply for chart recorder.

your chart recorder. When you are finally sure all the connections are made in strict accordance with the schematic shown in Fig. 2-9, connect a voltmeter to the output. Use a potentiometer as a voltage divider and make sure you have voltage in/voltage out. Make this check on both the summing and the differential sections of the amplifiers.

Now that all three sections have been checked out you are ready for the interconnecting. Refer back to the schematic shown in Fig. 2-6 and begin by connecting the pen motor to the output of the power amplifier. Connect the arm of the feedback potentiometer to the lead adjustment of the differential amplifier. Be sure to interconnect all ground terminals as shown on the schematic diagram and take the whole to ground only once, including the power supply. Don't shortcut by grounding each terminal separately.

Finally, center all potentiometers (except the bias controls and apply full power to the whole system. First center the pen on the chart paper by using the zero-adjustment control. If the control does not center the pen, reverse the polarity of the potentiometer and it will. With the pen centered, push it off the zero position with your finger and then let it go. Watch it quickly return to its zero position without overshooting. You say it didn't return smartly? Okay, then increase the loop gain until the pen oscillates and then back off just a little. Now when you flick the pen it should overshoot and oscillate a few times. You can now operate the lead adjustment control and find that turning it in one direction will stop the oscillations. You can now play with the loop gain and the lead adjustment controls and discover the optimal settings for yourself. When you are through tinkering the pen really will zap back pronto to the zero position without overshooting the mark by even a millimeter. When that state of nirvana is reached you are ready to record every electronic twitch and twitter of the plant kingdom.

HOW TO USE PLANTS AS A PARANORMAL LABORATORY

The plant detectors and recorders we have suggested so far will enable you to carry on a great deal of experimental work that will bring you new insights and maybe even help

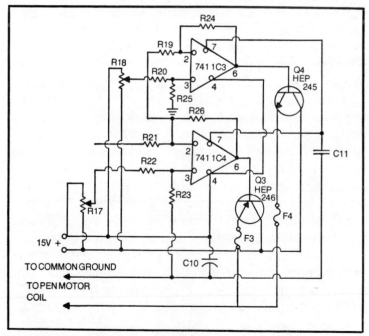

Fig. 2-8. Power amplifier for chart recorder.

you develop some new theories about the paranormal. By all means keep your monitors on during the times you are relaxing and talking and laughing with your friends. It never ceases to amaze me how many times my plants have joined in my personal conversations by reacting to things that were said about plant-related topics. Some of them have been far out. Such as the time my lovely Mimosa Pudica had a complete electronic fit when I read an article to my family out of *Newsweek* about the devestation caused by the use of Agent Orange on foilage in Vietnam!

You will soon find your plants are behaving in totally unscientific hilariously funny ways. My plants react to my thoughts about their well being and appear to sympathize with me and other members of my family. They react to the death of other living things around them. They appear quite anxious to please and "communicate" with me when I am alone with them, but get shy and shut up when strangers come around. You can believe this or not, but once when an acquaintance came around who was a plant pathologist and artist (she spent all of her time cutting up plants and drawing pictures of their anatomy) I could not get any kind of reaction whatsoever from any of more than a dozen plants I had wired up for communications at the time! It was as if they did not like this person and had all gone away the moment she came. When she left, her car had not cleared my driveway before the plants turned on again, making gay sounds and drawing squiggles on my chart recorder. I have had a Fiddle Leaf Philodendron "faint" (no signs of life, just a plain carbon resistor) when my son cut his foot and bled profusely. Many of my experiments would seem to indicate that plants can store information in a memory system somewhere. I had one that would sound a gentle alarm when one of my daughters was sleepwalking. I can tell you for sure that package of bean sprouts at the supermarket takes on a whole new dimension!

You may want to begin your experimentation by duplicating some of the clasic experiments of Cleve Baxter and others. You will find an extensive list of papers detailing these experiments in the extensive bibliography I have compiled in the back of this book.

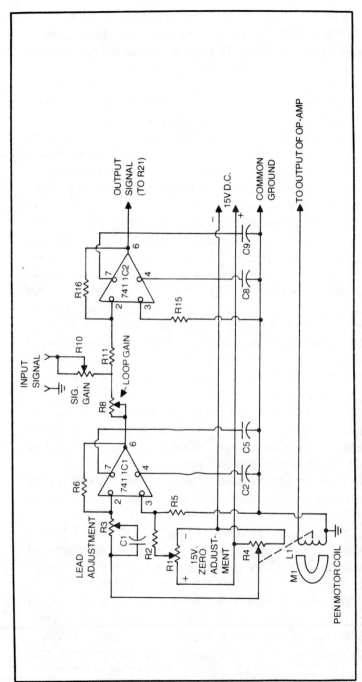

Fig. 2-9. Differential and summing amplifier for chart recorder.

73

There is something very satisfying about collaborating with plants that has to do with the connectedness of all things. And the collaboration seems to have something to say on all aspects of parapsychology—thought transfer, the effects of healing and psychokinesis, dowsing, the strange energy made visible by Kirlian photography, and even in the tricky process of stalking the wild UFO. Certainly, if you are interested in the problems of ecology our civilization has created, communicating with plants and allowing them a voice around your house can be tremendously rewarding.

Don't hesitate to talk to your plants a lot and expect some kind of response from them in return. Everyone knows about Luther Burbank and his amazing work getting plants to grow in great abundance and in unimagined and seemingly impossible combinations. I always thought he did these things in a very scientific way—and he did, of course, use all the help science had to offer. But I was amazed to find out when I did some serious reading about Burbank that he developed his new strains of plant life by visualizing exactly what he wanted—constructing a detailed mental model—and then sitting down with the plants involved and *telling them very carefully what it was he wanted* them to do! Burbank says he quite literally talked a species of cacti out of its thorns.

"You have nothing to fear," Burbank says he told the plant over and over again, "You don't need your defensive thorns, I will protect you." Slowly but surely the plant emerged into a thornless variety.

Luther Burbank stated his secret of success very plainly when he said, "The secret of improved plant breeding, apart from scientific knowledge, is love."

Most green thumbers will agree with that. I have a rubber tree plant that will agree, also. This one winks and flirts with many of my young female friends through the CR tube of an oscilloscope. One of these young friends, a lover of children as well as plants who teaches in a Montessori school, often comes and croons, "I love you truly" to this affectionate plant. When she does the plant makes a high-frequency, very rythmical tracing on the scope that looks for all the world like purring! The pattern of the tracing is nearly always the same whenever they do their little ritual.

In Findhorn, on a cold and barren sandy beach of northern Scotland just a short distance from the Arctic Circle, there is a whole community of people who talk to plants with amazing results. They appear to talk plants into proliferating as both vegetables and flowers on soil so barren little has ever grown there before. What they have grown there by loving communications are 40-pound cabbages, 8-foot delphiniums, and roses that bloom in the snow!

There is really no "magic formula" for communicating with plants. The best way is the way that makes you feel most comfortable. Two items of protocol, however, must always be observed. One is a kind of placebo effect. You must believe that it is possible for you to influence plants with your thoughts and words. And you can't fool them—Not even a dizzy little old daisy. You must be a true believer like Burbank. That is what appears to switch on the circuits between you and the plant world. The second item is that you must make a regular habit (daily, if at all possible) of caring for and talking to your plants. This is what "having a green thumb" is all about, of course.

Then there is the "brown thumb" syndrome, too, which is when your geraniums wilt and your ivy dies no matter how much you water, fertilize, weed, and mulch. The Delaware Laboratories in Oxford, England once asked its associates around the world to experiment with plants to see if withering, scornful thought, and other types of negative thinking could affect the growth and well being of plants. Among the hundreds of reports received confirming that plants do not grow well for people who dislike and mistreat them was one from a surgeon in South Africa who said he found he didn't have to outright hate his plant seeds to stop them from germinating. According to him, all he had to do was feed them a steady diet of discouraging words.

"It's too cold to grow. There isn't any sun," he told the beans he had planted in pots in his medical office. "It's no use trying to germinate," he continued. "You'll be sorry if you do." Every time he glanced up from his work, or returned to his office he repeated this litany of doom.

"I was surprised to find that I appear to be the devil's right-hand man . . . ," he reported. None of his beans sprouted.

Some plants like some people are pushovers for love and affection; some are not. I have found air plants to be quite sensitive, and there is even a little literature to confirm this. James Stegner, who is director of the University of Pittsburgh's Airglow Observatory, wrote that he worked for a time with a variety of air plant never to have been known to bloom and that after several months of intense daily conversation and suggestion, first one and then another lovely trumpetlike blossoms unfurled.

Dr. Paul Blondel, natural science professor at Blake College in California, has also written on this subject. He stated that he has found tomatoes, cabbages, and potatoes most influenced by loving attention and flattery (*sincere* flattery, we must assume).

Plants appear to be no strangers to the EPR effect. Distance seems to have little effect on their perceptions. Cleve Backster has conducted hundreds of experiments that seem to indicate that plants tune into or are somehow aware of their owners over distances of hundreds of miles at least. Plants not only seem to pick up thoughts sent to them but continue to have sympathetic responses to their owners regardless of the distance separating them.

Dr. Robert Miller's now famous experiments with spiritual healer Olga Worrall appeared to show that under carefully controlled conditions the growth of rye grass was influenced by Mrs. Worrall's prayers over a distance of more than 500 miles.

Other paranormal influences that plants seem responsive to which are produced by human beings are magnetic fields radio frequency magnetic fields and sound—especially music.

Dr. L. J. Audus of Bedford College in London writing in the prestigious scientific journal, *Nature*, reported in 1960 on experiments that showed plants to be very sensitive to electromagnetic fields. Magnetized seedlings showed some bending and more emphatic growth than unmagnetized control seedlings. Audus also related that it is possible to "quick-ripen" fruit with a small 900-gauss magnet. Tomatoes placed at various distances from the poles of the magnet (ranging from 3 to 17 in.) showed varying rates of ripening. Horticulturists have advanced the idea that the earth's magnetic field activates the ripening enzyme system inside fruits and vegetables. These enzymes can be triggered off artifically, they say, by placing the fruits and vegetables in a magnetic field.

The behavior of plants in strong radio frequency fields has not been researched in any depth but what little that has been done would indicate that plants must make some drastic adaptations of their d.c.-oriented biological mechanisms in order to survive in the vicinity of high-power radio transmitters.

The chairman of the Botany Department at Annanalai University in southern India, Dr. T.C.N. Singh, has demonstrated that plant protoplasm, when it becomes sluggish, gish, can be activated by rhythmic sound waves produced by a tuning fork, violin music, and dancing. He reported to the Horticulture Society in France that violins, flutes, and human song all quicken the growth and increase the size and yield of pepper plants, onions, petunias and tapioca. Singh's experiments showed that music brought about detectable chromosomal changes. In other words, plants so treated could pass on their traits for quicker growth and increased size to their progeny!

I find that my plants do well with classical music, especially Brahms, Bach, and Beethoven—even certain ballads by the Beatles. I have not tried it, but those who have, say that acid rock makes plants wither and die.

It will not take you long to discover that death is one event plants do take notice of. In a series of experiments Cleve Backster carried out under totally automated conditions brine shrimp were plunged to their deaths in boiling water at random moments determined by computer. As the tiny fish died, philodendron plants four and five rooms away (monitored by polygraphs) reacted sharply. This is an easy experiment to duplicate. I have also found that many of my plants will react to the death of yeast bacteria in much the same way that the Backster plants reacted to the death of brine shrimp.

Whatever your experiment, be sure you have a good base line before you start. Let your plant settle down to its normal routine of electrical activity so that you will know what a meaningful deviation looks or sounds like.

Some plants will show little movement from the baseline no matter what outlandish thing you do to it or around it. Some will show all kinds of reactions to nothing in particular and never seem to settle down to a consistent base line at all. Establishing rapport with a plant seems to be the key to getting it to wake up or settle down and pay attention. I had some Texas Bluebonnets that seemed to be reacting to something or nothing all the time. I worked with them every day for about 10 days—talking to them, welcoming them to my world, and explaining why it was important to me to have some wild flower helpers with my experiments. On the 11th day, the bluebonnets settled down and gave me two days of nice steady base line. On the third day, I went out and exterminated several nests of wasps that had made themselves at home under the eves of my house. All during the killing of the wasps, my bluebonnets were producing large spikes on my chart recorder. They were back to their baseline reading one hour later.

If you are getting nothing but baseline readings from your plants, check your equipment to be sure it is working properly. Then change plants. Some plants just don't react for some people—or under certain conditions. I was most embarrassed a few years ago when invited to bring my plants and their electronic extensions to a local psychic fair. My plants, including an old faithful philodendron, simply refused to produce anything but a steady baseline—even during a replay of the famous brine shrimp experiment. They just appeared to not like crowds—or at least *that* kind of crowd anyway. When I brought them back home I ran them through all the planned experiments, and they reacted in the manner I had expected they would at the fair.

One of the games I play with my philodendron and one which I almost never win is to have someone mix up one of my personal effects (such as a ring I wear all the time) with several of the other person's. I then ask them to show me the items one at a time in the presence of the plant and ask, "Is this yours?

When they come to the item that is mine, I lie and deny that it belongs to me. Almost invariably the trusty old phily will produce a wave on his ammeter and a spike on his recording chart, along with a sharp rise in his audio tone if that happens to be turned on.

A dual-channel tape recorder is a good device for monitoring experiments over distance. With a large reel of tape running slowly and with WWV time signals being recorded on one channel and the base line tone from your plant recording on the other channel synchronize your watch and go away somewhere. From time to time in a random fashion, think about your plant in a very concerned and loving way. Or if it has been successful at playing the "Is this yours" game, get a friend to do this with you. Make a note of the exact time these thoughts and events occur so that you can check for reactions on your tape at these times later. If your plant is sensitive to the death of brine shrimp, you might stop by a health food store and buy some yogurt. Mix it with some jelly that has a preservative in it. Eat it if you like. Why not? But eaten or not, the preservative in the jelly will kill the acidophili in the yogurt—they die by the thousands. Note the time you mixed the jelly and the yogurt to see if your plant back home took notice of what you did to the acidophili.

Some plants do seem to respond in some sense to the territorial imperative attributed to certain animals. For instance, there seems to be a certain range in which they react especially to the death stimulus. Plants seem to claim a certain amount of space that "concerns" them just as animals do.

Plants also tend to become conditioned to certain stimuli and after a time give no reaction to it. One exception appears to be that they seldom become conditioned to the death of human cells. A scratch on the arm treated with iodine will almost always bring a reaction from even the most conditioned of plants.

Another experiment you might like to try to duplicate is one that has been reported from the Timeryazev Institute for Photosynthesis and Plant Physiology of the Soviet Academy of Sciences. Researchers there report certain vegetables and flowers—they mention specifically potatoes, cucumbers, and buttercups—can remember certain rhythmic patterns of light (recalling the patterns for up to 18 hours). As usual, the news about Russian experiments in the field of parapsychology is lacking in details about just how they test for memory retention. Conditioning of plants has also been reported by the Russians (shades of Pavlov and his dog), with the use of light as the reward to reinforce the conditioning stimuli. It is said that some plants have been conditioned to recognize certain minerals by light reenforced conditioning.

My own area of interest at this writing is one that has little experimental precedent in the U.S., Soviet Union, or anywhere else that I can find. Rather than trying to get plants to do human things like recognizing one mineral from another, I am interested in eavesdropping on the secret lives of plants to see if I can get clues to what the various kinds of electrical activity going on really mean to the plants themselves. We tend to attribute our uniquely human reactions and activity to plants, and I am not at all sure that we have rightly interpreted what the plants are saying to one another and to their environments (if anything).

Early researchers of this secret life of plants, including J.C. Bose in England in the early part of this century and Bruce Scott in the U.S. in the late 1950s and early 1960s discovered that although electricity in plants is mostly of the dc (direct current) variety, there is often an ELF (extremely low-frequency) component present. Plants seem able to process information mediated by ELF radio waves (being both senders and receivers of such electromagnetic waves). In fact, one hypothesis about paranormal events taken most seriously by physicists is that all paranormal information transfer is mediated by ELF waves. These waves are not affected by sensory shielding, nor by the Faraday cage shielding which blocks higher frequency electromagnetic waves.

The ELF band is so little explored that I have had to make up most of the rules and design most of the equipment from scratch, so why not join in the exploration?

WAY-OUT PLANT DETECTOR

I define the extra low-frequency (ELF) band as those frequencies below 3 kHz, where the VLF band leaves off. As far as I know there are no transmitters made by man operating in this band. However, there are many biological systems, including man, operating at these frequencies. It may be that all life forms are connected in this band in the same sense that all ham radio operators around the world are connected by the short-wave band of frequencies.

My ELF "tuner" covers five bands by boosting and filtering. The first band is below 1 Hz; the second band is most sensitive to the range from 1 to 50 Hz; band three ranges from 50 Hz to 350 Hz; band four from 350 Hz to 1 kHz; and band five, 1 kHz to 3 kHz. Somewhere over the 3-kHz rainbow, the U.S. navy broadcasts its grunts and squeals to all the ships at sea. The Navy's powerful transmitters that propagate into salt water may well be picked up by your philidendron and passed on to you or transduced as its own. All the long-wave frequencies propagate through and around the earth, following its curvature. This means that you can get many a strange ac signal while eavesdropping on the ELF band. For example, weather conditions generate a lot of energy at those frequencies. From a purely theoretical standpoint, the ELF frequencies are ideal for mediating the connectedness that appears to be a feature of all life on this planet—perhaps, even, given the EPR effect, all life throughout the universe. At least this is an exciting theory to explore with our experiments. And whether we eventually prove or disprove it, we'll have a lot of fun learning along the way.

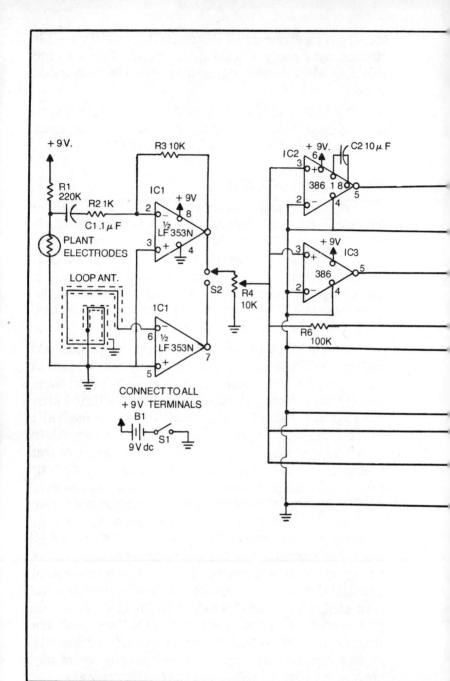

Fig. 2-10. Schematic for ELF receiver.

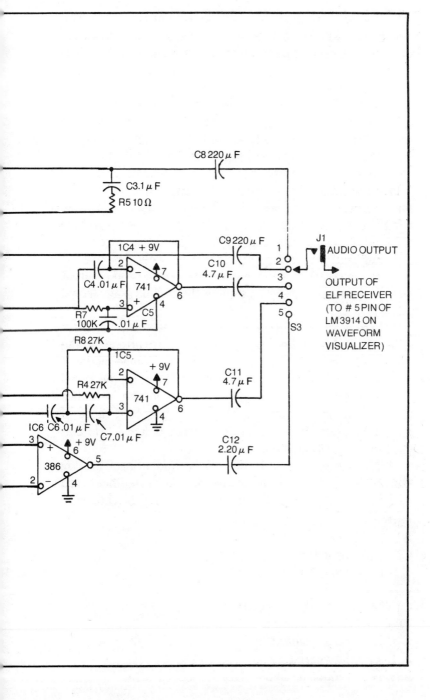

Figure 2-10 shows a complete schematic of the ELF receiver. Extra low-frequency (ELF) signals can be picked up either on regular plant electrodes, as shown in Fig. 2-1, or on a loop antenna. Regular audio microphone cable can be used to connect either to an rf amplifier stage. The amplified signals are fed through S2, with the source of your choice going through R4, the rf gain control, and then through one of five circuits very broadly tuned as described previously. S3 selects which of these circuits is desired and feeds the signal to a solid-state oscilloscope that uses 100 red LEDs in a 3-inch square readout module. Resolution is poor, but the wave forms can be visualized, and their frequency and phase relationships can be determined. Many of these signals are in the audible range, so audio output is also provided for listening and/or recording. The chart recorder described in the previous section can also be fed from the audio output jack for recording wave forms under the audible range (about 16 Hz).

Like most oscilloscopes the ELF waveform visualizer (Fig. 2-11) has a vertical gain control to attenuate the displayed signal to accommodate a wide range of input amplitudes; a horizontal sweep control to spread the signal over the full screen area; and a switch to choose either triggered or free running sweep. The triggered mode is especially useful when observing signals below 10 Hz that have low-repetition rates.

The use of type TLR-107 LEDs (Radio Shack catalog #276-033) is strongly recommended because these red LEDs are equipped with Fresnel lenses for high brightness.

Parts

B1 - 9 V battery
C1 - .1μF capacitor
C2 - 10μF capacitor
C3 - .1μF capacitor
C4, C5, C6, C7 - .01μF capacitors
C8, C9 - 220μF capacitors
C10, C11 - 4.7μF capacitors
IC1 - LF353N dual op amp
IC2, IC3 - LM386 op amps

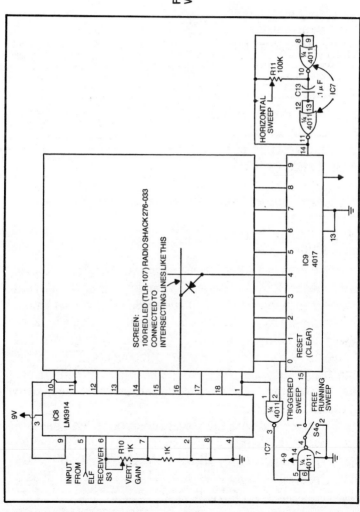

Fig. 2-11. Schematic for ELF Waveform Visualizer.

IC4, IC5 - 741C op amps
IC6 - LM386 op amp
IC7 - 4011 quad nand gate
IC8 - LM3914N dot/bar display driver
IC9 - 4017 decade counter/decoder
J1 - insulated phono jack, two conductor/closed circuit
LEDS - type TLR-107, 100 needed
R1 - 220K resistor
R2 - 1K resistor
R3 - 10K resistor
R4 - 10K potentiometer
R5 - 10 ohm resistor
R6, R7 - 100K resistors
R8, R9 - 27K resistors
R10 - 1K potentiometer
R11 - 100K potentiometer
S1 - spst off-on slide switch
S2 - spdt slide switch
S3 - single-pole five-position rotary switch
S4 - spdt slide switch
Misc. - aluminum cabinet approx 8-in × 6-in × 4-in, perf
       board, push-in clips, knobs, hook-up wire, wrapping
       wire, etc.

Construction

This project uses a lot of integrated circuits, so I used Radio Shack PC boards and wrapping wire. I inserted wrapping sockets in the board and made connections with a wire-wrapping tool. If you decide to go this route, Fig. 2-12 may be helpful. Apply wrapping wire directly to the leads of all capacitors, resistors, and other components. Then solder them firmly in place. All wiring should be carefully done, even though the receiver and visualizer are designed to operate at low frequencies.

Fabricate and wire the visualizer screen from a piece of ¼-in. masonite, drilled with 3/16-in. holes just far enough apart to accommodate the LEDs side-by-side. All 100 LEDs should fit inside a 3-in. square area. Wire each one in as a diagonal across the grid pattern (exactly as shown in Fig.

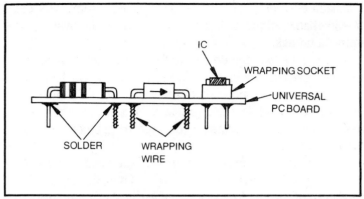

Fig. 2-12. Application of wrapping wire and solder to ELF construction.

2-11). When you have finished, you will have 10 leads coming off the bottom and 10 leads coming off one side of the back of the screen.

Now cut a 3-in. square hole in the middle of the front panel of the aluminum box and drill holes for mounting the potentiometers and switches that will go on the front panel (See Fig. 2-13). Mount the screen onto the panel by gluing it with Duco or similar cement. Next mount the potentiometers and switches on the front panel in the conventional manner. Cut a section of perf board to fit inside the cabinet, notched to accommodate the visualizer screen, and fit it into the box about halfway up. Two lengths of sheet aluminum bent into brackets can be used to mount the board and hold it rigid. Be sure to insulate all components from the aluminum box. Also, install serrated washers between the control bushings and the inside of the panel to ensure that the controls will hold their settings. Mount the jack for audio output and the terminals or jacks for connections to plant electrodes and the loop antenna on the rear of the perf board, drilling holes in the rear panel of the box to accommodate. Again, be sure these connectors are well insulated from the box itself.

Constructing the Loop Antenna

You will need four lengths of polyvinyl chloride (PVC) 2-ft. long × 1-in. diameter, two wood dowels 5-in. long (each of a diameter that will fit inside the PVC pipe, some 325-feet of #28 enameled magnet wire, along with some plastic tape and a phono jack.

Notch the wooden dowels and cement them together to form the core of the loop as shown in Fig. 2-14. Cut a ¼-in.× ½-in. deep slot on one end of each section of PVC pipe and slide the other ends over the wooden dowels. Put some plastic tape into the slots in the pipe to protect the wire winding.

Wind the antenna with 38 turns of the magnet wire and then cover with a layer of plastic tape. Over the tape, wind the electrostatic shield, as indicated in Fig. 2-15. Be careful to leave approximately 1-in. spacing between the shield winding turns. The electrostatic shield is wound using hookup wire, and one end should be connected to the ground lug of the photo connector. The other end needs to be taped to guard against accidental shorts. A good-quality phono cable should connect the antenna to the receiver input.

The antenna can be suspended from a length of nylon cord, or it can sit on a strip of Styrofoam or on a small wooden stool. It should be operated close to the plant so that its directional characteristics can help distinguish "plant talk" from ambient ac noise. Try using both the electrodes and the antenna on the same plant and compare the wave forms of the signals you get from each.

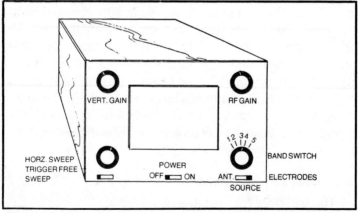

Fig. 2-13. Front panel layout of ELF receiver and Waveform Visualizer.

88

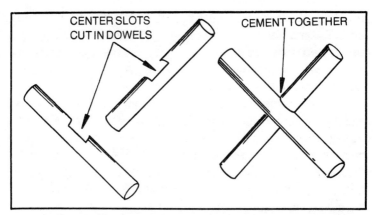

Fig. 2-14. Detail of loop antenna core.

Pay particular attention to the phase relationships of the ac signals you get from plants. According to recent hologramic theories of the way the mind operates*, it is phase relationships and not amplitude analogues that carry information and store memory. If you look for amplitude changes to tell you something, as in AM radio broadcasting, you may miss the message. It is apparently the phase relationships (as in FM radio broadcasting) that plants and possibly all forms of life use when transfering, processing, and storing information. Changes in the phase relationships of ELF waves as noted on the waveform visualizer, are what you are looking for to indicate meaningful reactions from your plants.

As you study the wave forms and their phase relationships broadcast by plants, you may want to ask yourself if this is just a reaction like one gets from iron filings sprinkled in a magnetic field, or does it represent the activity of a sensitive nervous system and some quality of consciousness? A long time ago, a great Indian scientist, Sir Jagadis Chandra Bose (he was knighted for his inventions and his work with plants) answered that question strongly in the affirmative. Working at the turn of the century with an amazingly sensitive device that he invented for magnifying and observing plant reactions, Bose concluded that plants are endowed with a nervous system that allows them to know love and hate, joy

*Read *"Shufflebrain, the quest for the Hologramic Mind"* by Paul Pietsch, Houghton Mifflin Company, BOSTON, 1981

and fear. He even demonstrated that plants get high on caffeine, and sway drunkenly on alcohol. He also demonstrated that trees are able to survive the shock of uprootings and transplantings much better if the uprooting is done under chloroform.

My own speculation, based on only a few years of reading and experimentation is that our puzzlement about plant-human communications comes about because of the great difference in time scale between us. When the activity of plants is speeded up in time as can be done with time-lapse photography, they seem to be as active and "alive" as we are. And I can imagine that to some being whose lives were scaled in nanoseconds, I might seem as lifeless as a rock. I believe the meaning of all that electrical activity in plants will become much clearer when we have enough changes in wave forms to make a kind of fast movie, or fast running tape. The information contained in the phase relationships of the wave forms could then be observed by us in a time frame perhaps more meaningful to us.

In any case, whatever the patterns of dc and ac coming to us from the plant kingdom may turn out to *mean*, they can be *used* to have the plants perform in useful and interesting ways. By operating sound-generating IC devices, music synthesizers, and by performing transducer duties, they can produce both entertainment and service to us who, hopefully, they view as their human friends.

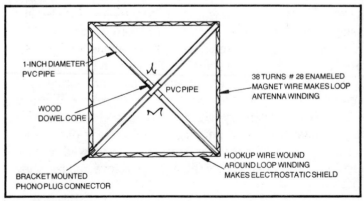

Fig. 2-15. Detail of loop antenna.

Once you have built these projects and become familiar with the kinds of signals produced by various kinds of plants, you will find yourself getting all kinds of ideas for further projects and for adapting the electronic projects suggested in other TAB books and current electronics magazines.

For starters I suggest you experiment with the SN76488 IC sound generator. With a few other parts out of a "junk box" and some imagination, you can create almost an infinite number of sounds in response to the electrical activity coming from your plants. The data supplied with the chip will give you an idea about what resistors and capacitors to use with the chip to produce certain kinds of sounds. Figure 2-16 will give you a schematic idea of the fantastic possibilities of this amazing IC device. It even includes a built-in speaker amplifier!

How about a snake plant that responds by hissing? The noise generator shown in Fig. 2-17 can be adapted to allow such versatile verbal behavior—and more. By changing a few components, the same plant can respond with the sound of a steam train or propeller-driven aircraft.

By using the auxiliary output of the op amp shown in Fig. 2-1 to operate a relay inserted in the speaker lead of the SN76477N noise generator, the plant will turn on the steady hiss produced by the generator when it is agitated. Snare drum sound can be had by tripping in a circuit that connects pins 25 and 26 to ground and pin 27 to +9 volts. Another circuit that can be activated by having the plant trip a relay contains a 1M pot from pin 20 to ground and a 1μF capacitor from pin 21 to ground. Depending on the adjustment of the pot, the noise generated will range from steam trains to propeller aircraft. To put these changing sounds under the control of a plant, use the plant leaf as the resistance between pin 20 to ground by connecting in the electrodes (as shown in Fig. 2-1) as the resistance.

Plants make good drummers. You can get them to produce all kinds of percussion sounds by using the percussion synthesizer shown in Fig. 2-18. Switch S1 can be replaced by the plant-activated relay, and electrodes on the

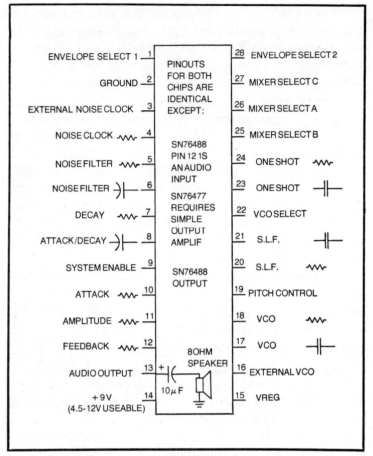

Fig. 2-16. Complex sound generator SN76477N/SN76488N (courtesy of Radio Shack).

leaves of several plants can supply the resistances that control decay, add exponential decay and slow attack, and control frequency and duration of sound. Several plants can be combined to form a symphony-sized percussion section.

Other plants can supply some melody lines for the percussionists among your plants—or out in your garden—by making them key electronic elements in the Universal Up-Down Tone Generator shown in Fig. 2-19. The plant-actuated relay (substituted for S1) will give an undulating tone that gradually decays and stops when the plant turns it on. Many different sound effects and musical effects ranging from siren to science fiction movie sounds are produced by this tone generator by changing the values of the resistors and capacitors connected to pins 16, 17, 18, 20, 21, and 22. These are the VCO and SLF components. And, of course, if you use electrodes on your plants for the resistances of these components, the plants themselves will change the quality of the tone as they react to your care or neglect, threats or loving thoughts, or perhaps to that approaching storm it picked up on the ELF band.

If you have a streak of Simon Legree in your soul, as I do, you can even press your plants into service as bio-androids and have them respond to your every thought by turning your electrical devices off and on. Figure 2-20 shows such a control circuit. The plant pulses are introduced through the trigger input which starts a timing process and trips the relay. The 1M pot and the 10-μF capacitor determine the length of time the device will stay on. If you wish to have the device operate continuously once the plant turns it on, use another relay which must be reset once it is tripped off. Keep in mind, however, that you must think in a "language" your plants understand and react to in order to get them to work for you. In keeping with the Simon Legree

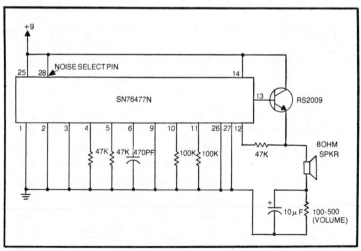

Fig. 2-17. Noise generator SN76477N.

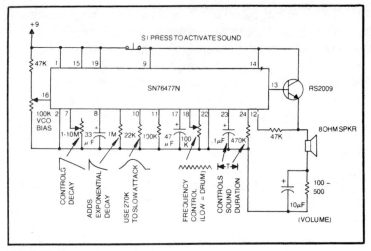

Fig. 2-18. Percussion synthesizer.

image, you might have to threaten the plant with injury to get it to turn on your reading lamp; it will never in this world turn on anything in response to a direct English thought such as, "Will you please be kind enough to turn on my reading light?" However, the threat route will not work either, unless you are serious and actually injure the plant, which puts you in trouble also.

This I have found to be the most fascinating area of experimentation with plants—how to communicate and get responses consistently. What I have found out so far is that it has a lot to do with the relationship one establishes with the plant. For example, my rubber tree plant that has this lovely thing going with my friend (the Montesori teacher), never fails to respond to her *feelings* about it. She turns the plant on and it will turn on *anything* for her. This same plant also seems to have a preference for turning on some things and not others in response to my loving and caring thoughts about it. It doesn't like to turn lights on very much, but it seems quite eager to turn them off. Furthermore, it seems to know whether or not I have the circuit hooked up to have it turn them *off,* instead of on. What it really likes to do is turn on a toy electric train. Working through my 555 control circuit with timer set for about 10 seconds (the train is stopped by

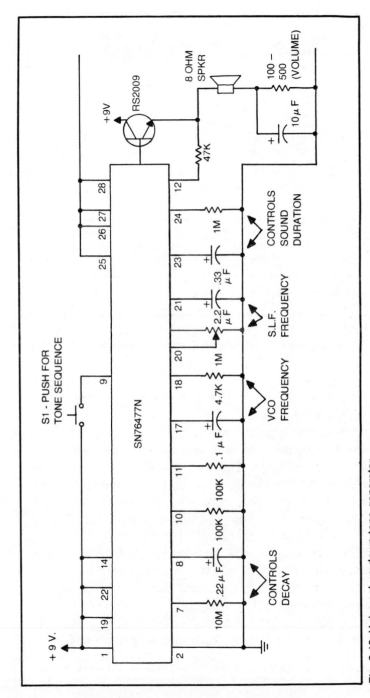

Fig. 2-19. Universal up-down tone generator.

95

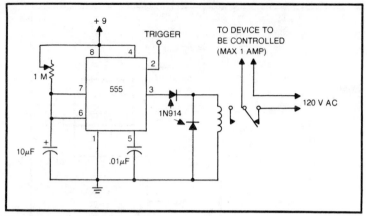

Fig. 2-20. Control circuit with timer.

the timer 10 seconds after being triggered to start), the plant will often restart the train time after time with no apparent prompting on my part!

I have an African Violet that appears to be conditioned to turning on its own "grow" light when my timer circuit turns it off. It also seems to know when it is hooked up to the light because it reacts with much greater frequency then that when not hooked up to any device or when hooked up to another type of device. The African Violet has never yet turned on my electric train.

One thing my plants have done for me throughout all my efforts to communicate with them has been to erode my Simon Legree image. They are teaching me to be more thoughtful and considerate of my total environment. Perhaps that is what they had in mind all along. I find I often ask myself, "Am I controlling my plants or are they controlling me?" "Who is the master and who the slave here?" After all, it is the plant kingdom that supports and sustains life on our beautiful blue planet. Would it be so surprising to find out that they therefore have something like care and concern for all the forms of life that they nurture?

Perhaps you can build some of these projects and help me to answer some of those really intriguing questions.

Chapter 3
Biofeedback
— An Electronic
Experimenter's Paradise

While the significance of electrical activity in plants is still open to many interpretations, the significance of electrical activity in animals, especially in humans is thought to be much better understood. At least when human beings get feedback on the various functions that these signals represent they are able to bring the functions under conscious control—to achieve what the famous American psychologist William James said was the greatest thing we can all do and that is "to make the nervous system our ally instead of our enemy."

The development of biofeedback training can be thought of as one of the most significant technological breakthroughs in the whole history of the science and the study of man. The breakthrough came about during the 1950s and 1960s as solid-state electronic technology advanced on all fronts. This wedding of psychology and physics presided over by the Yogis from the East has resulted in the necessity for rewriting all medical and most psychology textbooks.

What is being written into the new texts is the fact that new and exceedingly sensitive IC devices can now detect extremely small electrophysiological signals and amplify, filter, and display them with great speed. Thus subtle information about some ongoing activity under the skin can be fed back to us while the activity is going on. By making ourselves aware of, or more sensitive to, these psychophysiological processes, we can develop some measure of voluntary control over them. As Dr. Elmer Green of the Menninger Foundation has said, "Biofeedback training is a tool for learning psychosomatic self-regulation."

By the early 1980s, the diverse bodily functions brought under control by biofeedback training with electronic devices included heart rate, blood flow, blood pressure, brain waves, gastrointestinal functions, and air flow in bronchial tubes (to alleviate asthma). Control of paralyzed and spastic muscles was also being demonstrated.

We were also having to admit that this was nothing new to mankind, only new to Western culture. From earliest times Eastern Yogis made use of several forms of noninstrumented biofeedback to check on the learning progress of their pupils. One of the goals of this teaching was to teach the body to be quiet, by which they brought the body's basal metabolism rate under control. This was accomplished by slowing the breathing rate to a very regular one breath per minute. The resulting anoxia causes an involuntary jerking of the diaphragm which gave feedback to consciousness of a normally unconscious process. When the student could bring the jerking under control and his diaphragm no longer convulsed, the yogis knew that learning was proceeding correctly.

The first instrumented biofeedback that I am aware of is that used by one J.H. Bair and described by him in a 1901 report called "Development of voluntary control." Bair apparently used a mechanical feedback device to train people to acquire control over the muscles that wiggle the ears.

In 1938 O.H. and W.M. Mowrer developed an alarm system triggered by urine that gave feedback to bed-wetting children and enabled the children to bring their enuresis under control. In 1943 Dr. Lawrence Kubie was feeding back amplified breathing sounds to his patients to get them into a state of hypnagogic reverie so that they could get information from their unconscious minds.

Three psychiatrists (the team of Haugen, Dixon, and Dickel) in 1963 made some impressive use of biofeedback to cure their patients of anxiety tensions by feeding back their muscle tensions to them in the form of wave patterns on an oscilloscope.

About that same time, a researcher by the name of Joe Kamiya seemingly caught everyones attention with his work teaching college students to regulate their brain wave patterns by feeding back the wave patterns to the students from an EEG machine.

Since the mid-1960s there have been lots of researchers exploring the use of biofeedback training and techniques and among the leaders have been Elmer and Alyce Green of the Menninger Foundation, and Barbra Brown, author of *New Mind, New Body* (1974).

As with all other things parapsychological, biofeedback control is better and more effective if you have fun with it. So the best way to get started is with an emotional "hang-up" meter that is very similar to the "lie detector" you build for your philodendron in Chapter 2.

HOW TO BUILD A "HANG-UP" METER

The Hang-Up meter not only detects your emotional hang-ups and (by providing feedback) enables you to achieve more control over them, it also makes an excellent lie detector since it displays variations in the electrical resistance of one's skin. The variations in skin resistance are related to several physiological fluctuations caused by emotional stress that are usually under the control of the "autonomous" nervous system. But by increasing your awareness of these subtle fluctuations you will be able to bring them under the power of your will. You will find that there are many complex physiological responses you have that are reflected in meandering skin resistance. You'll find it very rewarding as well as lots of fun to build this GSR (Galvanic Skin Response) monitor. By using it for just a few minutes a day as a relaxation trainer you will be able to accomplish what yogis take weeks to teach on remote mountain tops.

Parts
B1, B2, B3 - 9 volt batteries
B4 - 1.5 volt battery

C1 - .05μF capacitor
C2, C3 - 50μF capacitors, 10-volt eletrolytic
C4 - 220pF capacitor
C5 - .01μF
C6 - .005μF capacitor
D1, D2 - silicon diodes, IN4004
IC1 - 741C op amp
I1 - 2.2-volt lamp #222
M1 - 0-1 mA meter
Q1 - SK3011 transistor
Q2 - SK3003 transistor
R1 - 75K resistor
R2 - 100K potentiometer
R3, R4 - 1K resistors
R5 - 240K resistor
R6 - 1M potentiometer
R7 - 82 ohm resistor
R8 - 470K resistor
R9 - 3,3K resistor
R10 - 10K resistor
R11 - 470K resistor
R12 - 1K resistor
R13 - 4.7K resistor
R14 - 100-ohm resistor
J1 - closed circuit jack
J2 - open circuit mini jack
S1 - spst switch
S2 - dpst switch
S3 - normally open push-button switch
S4 - spst switch
Misc. - suitable chassis and cabinet, battery holders, pilot
       lamp mounting assembly, 2 pieces ⅛-inch thick 1-inch
       square copper electrodes, 2 bicycle pants clips, 2 to
       4-feet shielded audio cable; pillow speaker with built in
       volume control (Radio Shack 33-207 or equivalent),
       etc.

Construction

The schematic in Fig. 3-1 shows the basic GSR device
with both visual (meter) and audio (pillow speaker) feedback

devices. The main elements shown on the schematic include a Wheatstone bridge input, an op amp guard circuit that can be disabled by opening S1, a dc op amp with large signal gain of the order of 100,000, and an audio tone generator whose frequency varies with the skin resistance.

Assemble the circuit on perf board but be sure to avoid heat damage when soldering the IC and other semiconductors. Double check and be sure that the electrolytic capacitors are wired in with the correct polarity. The + side of C3 is wired to pin #7 of the IC, while the + side of C2 goes to the common ground with the *opposite* lead connecting to pin #4. A well filtered 9-volt power supply may be used for the power source in place of the 9-volt batteries if you prefer. Be sure that J1 has one contact that closes when the plug is inserted connecting the electrodes into the bridge.

The electrodes can be cut from ⅛-inch copper sheet. Work the copper with a ball-peen hammer a bit to make it slightly convex for a better fit into the palms of the hands. Solder small U-shaped brackets to each electrode on the concave side. Remove the spring tempering from one end of each of the bicycle pants clips by heating one inch of it with a propane torch and allowing it to cool. Insert the heat treated end under the bracket and bend it so that the clip is firmly attached to the bracket, but is still free to pivot. Be sure to insulate each of the former bicycle clips, now electrode clips by covering them with cambric tubing. This will also make them more comfortable to wear.

About four feet of two-wire shielded microphone cable can be used to connect the electrodes to the bridge. Strip away the shielding and separate the two wires at one end for about one foot so the lead can go comfortably one to each hand. Solder one wire to each electrode and solder the other end to the terminals of the male plug that mates with J1. Wiring polarity is not important. Tape the wire to the clip to secure the soldered joint.

Testing and Operation

When the electrodes (one from each hand) are plugged into the bridge circuit it is automatically energized by the jack (J1) as it closes the circuit from B1. To keep battery drain to a minimum the electrodes should be unplugged whenever the "Hang-Up" meter is not in use. The amplifier section will have no output unless the bridge is energized so don't forget to turn S2, the power switch off when you pull the plug on the electrodes. Power to the audio oscillator is supplied by closing S4.

To test the system clip a fixed resistance of about 75,000 ohms between the electrodes and plug them in. Place the 100K null control (R2) near mid scale. When you turn on S, rotating the null control should cause the needle on the meter to swing through its full range. With S4 closed the tone from the oscillator should go through a wide range of pitch change. These changes, of course, are produced by the off-set signal from the bridge which is amplified by IC1.

The IC, by the way, is guarded by diodes D1 and D2. This is necessary because sweaty hands can sometimes produce large currents before the bridge is nulled. When S1 is closed, the diodes automatically limit the input voltage to the IC to a safe value. S1 can be safely opened to achieve maximum sensitivity once the circuits are operating properly and the meter has been nulled.

The meter indicates the output from the op-amp which changes as the skin resistance of the subject changes. The output of the amplifier also controls the frequency of the oscillator (Q1 and Q2) as a function of the dc output, thus making the tone an analogue of the subject's skin resistance. When the skin resistance changes, the bias on Q1 changes to alter the pitch of the oscillator. Indicator lamp I1 lights if the battery voltage in B4 is okay. The test is made by momentarily depressing push-button switch S3. This will also increase the pitch of the oscillator tone.

If everything has checked out okay so far, reduce the value of the test resistor by pinching both sides with the thumb and forefinger of each hand. This should make the meter read farther up scale. If the reading is down scale you will need to reverse the polarity of the meter connections or the bridge energizing battery. Rotating R6 should increase and decrease the gain of the op-amp IC1.

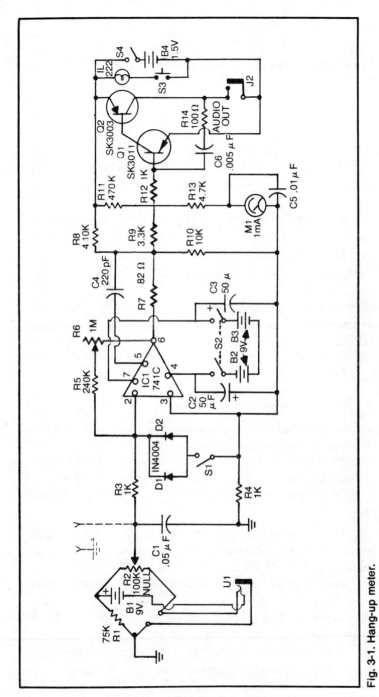

Fig. 3-1. Hang-up meter.

103

To use the Hang-Up meter as a biofeedback training device (and get rid of your hang-ups) clip an electrode to the palm of each hand and plug in the electrodes to J1. With S1 in the "on" position turn the power on to the amplifier and set the null control (R2) to bring the meter needle to a point just above zero. Plug in the pillow speaker and seat yourself comfortably where you can see the meter while resting your head on the pillow speaker or on a pillow covering the speaker. Adjust the volume control on the speaker to a comfortable level and begin to relax as much as you can. You might practice the autogenic exercises suggested in Chapter one. Or you might day dream a while and imagine yourself in some favorite relaxing spot, lying in the warm sunshine. As you relax your skin resistance will rise and the needle on the meter will also rise. Notice, also how the pitch of the tone changes as the needle rises. If you find it difficult to relax with your eyes open looking at the meter, you can close them and just listen to the tone which will tell you by its changing pitch that you are becoming more and more relaxed. Your task is to get the meter to rise to a full scale reading by your thoughts and daydreams alone—and/or to change the pitch of the oscillator to the frequency corresponding to a full scale reading on the meter. You can then further reduce your tensions and increase your relaxation by nulling the meter again and starting all over from a lower base line. This will teach you what deep relaxation feels like and you will be able to reach this state quickly on your own without the Hang-Up meter. This will mean that most of your hang-ups will be gone!

The level of ones skin resistance at any particular time appears to be a measure of ones general activation or arousal. In biofeedback circles this is usually expressed as *Base line conductance*. (Conductance being the inverse of resistance.) High base line conductance indicates a wide awake state of relatively high tension throughout the body. A low base line conductance indicates a day dreamy, relaxed, even drowsy or sleep state of the body. However, the mind can be quite alert in a low base line state of conductance.

One tends to go to a high base line when under emotional shock or tension. For this reason the GSR measurements are often used as "lie detectors", on the theory that the emotional tension created by lying results in a jump in base line conductance. This is an oversimplification but it can be used for fun and games such as the one suggested in Chapter 2 where you use a human friend instead of a plant to see if a person is as good at detective work as a plant.

A variation on the game is to have someone pick out a card from a deck, replace it, and then have him lie about which card he/she picked. Did the Hang-Up meter give him/her away?

Of course these "lie detector" games are based on the old premise (that we now know to be false) that these variations in a person's skin resistance are "autonomous"; in other words, beyond one's conscious control. But if you train yourself in biofeedback, you can lie to the lie detector and make it indicate that you are telling the truth when in fact you are lying, and vice versa!

You can, however, use the Hang-Up meter to explore your emotional reactions to all kinds of situations to find out what things turn you on or off or make you extra "up tight." You can then use the device to train yourself to relax, or just not be bothered by these situations. From the perspective of parapsychology you are really achieving "mind over matter"—using your mind to control your circumstances rather than letting circumstances alter your state of mind.

THE ELECTRONIC MONASTERY

To become a true yogi/of the technological age, one needs to establish an electronic monastery consisting of a recliner chair and a brain wave monitor that will change brain waves into audible tones which one can then learn to use to achieve control over the electrical activity of the brain. The nonmedical uses of brain wave biofeedback training are many, varied and fascinating. BW feedback can be used to improve your attention span, to achieve deep relaxation and deep meditative states of mind, to enhance creativity and problem solving abilities, and to amplify and intensify ESP abilities. The latter use has been taken quite seriously by the National Aeronautics and Space Administration (NASA) in that they have funded research at the Stanford Research Institute, and by the former Newark College of Engineering where BW biofeedback training is being used to teach executives how to develop and use their intuition more effectively in the decision making process.

Elmer Green writes in *Beyond Biofeedback* (Dell Publishing Co., 1977) that many ESP experiences have surfaced in their experiments into Theta Training in imagery and creativity. Dr. Green mentions these incidents because he says he believes that such events are not rare, but almost commonplace. My own experience and experiments tend to confirm that opinion. And I have noticed in my job of reporting on scientific research that most researchers pass these events off as coincidence and do not include it in their data. Sooner or later, though, they will have to start including *all* the data if we are to come to truly understand ourselves and what place ESP experiences have in the scheme of things. Coincidence is, after all, the most far fetched, unlikely and unscientific explanation of anything. So welcome to the monastery!

THE BRAIN AND ITS WAVES

Our electronic monastery does not demand either the time or the discomfort of monasteries inhabited by Tibetan monks high in the Himalayas. We will not claim that our technological short cuts are better or that they are even as good. I have not been able to pass the thousands-years-old graduation ritual of these monks, who, on the coldest night of winter spend their time dipping robes in water letting them freeze, then draping them around their bodies to be melted in seconds. The best students are also able to melt considerable snow with their bodies also. However, I have learned to warm or cool either one of my hands by 20°F and while that doesn't melt much snow or unfreeze many white robes it does keep my blood pressure low and my body free of knots and tension, and enables me to do a lot of yogi ESP things like run a psychotronic engine—as we will explain in the next chapter. It's all done with brain waves, but before we begin our brain wave monitor project let's look at the electronics of the human body-brain system.

THE ELECTRONICS OF HUMANS

Bio-potentials are the tiny voltages developed by all living organisms and originate at the cellular level. Each and every living cell is also an electric battery. When we measure these voltages, however, we get an additive effect and actually measure the electrical activity of an entire body subsystem. Our GSR measurements, for example, were largely measurements of the electrical activity of the subsystem of muscles. These measurements are often called electromyograms (EMG). The recording of the electrical activity of the heart is an electrocardiogram (EKG) and the voltages produced by the sum total of a group of brain cells is an encephalogram (EEG).

EEG signals have to be picked up on the scalp, of course, and, due to the high impedance of the human body, are quite minute—on the order of 10 to 100 microvolts (ten to a hundred millionths of a volt). It takes only a little noise or interference to drown out these signals entirely. The worst source of interference nowadays is the electromagnetic field from power lines that are nearly everywhere. These fields can induce potentials a million times stronger than the ones produced by the brain.

It is only through solid state technology that these problems can be overcome. The interfering fields can be screened out, precisely because they are so much larger than the brain wave signal, by a differential amplifier. This device rejects any extraneous voltage common to two inputs while boosting the small difference signal between the two inputs (see Fig. 3-2).

Since the human head runs a high impedance in the range of 1000 to 10,000 ohms, the amplifier requires a very high input impedance so as not to load the signal source. Of course, the amplifier itself must generate very little noise and this dictates your expensive type amplifier referred to in electronic circles as an instrumentation amplifier.

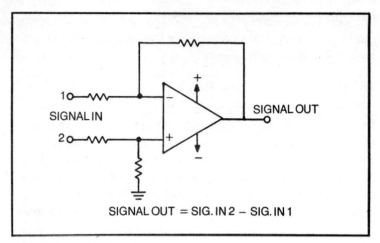

Fig. 3-2. Difference amplifier.

In addition to the high-quality amplifier needed for brain wave biofeedback, some way of using the amplified micro potentials from the brain need to be included. The brain waves of greatest interest fall in the 3 to 14 Hz range which is below the range of the human ear. Of course, the information on brain wave frequency could be presented to any sense, including the visual, but experience has shown that audio feedback is most effective when learning to control ones brain waves. Accordingly, the amplified brain waves control a second signal source having a frequency range well within the ability of the ear to hear, and it is this analog of one's brain waves that one hears and manipulates. It is this mental effort to change the pitch of the sound one hears that completes the feedback loop back to the brain. Thus once you have control over the sound pattern you hear, you have control over the electrical activity of your brain, which, in turn, appears to be related to states of consciousness. Table 3-1 gives some details about the relationship between brain wave activity and states of consciousness. Figure 3-3 shows typical EEG patterns obtained off my chart recorder during efforts to achieve the various states of consciousness.

The four major types of brain wave patterns are alpha, beta, delta, and theta. The lowest and slowest so far detected range from below 1 to 4 Hz. This is the delta band.

People are generally asleep or unconscious if they are producing delta waves in any significant amount. At least this is the case with "normal" untrained people. Yogis have, in the research laboratories, been able to produce predominately delta waves while in a deep trance but still quite conscious. The next higher band is the *theta band,* which includes frequencies of from 4 to 8 Hz. These are the waves normally produced by people about to fall asleep. The state of consciousness is subliminal and we often see dreamlike images called hypnagogic images in this state. These images are not daydream type thoughts or images but projections from unconscious sources in our mind. They are often surprising and startling because they appear seemingly out of nowhere.

The Alpha rhythm band, from 8 to 13 Hz, is associated with a state of greater awareness than the theta state. Unless you have trained yourself to do so you cannot hold on to full consciousness in the theta state, but everyone maintains awareness during the state signaled by the predominate production of Alpha waves. These waves do appear in much greater profusion with the eyes closed, however, in fact, all that is required to produce brief bursts of alpha waves is to

Table 3-I. Typical Brain Waves.

Brain Wave Designation	Frequency Range	Associated State of Consciousness
DELTA	0.5-4Hz	Unconscious, deep sleep or other non-REM sleep state.
THETA	4-8Hz	Reverie state, drowsy, near unconscious & aware of dreamlike or hypnagogic images.
ALPHA	8-13Hz	Alert and aware but unfocused on outside world. Attention directed inward.
BETA	13-26+Hz	Alert and focused on outside world. Concrete thinking and observing state.

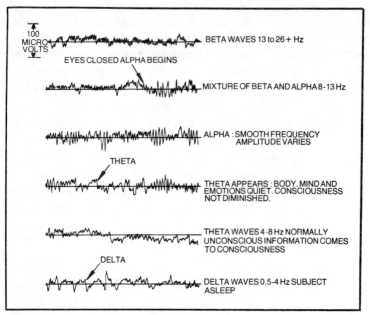

Fig. 3-3. EEG patterns from strip chart recorder.

close your eyes for a second or two. Even with the eyes open if the focus of your attention is on some daydream or other interior image you will produce lots of alpha. You will not, however, be paying attention to what your eyes are pointed at and your eyes will appear to others to be glazed. There is often heightened awareness during alpha production in spite of it being a tranquil, meditative state of consciousness.

The beta band, from 13Hz up, is nearly always associated with an active state of consciousness where attention is focused on the outside world and thinking is quite concrete, even mathematical. Whatever state a person is in as soon as you ask him/her to do some simple mental arithmetic like subtract 18 from 48, the brain will shift immediately into beta to do the job. Although, if you give a person a task to do in his head and he cannot remember how to do it, he will go into an alpha state while searching his memory.

In summary, to keep it simple, then we can say that ordinary people produce beta waves when alert and focused on a task, alpha when alert but not focused, theta when drowsy or in state of reverie, and delta when deeply asleep.

When dreaming we are in a state of consciousness that has been termed REM (for rapid-eye movement, which always occurs during dreaming when the eyes dart rapidly back and forth) and in that state the brain waves appear in patterns that would look like an awake brain, with beta, alpha, or theta activity depending on what was being experienced in the dream.

It is interesting to note that a widely reported 1963 study of the brainwave activity of Japanese Zen monks, some of whom were masters of *zazen,* the Zen way of meditation, showed that as they began to turn their attention inward long trains of alpha appeared on the recording charts. As more time passed the brain waves decreased and hovered at the alpha-theta border line, around 8 Hz. Those who were considered to be most talented at reaching a deep state of meditation produced long trains of theta waves. The Zen Buddists identify this state of consciousness with a state of "knowing," rather than "thinking."

This is especially interesting because Dr. E.D. Dean trains his business executives to produce these long trains of theta waves in order to reach a state of consciousness in which they can tap their intuitive faculty and heighten their ESP functioning.

Alyce Green, working at the Menninger Foundation, in her extensive studies of creativity has found that many artists and scientists who have been unusually creative in their fields describe a kind of near dream state of reverie where intuitive ideas appear to come to them often in the form of hypnagogic images. From these clues she and her husband, Dr. Elmer Green developed their now famous "psychophysiological training for creativity," which involves deep relaxation plus the feedback of theta brain waves to increase their production. With your own brain wave monitor able to feed back alpha and theta waves you can certainly, with a good dose of consistent practice learn truly how to relax and increase your intuitive and creative abilities. This will also raise your PSI-Q, or ESP abilities many fold.

HOW TO BUILD A SIMPLIFIED
ALPHA-THETA BRAIN-WAVE FEEDBACK MONITOR

The schematic shown in Fig. 3-4 details the circuit for this simplified machine for brain wave feedback. It is designed for nonmedical uses and so does not need a lot of the electronics found in medical EEG amplifiers and recording devices. While an output is provided for the chart recorder described in Chapter 2 to make this a complete EEG machine, the feedback is provided by either an amplitude-or frequency-modulated fixed tone available by adjusting the tone-threshold control. The frequency modulation is included because of my aforementioned idea that phase relationships are more important than amplitude changes in things of the mind.

Electrodes for picking up the mini currents and potentials from the scalp are much more critical than those used in previous projects concerned with the resistance of plant leaves and human skin. Requirements for EEG electrodes include that they should not generate tiny noise spikes or drift voltages. Stainless steel is not a good choice of electrode material because it tends to do both of the above. Silver electrodes can be used if coated with chloride. Any medical supply house can supply so-called disposable EEG electrodes of the chloride coated silver type (Ag/Ag-C1). With care and good cleaning they will last a long time before the chloride coating wears off. At this writing a set of these electrodes could be had for about five dollars from Extended Digital Concepts, P.O. Box 9161, Berkeley, CA 94709. Much more expensive but trouble free and lasting forever are the pellet-type Ag/Ag-C1 electrodes. If you have a lot of friends who will bug you for free alpha-theta training these might be a good idea for the long run.

The electrodes in our monitor are direct coupled to a differential op amp of the instrumentation type using two low bias ICs providing good rejection of interference and erroneous signals.

The output of the op-amps feeds into a network of filters designed to separate out alpha, beta and theta frequencies. A four pole, three position switch will pass your choice of frequencies on to modulate the audio oscillator. Modulation—either AM or FM, can take place either in the direct or integrated mode. In the direct mode the brain wave form modulates an adjustable tone which gives one the feeling of being in direct touch with the brain—actually tuning in on the brainwaves themselves. It also subjects you to a continuous sound. By setting the oscillator just below its threshold point only the peaks of the brain wave forms will trigger the tone which integrates the wave form over time and gives a discontinuous sound which most people find less objectionable than listening to a tone constantly.

Finally, the modulated audio signal is amplified and fed to a pillow speaker, or a regular speaker, or a headset, if that is preferred through a headphone coupler from the speaker terminals. An auxiliary output is provided for a chart recorder.

Parts

B1,B2,B3 - 9 volt batteries
C1 - 1μF metalized film capacitor
C2 - .01μF disc capacitor
C3,C4 - 0.2μF metalized film capacitor
C5 - .001μF metalized film capacitor
C6,C7 - 0.2μF metalized film capacitors
C8,C9 - 0.1μF metalized film capacitors
C10,C11 - 100μF 2-volt electrolytic capacitors
D1,D2 - IN4003 silicon diodes
Headphone coupler-Radio Shack 33-1009
IC1,IC2 - N5556 op amp (Signetics)
IC3,IC4,IC5,IC6,IC7 - 741C op amp
J1 - contact 3-wire polarized socket
J2,J3 - contact 2-wire polarized sockets
Q1 - TIS58 field effect transistor
Q2 - 2N4250 transistor
Q3 - 2N3565 transistor
(note: all fixed resistors ¼-watt, 5% tolerance)
R1 - 1K resistor
R2,R3 - 47K resistor
R4,R5 - 3.9K resistors

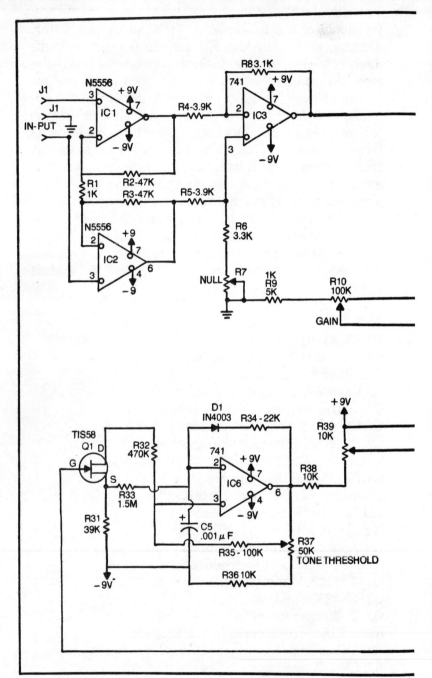

Fig. 3-4. Brain wave monitor.

114

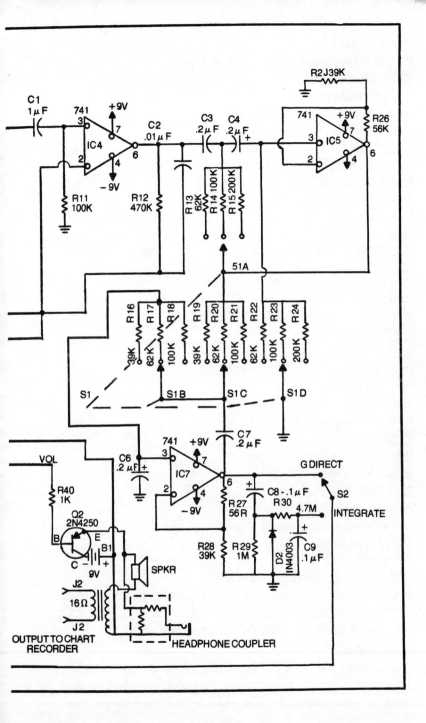

115

R6 - 3.3K resistor
R7 - 1K potentiometer (PC trimmer type)
R8 - 3.1K resistor
R9 - 5K resistor
R10 - 100K mini potentiometer
R11 - 100K resistor
R12 - 470K resistor
R13, R17, R20, R22 - 62K resistors
R14, R18, R21, R23 - 100K resistors
R15, R24 - 200K resistors
R16, R19 - 39K resistors
R25 - 39K resistor
R26, R27 - 56K resistors
R28 - 39K resistor
R29 - 1M resistor
R30 - 4.7M resistor
R31 - 39K resistor
R32 - 470K resistor
R33 - 1.5M resistor
R34 - 22K resistor
R35 - 100K resistor
R36 - 10K resistor
R37 - 50K mini potentiometer
R38 - 10K resistor
R39 - 10K mini potentiometer
R40 - 1K resistor
R 41, R42 - 22K resistor
R43 - 5K resistor
S1 - shorting rotary switch, 4-pole, 3-position
S2 - spdt switch
S3 - spst switch
SPKR - 8-ohm mini or pillow speaker
Misc. - electrodes, electrode cream, earclip, headband, 4-6
    feet shielded flexible cable, 2-wire; metal cabinet, PC
    board, knobs, battery holders, hardware, etc.

Construction

Constructed on a PC board the parts lay out for easy construction for this project. Just be careful to observe the notch and dot code of the ICs. Double and triple check your wiring of the diodes and transistors to be sure the lettered terminals correspond to those on the schematic.

Install the three potentiometers as well as the three switches on the front panel. Solder all resistors connected to the rotary switch (S1) directly onto the terminals on the switch with fine solder and a low-powered soldering iron.

If you use a mini speaker, cement it to the front panel and drill a few holes to let the sound come through. If you use a pillow speaker, mount a connecting jack on the front panel. No reason why you can't use both with a jack to take the speaker out when the pillow speaker is plugged in.

The ear clip should be soldered to the shield on the two-wire cable and grounded through the three way socket (J1) to the monitor. Remove about a foot of the shielded covering on the electrode cable by unwinding it. Twist it into conductor form and solder it to the ear clip. Then remove about ½-inch of insulation from the two insulated wire leads and solder to the electrodes.

The power supply is battery with a source follower (Q3) to create a low-impedance ground about half way between the plus and minus 9V. supply (see the schematic of Fig. 3-5).

Under no circumstances should you operate this or any other biofeedback equipment with an ac source through a battery eliminator, hooked up to an oscilloscope or other equipment operated from the conventional ac powerline source. The battery operation of this, as well as most commercial machines is to prevent shock should the power line source short to the inputs. Any time that ac equipment is hooked up to EEG monitors in the laboratory light coupling systems are used to isolate the power line from the subject or patient. Operating on 9 volt batteries the device is completely safe no matter what. To avoid feedback a separate battery is used for the Q2/speaker circuit. This circuit does not need the plus and minus 9V supply (see the schematic of Fig. 3-5).

Testing—Alpha, Beta, Theta

With fresh alkaline batteries installed, turn the power switch (S3) on and adjust the tone threshold control (R37)

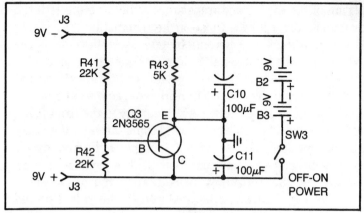

Fig. 3-5. Power supply with low-impedance ground.

until a tone is heard. Set the brain wave select switch (S1) to
the theta band (4-8Hz) and with S2 select the direct mode
position. Clip the ground lead to one of your earlobes (don't
forget to use a little electrode cream) and (using plenty of
electrode cream) hold one electrode in each hand. You
should now be hearing a beep, beep, beep, which is the beat
of your heart. This pulse signal picked up from your hands is
a very strong signal compared to the signal you will get from
your brain even in the high amplitude alpha and theta bands,
so if you do not hear your heart beat, go back to the PC board
and check your wiring. If you use a scope and signal
generator to check out your wiring, the dc output of all op
amps should be near zero when feeding an attenuated signal.

Once your monitor tests out okay, your differential
amplifiers need to be balanced to assure maximum noise
rejection. To do this job by ear, ground the electrodes
through a 10,000-ohm resistor and then touch the common
leads. You will hear ambient ac noise picked up by your body.
Adjust R7—the noise null control—for a clear tone with
minimum noise. The noise null control is a kind of trimmer
pot to trim the gain of one side of the differential amplifer so
that the gain of one side is exactly the same as the gain of the
other side. When they are in perfect balance noise rejection
is maximum. If you have a VTVM or scope, feed it with the
output of IC4. Feed a common mode signal of about 4 volts

into both inputs tied together across a 10,000-ohm resistor. Now adjust the null control (R7) for the weakest signal. Now you are ready for the brain wave pick up.

Hooking up the Monitor

The best contact is made with your brain if you float your electrodes on cream just above the scalp. Wrap a soft cloth band around your head so that it crosses the widest part of the back of the head and covers the eyebrows in front. Coat one of the electrodes with cream and tuck it under the band just above the eyebrow on either the left or right side of your head. Use a bit more cream on the second electrode and place it at the rear of your head *directly in line with the front electrode*. Spread your hair apart so that good contact with the scalp is had through the electrode cream. With this place-ment you will be picking up on your occipital brain waves. Brain waves from this source are the ones most widely used for bio-feedback training. Both electrodes can be placed on the forehead to pick up waves from the frontal lobes of the brain. In deep states of meditation alpha and theta production also increases from this area of the brain. However, if you are a beginner you will find it easier to control the waves eminating from the occipital area of the brain.

You will want to train yourself to produce alpha brain waves before you try for the theta band, and since you will be mostly in the beta state as you settle down to use your monitor, switch your brain wave select control to Alpha (8 to 13 Hz range). With the mode switch in *direct* turn the gain all the way down and adjust the tone volume to a pleasing level. You should hear a bleep when you blink your eyes. Slowly advance the gain control and with your eyes open and focused adjust the gain for a fairly steady tone. You will not be producing much alpha yet and, of course, the beta waves are being filtered out so you are not hearing them. Now, sit down and make yourself comfortable (I like a recliner chair and speaker pillow at this point), close your eyes and listen for a rhythmic modulation of the tone. *Do not make any effort to produce this rhythmic modulation*—you cannot control your brain by will power. Let your mind go free wheeling along and just *listen* for this modulated tone to happen. Expect it to happen, but don't try to make it happen. This process was aptly described by Ogden Nash in his little poem about inspiration:

"Inspiration is like a cat,
Pursue it and you don't know where you're at,
Try to shoo it out of the house
And it brings you an inspiration mouse!"

I find going through the Autogenic exercises suggested in Chapter 1 (see Table 1-1) gets me started producing alpha brain waves. Once I hear them beginning to modulate the tone, I conjure up a great Science Fiction daydream about traveling out through space. By the time I have propelled myself out to the asteroid belt and start playing around with a comet or two, I find I am producing trains of alpha waves.

Once you are confident you are producing some alpha waves you can flip your mode switch (S2) to *integrate* and adjust the tone threshold control (R37) so that no tone can be heard when you are in an eyes-open-adjusting-the-equipment mode. Now close your eyes and see if you can turn the tone on. The more alpha you produce the more often the tone will come on. This is called percent training. When you get pretty good at that you can try increasing the frequency of the tone which is amplitude training.

I have found amplitude training to be most useful in the theta band which you will want to graduate to when you have mastered the alpha state of consciousness. Repeat all of the above steps with your brain wave select switch on the theta band (4-8Hz), then go after those hypnogogic images that tend to sneak into your meditative mood when you are into your alpha level. Very often these will be faces of all sorts of strange folk. They will zoom in and out and move across your closed eyelids. It will take you a while to become aware that they are there. Sometimes you will only see designs or patterns and always they will be quite elusive. The more you concentrate on seeing what they are the faster they disappear like zooming out through the wrong end of a telescope. Don't be discouraged if you find that you fall asleep while in the alpha state of consciousness and skip down to delta without being aware of your theta state. That is a usual experience. Those of us who meditate don't like to admit it but we really do spend a lot of our meditative time sleeping! Once you begin to get control of your brain, however, instead of always letting your brain control you, you will find you are able to keep yourself in that delightful "twilight zone" between being asleep and awake for longer and longer periods of time. One way I find of keeping myself in this state of consciousness and of increasing the amplitude of my theta waves (by increasing the frequency of the tone) is to expect that the tone frequency will increase and be accompanied by flashes of inspiration about novel ways to solve problems and new things I might create. I use my imagination and pretend that these things will come to me in literal flashes of light, like lightning revealing a whole countryside on a dark and stormy night. Sometimes, this really does happen, and I see revealed in the briefest instant a whole solution to a problem, an entire design, a new book, or a completely new system of electronics.

This is not a thinking man's solution; it is as the Zen monks have termed, "a knowing state of consciousness." It is often accompanied by a sharp increase in tone on the feedback monitor indicating a burst of high amplitude theta waves accompanying the inspirational flash as a clap of thunder accompanies a flash of lighting. One sees wholes and not parts and, of course, you have to later take your inspirational whole apart and put it into a linear time frame to make reality out of your vision. Sometimes there will be no vision at all, but only a strong hunch that something is true or that something ought to go together in such-and-such a way.

I find, too, that sometimes I can't remember this great thing I saw in detail. Like the writer of the lyrics of the song, "The Lost Chord" relates, he remembers hearing this fantastic musical chord but can't remember how to play it again!

Seated one day at the brain wave monitor, I had a very similar experience while doing amplitude training in the theta band. I was tooling along through the darkness expecting the tone to increase in frequency, which it was doing very slowly, when I got a sudden image of a winding stairway. The view was from the top, and at the bottom was a colorful luminous mosaic—like an inlaid stain glass window in the floor. The colors were breathtaking and more luminous than anything I had ever seen in real life. The pattern was fantastic, and I caught the motif. The whole scene faded away very slowly, and the tone in my ears warbled in the high register. I still have to say it was the most beautiful thing I have ever seen, and while I remember the *experience* and the thrill of seeing such beauty, I could not, five minutes after or still to this day, begin to construct such a design in reality, though I have tried many times to make a mosaic of ceramic tile that would approach it. So don't be too disappointed if you lose a chord, or a stained glass window in the floor, occasionally. Your Alpha training will pay off in enabling you to truly relax, and your theta training will pay big dividends in creativity. And both will likely raise your PSI-Q many, many points. While you are in the process of training yourself, be alert for ESP type experiences, they happen with much greater frequency when one is in the state of consciousness characterized by the production of large-amplitude theta waves.

Chapter 4
The Control of Psychokinetic Energy

A funny thing happened to me on my way to trying to understand the wild an wooly world of psychokinetic energy. While stalking the wild Hieronymus machine (the schematic diagram of the machine works just as well as the machine itself!), the peculiar power of pyramids, the psycho behavior of psychotronic generators, and the well documented apparent ability of the mind to alter the randomness of radio activity at the subatomic level, I stumbled on to the secret of the control of psychokinetic energy. I shall reveal it here for the first time.

I surely hope you have a sense of humor, for if you do, you will get some great insights from what I am about to reveal to you—and you will have a ball with these projects which really do run and work under the control of your mind. If you do *not* have a sense of humor, you will probably brand me a smart alec, a spoil sport, or worse. At least you will think I am pulling your leg, but I'm not really. For while these projects do, as I said, operate under the control of your mind, they do not do so in the occult way we have all been led to believe (or perhaps hope?) they might.

As I said, a funny thing happened to me. I had spent a couple of years researching this strange energy that everyone seemed to have a different name for. In approximate order of historical appearance, I made a list that looked something like this:

Ancient Hindu	Prana
Alchemists of Old	Vital Fluid
Anton Mesmer	Universal Fluid
Baron Karl von Reichenbach	Odic Force
Dr. William Reich	Orgone Energy
George de la Warr	Prephysical Energy
T. Galen Hieronymous	Eloptic Energy
Robert Pavlita	Psychotronic Energy
Various Soviet Researchers	Bioplasma
Dr. Robert Miller	Paraelectricity
Everybody who isn't anybody	Psychokinetic or PK Energy

I had also acquired a list compiled by Sheila Ostrander and Lynn Schroeder (authors of *Psychic Discoveries Behind the Iron Curtain,* Prentice-Hall, 1970) which described some of the commonly agreed-upon features of the mysterious which was supposed to help me recognize it, should it suddenly appear to me.

PROPERTIES OF THE ENERGY OF A THOUSAND NAMES

It permeates all things to a greater or lesser degree. It accompanies sunlight and probably other forms of light. It has properties similar to other forms of energy but is a distinct energy. It accompanies magnetism but also appears separately. It is polarized and can be reflected by mirrors. It emanates from the human body and has been particularly noted at the fingertips and the eyes. It can heal or, used negatively, can harm living creatures. It can be conducted by such things as copper wires and silk threads. It can be stored in inanimate materials such as water, wood and even stone. It can fluctuate with cosmic and weather conditions. It can be controlled by mind. It can cause things to happen at a distance and enters into the dynamics of many paranormal phenomena.

In addition, this energy is claimed to be cosmic in nature, yet very personal. We all have it; we just have not learned how to control it consciously. Those few who have—the gurus, healers, and PK psychics—are able to bend spoons and work other "miracles." In fact, I have read a statement made by the Russian physiologist, Dr. Leonid L.

Vasiliev (said to be the father of Soviet parapsychology) to the effect that: "The discovery of the energies associated with psychic events will be as important, if not more important, than the discovery of atomic energy."

So what about that funny thing that happened? I picked up my copy of *Scientific American* one month and, as I always have, I turned first to my favorite feature, Martin Gardner's column on mathematical and scientific fun and games. Gardner is neither a mathematician nor a scientist, but he is a marvelous writer and editor with a great sense of humor (he became famous as the editor of *Humpty Dumpty's Magazine* for children). But little did I suspect on that fateful day that he was—because of these qualities and this background— eminently qualified to stumble unknowingly onto the secret of the ages. I think the principle is that "Ye must become as little children" to arrive at the ultimate wisdom, or something like that.

Gardner's column that month was one of many in which he has aimed his barbed wit slingshot at parapsychology and its myriad of false prophets; in fact, Martin Gardner has probably ripped the sheep's clothing off more psychic wolves than even The Amazing Randi. This column, however, was especially funny after what I had been trying seriously to figure out what made Czech researcher Robert Pavlita and his psychotronic engine run.

With his best poker face forward, Gardner's column announced a motor that would run on your psychic energy. It was, he related, an invention of Dr. Robert Ripoff, founder of the "Institute for the Investigation of Mammalian Auras."

To build the psychic motor, one was supposed to cut a rectangle from heavy paper, bend it into a cylinder, and then cut two slots on opposite sides of each other one-half inch from the top (see Fig. 4-1). Push a needle through a smaller strip of paper and insert the ends through the cylinder slots. Balance the whole apparatus on top of a bottle with a hard cap (Fig. 4-2).

I must now give you Gardner's verbatim instructions on how to operate the motor: "Place the little motor on a copy of the Bible or *I Ching*, with the book's spine running north and

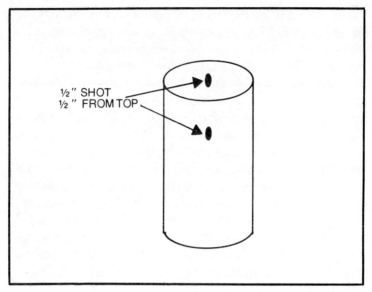

½" SHOT
½" FROM TOP

Fig. 4-1. Bend 5½" × 8½" cardboard rectangle into a cylinder.

south, and hold your hand close to the cylinder without actually touching it—make your mind blanker than usual." After about a minute, Gardner promised, the cylinder will start to rotate.

After wiping the tears of laughter from my eyes and settling down to a low rumbling series of chuckles I got out my scissors and paste and constructed the Ripoff Motor. In best *Humpty Dumpty's* tradition I simply cannot resist doing any project suggested by Martin Gardner. It just happened that I had a copy of the *I Ching* lying about, loaned to me by a friend who knew I was interested in the far out pursuit of wisdom, ancient and modern. I even had a good north and south orientation marked on my work table because I had been fooling around with pyramids.

After all was cut and pasted, oriented and mounted, of course the little engine could and did work. But alas, as Gardner ultimately pointed out, it was driven not by one of the thousand names of psychic energy, but from convection currents set up by the heat of the hands. As I sat hunched over my little motor running by the mundane laws of physics, playing with my latest toy, I ruminated over my first experience with what was called the *PK effect* by my first instructor in my first formal course in parapsychology. The instructor had us construct something similar to Gardner's machine, although it was simpler. It was a soda straw bent in the exact center and balanced on a needle stuck in a piece of cork (see Fig. 4-3). The instructor called this a PK trainer and indeed gave us instructions very similar to the instructions one receives when undergoing biofeedback training.

"Don't try to will the straw to turn," the instructor had told us, "just expect it to and, holding your hands close to but not touching each end of the straw, try to engage in some playful mental activity that will start the straw turning. You will soon teach yourself what you have to do in order to control the direction of and speed of motion."

After suspecting that some of my classmates were running their trainers on surreptitiously exhaled breath but taking pains to make certain mine was not running that way, I concluded at the time that I surely must be tapping that mysterious energy of a thousand names. Now I had been

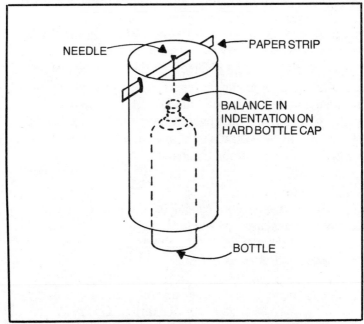

NEEDLE — PAPER STRIP

BALANCE IN INDENTATION ON HARD BOTTLE CAP

BOTTLE

Fig. 4-2. The Ripoff Psychic Motor (A Martin Gardner Spoof).

127

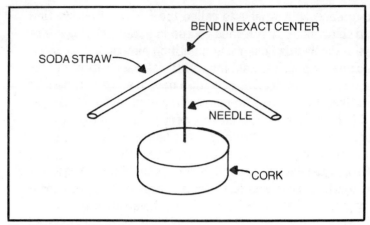

Fig. 4-3. Simple PK training device.

enlightened. It was just plain old, Gardner variety thermal energy making waves in the air. I'll admit I felt a tinge of disappointment. And then the lightning struck me. I must have given off an unprecedented burst of high-amplitude theta brain waves. My wife said at the time that my eyes were indeed glazed over, for it occurred to me that it was actually thermal energy I had learned to control in biofeedback training. I could, *using my mind alone*, run my hands through a 20°F variation in temperature. And was it not *thermal energy* the monks of Tibet learned to manipulate on those cold and dark mountain tops? To be initiated into the club these candidates for psychic honors would spend the night by a frozen lake clad only in their thin orange robes. Slipping out of these they would dip symbolic white robes into the icy water and drape the instantly frozen robe around their nude bodies. And how did they keep score? Who was the mightiest psychic?

The number of robes a candidate could melt in a single night gave his teacher a reading on the level of the candidate's spiritual development! Mind over matter brought to you by thought control over heat!

Quickly I dug out my list of "Properties of the Energy of a Thousand Names," and asked myself if thermal energy would not answer each and every criterion. Go try it. Our suspect fits all the clues!

When I got down the list to the one that reads, "It can fluctuate with cosmic and weather conditions," I thought of my lawn chair out on my patio. I had just looked out through my sliding glass door to see it moving seemingly by some unseen force, scooting across the patio. And although I could not see or hear the wind from where I sat, I knew, of course, that the light aluminum chair was being pushed by the wind. But was not the wind a result of thermal energies playing in the atmosphere? The moving chair gave the appearance of what has been described in the literature as the *Poltergeist phenomenon*. That's when pieces of furniture, dishes, and such go tumbling about or sailing through the air—often accompanied by "cool draughts of air." Could it be, I wondered, that even these manifestations of psychokinetics (PK) are due to mind-affecting thermal energies which in turn react on atmospheric pressures to push and shove things about? After all, it takes only a slight difference in air pressure between the upper and lower surface of the wings on a Boeing 747 to levitate it right up into the wild blue yonder. It would take even less of a pressure difference to levitate a table or a yogi a few inches off the floor. And we know that small differences in temperature between layers of air can trigger the awesome distructive power of a tornado. If you placed your hand in slipstream at the top of the wing of a flying aircraft you would feel the blowing wind. And if you felt the slipstream on the bottom of the wing you would also feel the same amount of wind. You would not likely be able to feel the slight difference in wind velocities that was keeping the craft air borne even though the aircraft might weigh several tons. Perhaps the physical events taking place around PK phenomenon are just as subtle. Not knowing the physics involved, we would attribute the wind on the wings of an aircraft to its forward motion—and we could prove that we are correct. We might easily overlook the fact that the air was moving ever so much more slowly over the curved top surface than over the straight bottom surface and that it was this little bit of difference that keeps tons of metal and glass and plastics and people flying about all over the world. Just as I was about to overlook the fact that it was indeed my mind that kept my hands warm that made the convection currents that turned the straw or the cardboard cylinder and therefore we did have a legitimate "psychic" device. Not only that, by changing the temperature of the skin of one's hands, or by making one hand cold and the other warm the *movement* of the convection currents could be changed by thought alone and thus movement of the device could be brought under mental control. Won't Martin Gardner be surprised? Perhaps he will now want to put out his own magazine of cut-and-paste psychic motors.

It also occurred to me in that great burst of theta lightning that it is thermal energy that not only makes the world go round but that keeps the sun shining and all living organisms living. And after all, what is "atomic" energy but thermal energy generated in huge amounts in short time spans?

Vasiliev was right about the energies associated with psychic events being more important than the discovery of atomic energy (if I am right in my insight that it is thermal energy) but he was wrong in assuming that it had yet to be discovered. After all, Lord Kelvin tumbled to it more than a hundred years ago, and Maxwell's Demon played psychic for years after! The laws of thermodynamics apparently haven't recovered yet.

About all that remains now is for us to invoke Bell's Theorem and keep in mind the EPR effect (see the "Introduction") and perhaps a few other scraps of quantum mechanics and we can begin to explain and predict a whole universe of PK events. After all, if an electron can know that its distant twin has changed spin and turn around with no further prompting, perhaps molecules can know what other molecules are doing and change velocities on cue, too. The thermal energy of any substance is a factor of the average speed of its constantly moving molecules. By using my mind to change the speed of the molecules in my own body what effect might I be having, or be able to have on molecules elsewhere? How might the power of my changing molecular speeds be multiplied through resonance effects?

What might my thermal energies do if I can keep the

waves all in step? As I think I have mentioned before it appears to be the *phase relationships* (not the *amplitudes*) that we need to pay attention to to perform "miracles" and to understand them. After all, it is not intensely *bright* light that drills through steel. It is rather a dim light, as a matter of fact, but a light whose waves are in a very special phase relationship. And so what really leaves me awe struck from this funny thing that happened to me on my way to trying to understand psychokinetic energy that day, is to wonder what fantastic feats of physical events I might be able to trigger off with my simple ability to change the temperature of my hands by a couple dozen degrees F? You see, when you come up with an answer of some kind, what happens is that you raise all kinds of questions you never had to deal with before you got so smart! But they are all questions that sent me back to the electronic drawing board because they are all the kinds of questions our solid state technology can help us answer.

CONSTRUCTING TRAINING MACHINES FOR THE DEVELOPMENT OF PK ENERGIES

One of the best training machines is still the soda straw on a needle device (Fig. 4-3). The straw floats on an almost frictionless bearing—the needle point—and is sensitive to the slightest convection currents. With out new enlightenment, however, we now know that we need a temperature probe for our hands to give us some feedback on the amount of thermal energy we are generating from our hands. Keep in mind that to achieve good control of the PK training device you will need to learn to cool your hands as well as heat them and to heat one and cool another. These changing thermal conditions will generate a variety of convection currents around your hand which will enable you to control both the speed and direction of rotation of the soda straw. One of the most useful temperature probes I have found for use in PK experiments is a 1N914 silicon diode used as one leg of a Wheatstone bridge connected to a digital multimeter.

DIODE TEMPERATURE SENSOR

The voltage drop across the diode junction of any conventional silicon diode changes at the rate of approximately 1¼-mV per degree F when a small forward bias is applied. Any diode, then, such as the low-cost readily available 1N914, can be used as your temperature probe.

Figure 4-4 shows a schematic diagram for the bridge circuit I use to feed into my DMM. It gives me accurate temperature readings from 32°F (0°C) to 212°F (100°C) on the 200-mV (for low temperatures) and the 2-volt (for high temperatures) dc ranges. And the displayed digits are the temperature—no conversion needed. Figure 4-5 shows the same circuit with different resistor values in case you want your temperature readout in degrees Celsius. A bypass capacitor is used across the diode leg of the bridge to get rid of any stray signals that might be picked up by the leads.

Parts

B1 - 1.5-volt battery
C1 - 0.01μF disc capacitor
D1 - 1N914 silicon diode
R1 - 33K ½-W resistor
R2 - 82K ½-W resistor (12K for C°)
R3 - 1K potentiometer
R4 - 56K ½-W resistor (68K for C°)
R5 - 10K potentiometer
R6 - 49K ½-W resistor (120K for C°)
R7 - 220K ½-W resistor (100K for C°)
Misc. - battery holder, flexible two-conductor cable, solder, etc.

Construction

Assemble the project on a small perforated board with wirewrap and solder. You will need a pc pad or wirewrap pin to make the connections to the remote diode sensor. The diode can be taped to your index finger with a small adhesive bandage to read hand temperature.

The ratios of the resistance values in the bridge are critical, while the values themselves are not. To calibrate your diode temperature probe, keep in mind that potentiometer R3 is the one that balances the bridge to indicate the freezing point. When the probe is submerged in crushed ice you will adjust R3 so that the digital readout from your multimeter reads 32 or 0, depending on whether you are interested in reading Fahrenheit or Celsius. R5 is then used to reduce the 1.25-mV/°F (it is 2.24-mV/°C) to exactly 1mV per degree. R5 is also used to set the upper range point. The diode will need to be floating on the surface of boiling water with the DMM switched to its 2-volt range when R5 is adjusted to give a reading of 212 for degrees Fahrenheit or 100 for degrees Celsius.

The boiling point of water is just about the limit for the plastic insulation used for diodes leads so do not submerge the diode completely in the boiling water for more than a few seconds to make this calibration adjustment. You can get an accurate adjustment by surface to surface contact only between diode and water surface. If you wish you can make the diode safe for immersion simply by slipping a short length of vinyl tubing filled with epoxy up around the diode leads and over the ends of the diode to protect the insulation. Be sure the epoxy has cured for at least 24 hours, however, before you dunk the diode in boiling water. Heatshrink tubing will also work and can be shrunk for a tight fit.

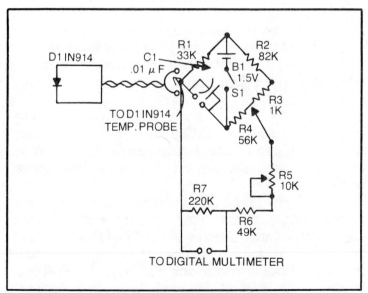

Fig. 4-4. Schematic diagram for bridge circuit to feed DMM.

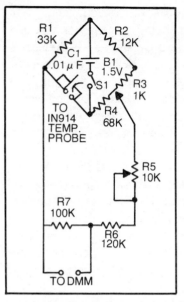

Fig. 4-5. Bridge circuit to feed DMM for Celsius readings.

For uses in training exercises to learn to control psychokinetic devices, or to make demonstrations of "psychokinetic" energy you will be mostly concerned with dry contact temperature measurements in the 65°-95°F (18°-35°C) range.

Another device that can be used as a temperature sensor is the LM334, an IC that looks more like a transistor (Fig. 4-6). The IC is ideal for an analogue type thermometer since its output voltage varies 10 millivolts per degree Celsius.

Figure 4-7 is the schematic for a basic analogue thermometer using an LM386 as a voltage amplifier. Amplification up to 200X is controled by R3. R4 can be adjusted to give a narrow or wide range of temperature readings.

To calibrate M1 for the narrow band most useful in our thermal training exercises we need to be able to read changes in fractions of degrees. For this kind of narrow range accuracy, I recommend the use of finger temperature indicator utilizing thermochromic liquid crystals. Bio-Temp Products, Inc., 3266 N. Meridian, Indianapolis, Indiana, 46208, distributes these handy little devices under the brand name of Biotic-Band for about $5 including postage. The range is 78°F to 98°F with color changes indicating a change of as little of ½°F. Your LM334 analogue thermometer can be calibrated directly by taping the LM334 to your finger beside the Biotic-Band. Once calibrated temperature changes much smaller than ½°F can be read on the meter, M1.

Parts

B1 - 9-volt battery
C1 - 10μF capacitor
C2 - 0.1μF capacitor
IC1 - LM334 IC, Radio Shack cat. #276-1734
IC2 - LM386 IC
M1 - 1mA meter
R1 - 220-ohm resistor
R2 - 10K resistor
R3 - 10K potentiometer
R4 - 10-ohm resistor
R5 - 25K potentiometer
Misc. - small pc-board, battery holder, two-conductor shielded cable. solder, etc.

Construction

Construct on pc-board or perf-board using wire wrapping soldering. Solder LM334 to two-conductor shielded cable for #3. Connect to board with push-in terminals. Be

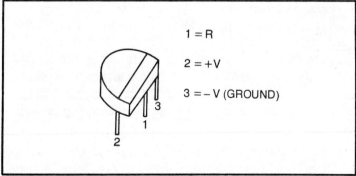

1 = R

2 = +V

3 = - V (GROUND)

Fig. 4-6. The LM 334, an IC that looks like a transistor.

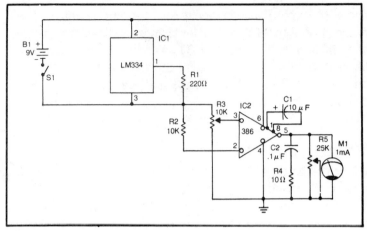

Fig. 4-7. Basic analogue thermometer.

sure to label wires and terminals so that 1 is always connected to 1, 2 to 2, and 3 to 3 (Fig. 4-8).

AN ELECTRONIC PSYCHOTRONIC
MACHINE YOU CAN RUN ON YOUR OWN PK ENERGY

The analog thermometer just described can be made into a dandy psychotronic machine that will run on your own PK energy with just a few variations in circuitry. The major change is to substitute a small hobby motor for the mA meter. Figure 4-9 gives the revised schematic diagram for this machine. I am sure that it is the world's first such device, a true psychic motor which you can start, stop, speed-up and slow-down by the use of thought gymnastics! It also makes a marvelous demonstrator of the interplay of forces that probably go to make up what is commonly called *psychic phenomenon*. If you use a model airplane propeller on the shaft of the motor, for example, you can stir up the air and create poltergeist-type effects (including levitation) in miniature. A kind of psychokinetic wind tunnel, maybe? Many different kinds of models can be run psychokinetically with your device.

Parts
B1 - 9-volt battery
C1 - .001μF capacitor

136

C2 - 10μF electrolytic capacitor

C3 - 0.1μF capacitor

IC1 - LM334

IC2 - LM386

Mo1 - 1-6VDC hobby motor (Radio Shack Cat. No. 273-206)

R1 - 220-ohm resistor

R2 - 10K resistor

R3 - 680-ohm resistor

R4 - 10K mini potentiometer

R5 - 10-ohm resistor

Misc. - perfboard, battery holder, 2-wire shielded cable, small box, hardware, solder, etc.

Construction

Construction is basically the same as the analog thermometer except that your perfboard can be mounted inside a small box with gain control knob and off-on switch on front panel of box and the motor mounted on top of the box, with clearance for model airplane propeller to go on shaft of the motor. Be sure that connector terminals for the LM334 are wired into the circuit properly and double check all wiring and capacitor polarities before switching on the power.

Operating the Psychic Engine

With power on and the LM334 temperature sensor taped to your hand (finger or palm), adjust R4 until the motor starts. Unless your hands are ice cold the motor should run

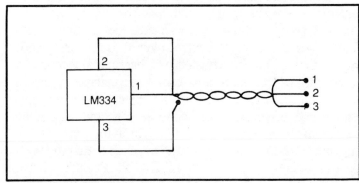

Fig. 4-8. IC temperature probe.

on the ambient heat of your hands with the pot wide open at least. This is your threshold control, so back it off until the motor stops. Next, go through your relaxation exercises and whatever imagery works to raise the temperature of your hand to the point where the little motor starts running. In the beginning it helps to have some temperature feedback to help you heat up your hand. A Biotic-Band is ideal for this purpose. You will want to practice both the warming and cooling of your hand so that you can mentally switch the motor on (by warming) and increase its speed and switch it off and slow it down (by cooling) without touching the threshold control.

Once you have achieved control over the motor with your thoughts you can then demonstrate the usual psychokinetic effects by placing objects in the slipstream of the propeller attached to the motor shaft. You can move doll furniture around in poltergeist fashion and even demonstrate table levitation of the type reported to take place during typical 19th century séances. You will need very careful adjustment of the slip stream so that it moves across the top of the table, but not underneath. The decreased air pressure on the top surface of the table will cause it to rise slightly, which, of course will put the bottom surface of the table into the slip stream and it will plop down again. Thus the table will actually jump about in just the fashion reported to take place in these feats of psychic levitation and object moving. The table will probably even tumble over from time to time. By mounting the motor on a swivel one can get a bit more control over the effects produced.

This psychic engine makes an excellent training device for learning more direct control over these psychokinetic effects. You not only teach yourself what mental gymnastics to go through to heat and cool your hands to create convection currents that move light objects about, you also demonstrate to yourself that it can be done and developing this firm belief seems to be a key factor in the repeatability and control of these macrocosmic psychokinetic effects. If we can believe the reports of Dr. V. Pushkin of the Psychology Institute of the Moscow Pedagogical Institute,

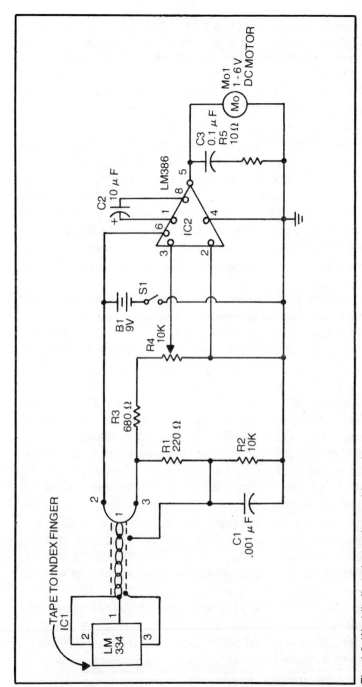

Fig. 4-9. World's first electronic psychic engine.

139

who has trained many people to do PK effects, it is possible to achieve some control over where and how the currents move. One of his students, for example, can allegedly cause a book to hang in the air on its own. This could be explained if there was a current of air moving over the top surface of the book but not over the bottom surface of the book. You might try that one for a graduation exercise.

Meanwhile, begin with light movable objects, preferably something that rolls easily. Favorite objects for me are light metal cigar containers, cigarettes, pingpong balls, lipsticks, and mobiles, in addition to Mr. Gardner's motor and my own balanced soda straw device. Keep your hand from touching the objects but place them near the object and try to attract or repel them with little convection currents generated by the heating and cooling of your hands. Use one hand or both.

As you progress with your experiments, and play with your electronics, it will become obvious to you that more is involved in the PK effect than convection currents. Those are only one of the secondary effects of the control of thermal energy. It appears quite possible to heat objects at a distance—to somehow bring distant molecules into resonance with the molecules in your own body and have them respond as if thermal energy is being induced from a distance. This heating effect is reported in almost all of the Russian experiments into psychokinesis but it is always interpreted as a side effect. So far as I know no one has considered the thermal effect as the primary effect of "mental control" and the PK effects or psychic events to be caused by the end of a chain of secondary effects. After all, thermal energy is easily converted into electrical energy, and vice versa. It may be that PK effects are difficult to bring about precisely because they are effects removed by several generations from the primary thing the mind is doing—they are, perhaps, "Rube Goldberg-type" chain reactions, difficult to control because of the many steps between initial mental effort and final effect. But nothing more mysterious than the mundane laws of physics along with some quantum mechanical effects in the macroscopic level is actually operating. Bell's theorem, for example would indicate that with a basic hologramic structure to the universe, no new "energy" or occult forces need be postulated to explain psychic phenomena. At least, if we give up the doctrine of Einstein separability that assumes that the world is made up of objects whose existence is independent of human consciousness, and go with the implications inherent in quantum mechanics and with facts established by recent experiments we do not need to discover any new form of energy or unmask any hidden forces. We need only change some of our basic assumptions. For example, if I had held on to the assumption taught in medical text books that I could not consciously control the temperature of my skin I would have concluded that the demonstrable control of our balanced soda straw PK device was "impossible by all the known laws of science." The fact is, of course, that there are many "laws of science" not yet known to us (otherwise what will our 21st and 22nd century physicists have to do?) and other "laws of science" that are simply in error, as recent experience in bio-feedback has shown.

Although scientific proof is always hard to come by, it is not at all hard to satisfy yourself of the fact that the world of objects "out there" and the world of mind "in here" is somehow inexorably connected. The best of devices for doing this job is the simple electronic coin tosser.

It is always possible, when tossing coins by hand, to influence the outcome of the toss by the way one handles the coin. So if you try mentally to influence the outcome and get a result that is better than 50-50 chance would allow, there is always the possibility that your influence was more kinetic than psycho! However, if you leave the coin tossing up to an impartial electronic circuit and the outcome is different from what the laws of chance allow, you can soon demonstrate, to your own satisfaction at least, that there is some connection between the electronic circuit and your mind.

ELECTRONIC COIN TOSSER

The schematic diagram of Fig. 4-10 illustrates an easy-to-build and inexpensive coin tosser that can be used

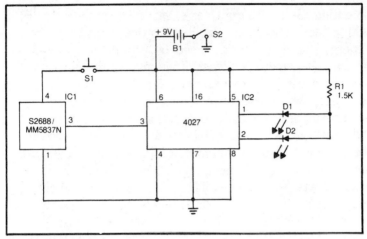

Fig. 4-10. Electronic coin tosser.

for many kinds of PK testing and experiments. If you care to build two of them you can play an electronic version of the famous Australian gambling game of "Two Up." When switch S1 is held down both diodes (D1 and D2) light up. When S1 is released one or the other will stay lit. Which one is a purely random event, like the toss of a coin. For playing two up, S1 on each coin tosser is released at the same time after betting on whether or not the same LED on each tosser will remain on.

Parts

B1 - 9-volt battery
D1, D2 - TLR-107 type LEDs, one red, one green
IC1 - S2688/mm5837N random generator IC
IC2 - 4027 dual JK flip flop IC
R1 - 1.5K resistor
S1 - momentary contact, normally open switch
Misc. - small perfboard, IC sockets, battery holder, hook-up
     wire, solder, etc.

Construction

Construction couldn't be simpler. You might wish to enclose it in a small cube with the LEDs, and S1 on top—make it a black box device. Double check your connections to the ICs and be sure to ground the inputs of the unused half of the 4027. This means grounding pins number 9, 10, 11, 12, and 13. If you build the Australian version you will be able to use the other half of the 4027 in conjunction with another S2688/mm5837N as the flip flop.

Operation and Control

The randomness of the coin tosser is assured by the IC1 chip which produces broadband white noise of a very uniform quality. It is produced by a 17-bit shift register which is clocked by an internal oscillator. It is this internal oscillator that you try to interfere with when using your PK on the sub-atomic level—the easiest level on which to push things around, because there is so little mass to contend with. On the other hand, you may be able to influence the oscillator on the molecular level by inducing heating. However, this can damage the IC if overdone, so keep your thoughts on the EPR effect at the subatomic level. Tell yourself that your mind and the oscillator are interconnected. Feel that they are as you push S1 to load the flip flop. As you hold the switch closed pretend that it makes a direct connection between your mind at the 4027. Instruct it to turn on the red light (or green, if that is your preference) and believe that your instruction will be followed as surely as your finger will follow your mind's instruction to release the switch. Each time your choice lights up congratulate yourself, give a cheer, be joyful about the event—have a thrill, like you won the Irish Sweepstakes. If you get bored with the process, or take it too seriously, any psi effect you might trigger will quickly extinguish itself. It was this fun and games aspect of PK that first got me interested in the strange energy events said to take place in a pyramid.

HOW TO BUILD AND USE PYRAMIDS

My father-in-law, Joseph Reiner, was a Czech who spend the first half of his life in central Europe. This included a stint of military service. Joseph apparently enjoyed his military service because he was always full of funny stories about the jokes constantly being played on and by him. At that time soldiers still used straight razors with which to shave. One of their gambits to tease someone and get them really angry was to put the man's razor on the window sill at night so that it was in the light of the full moon for many hours. This made the razor quite noticeably dull. Joseph's stories, of course, always dwelt on the reactions of the individuals to this prank and the fact that moonlight could dull the edge of a sharp razor blade was taken as a fact with which everyone must be familiar. I thought nothing of this "fact" so incidental to an amusing story until the day my parapsychology teacher broke out the pyramids and claimed that razor blades could be sharpened by placing them under a pyramid—provided the pyramid was constructed in exact scale to the great pyramid at Cheops and that one base line was oriented along a north-south line. Shades of Robert Ripoff!

But I dutifully did my homework in pyramidology, for I had promised myself that I would try with an open mind anything that parapsychology might claim no matter how ridiculous it might seem to my logical mind. My homework paid off with some 35 shaves from a Gillette "Blue Blade," which was some 30 shaves more than I could get from the same blade stored in a rectangular box made of the same cardboard as my pyramid. This was no where near the *hundreds* of shaves from the same Zenith blade claimed by Karel Drbal of Prague, holder of patent number 91304 on the Cheops Pyramid Razor Blade Sharpener, but it was enough to whet my curiosity about this obvious sharpening effect and to make me recall my father-in-law's stories about his pranks in the army. Were the Czechs now teasing their army buddies by putting their razors under pyramids to make them super sharp? And what about moonlight blunting a razor blade? The one thing seemed about as inane as the other. So the next night of the full moon I broke open a newly purchased package of razor blades (Gillette Thin-Blades this time) and placed two of the blades on a wooden potting table in my back yard where they would get moonlight all night long. The next morning I tried to shave with them and found that, sure enough, they were very dull. A third blade out of the same package, which I had kept in the dark all night, whisked my whiskers off with ease.

With silent apologies to my father-in-law for thinking all these years that he had probably just made up the stories involving the dulling of razors with moonlight, I went to see a friend of mine who was a rather broadminded physicist knowledgeable in metalurgy and ask him if he had any idea how moonlight could dull razor blades. (I did not mention the pyramid sharpening of blades—he was not THAT broadminded!) He did not have a ready explanation but he also did not seem to think it was so odd, after all. He pointed out that moonlight is reflected sunlight and as such is polarized. Polarized light, he said, falling on polished metal, often changes rectilinear polarization to elliptical, and that elliptically polarized light could have an effect on the crystalline structure of metallic molecules, especially iron. He then asked if the Czechs ever used a magnet to hasten the dulling effect of polarized light. I had to reply that magnets had not entered into any of my father-in-law's stories. He suggested that perhaps the *Faraday effect* might have something to do with solving the mystery. That effect he informed me, was one involving the rotation of light waves along the lines of force of a magnetic field in some substances that would otherwise not be affected by polarized light.

None of this seemed to shed much light—polarized or otherwise—on the parapsychology of pyramids until my encounter with the Gardner spoof honed my newsman's hunches to the fine edge of thermal energy. Pyramids were supposed to be collectors, storers and focusers of some mysterious cosmic energy that not only resharpened razor blades but also mummified organic matter—a kind of quick dehydration effect that could preserve foods in a jiffy just like a microwave oven could cook foods in a jiffy. Well, why not? Here is this Cheops pyramid—13 acrea of limestone, a 1,000 yards around the base—sitting in the middle of a desert at near equatorial latitudes. What a device for/collecting and storing that great cosmic energy, heat. It would certainly have a superb thermal flywheel effect, reradiating infrared heat energy inside and with its slanting walls not so much focusing the energy in the sense that elliptical geometry focuses microwave energy, but *polarizing* the infrared radiation by the angle of slant of the interior walls. Would polarized infrared "light" waves act as jiffy dehydrators and honers of tempered steel? What about the dulling effect by moonlight? Would you believe that razor blades exposed to moonlight in the presence of a magnetic field—provided the edge of the blade lies along the axis of the lines of flux—will stay nice and sharp? The antidote to the razor in the moonlight prank, then, would be to tape a magnet under your window sill! It appears that polarized light—and especially infrared light shakes up a thin layer of molecules. Magnetic field seems to line them all up again.

What does one's own energies have to do with the care and feeding of pyramids? The Czechs and the Russians seem to have much better luck keeping their razor blades sharp than we Americans do. There are lots of people I have talked to who can't seem to turn on any pyramid power at all. I find these to be the overly serious and doubting Thomas investigators with little or no sense of humor. The Czechs and the Russians were having great fun and joy with their little wonder Cheops Pyramid Razor-Blade Sharpeners. As one Czech put it, "You couldn't get imported razor blades, then, so you see the sharpener was working miracles with our inferior Czech blades!" In the Soviet Union, where the sharpeners were set up by the thousands in soldier's barracks, getting a decent razor blade in the USSR was so difficult that soviet newspapers and satirical magazines were full of jokes and cartoons about the quality of their home grown razor blades. I am convinced from my own experiments that this joking and lighthearted humor is part of the dynamics of our "toy" pyramids. It must be that we project our own thermal energy to the pyramid, which then collects, stores and polarizes it—reflecting it into the "Pharaoh's chamber" where it starts a chain reaction on the molecular and/or atomic level which results in the many reported Pyramid effects.

I must caution you again that you must not take your pyramid too seriously or you will attenuate the effect. The electronic pyramid will work for anybody. I invented it for sour pusses of all persuasions—and those who otherwise have trouble joking. Also those who have trouble letting go of their own thermal energy will find the use of a heat lamp over a pyramid of any construction will enhance their psychic performance.

There are several ways to go about constructing and experimenting with pyramids, but in all of them geometry is the critical factor. The slant of the walls has to do with the angle of polarization of infrared radiation among other things. And I am sure there are things still unknown that you may well discover about the dynamic effects of pyramid geometry.

Constructing a Pyramid From A Pattern

For those who would like a small pyramid, the easy way is to enlarge the pattern presented in Fig. 4-11. By bringing up each base line to approximately 6 inches, you will have a pyramid large enough to sharpen razor blades and dehydrate small bits of organic matter.

Your choice of material will be important in the construction of your pyramid. Material that is efficient at storing and reradiating heat is what you are after. Cardboard—compressed not corrugated—is quite good, and so is solid wood (better, by far, than plywood), and styrene plastic. Styrofoam is not a good material. For a large out doors, pyramid 6 or 8 inches of dirt is great sandwiched between plywood forms.

If you do not have a pantograph handy for enlarging Fig. 4-11, you can duplicate the pattern by scribing a circle 5-⅞-inches in diameter. Draw a line from the center of the circle to the circumference. Set your compass on 6-inches and mark off 6-inch lengths around the circumference, scribing a pentagon as shown in Fig. 4-12.

Cut out the shape along the solid 6-inch base lines and fold at the dotted lines. Tape the flap to the underside of the adjacent side. This will yield a pyramid about 4-inches high with a six inch base.

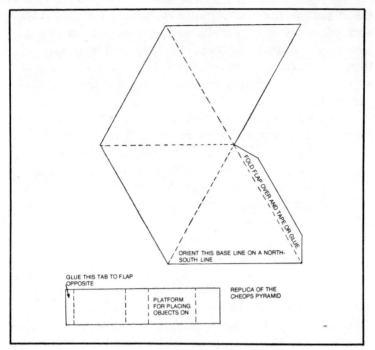

Fig. 4-11. Replica of the Cheops pyramid.

If you want a pyramid that measures in feet instead of inches, construct a wooden trammel from a yard or meter stick or other narrow slat slightly longer than the radius of the circle you wish to draw. Drill two holes, one near each end of the stick separated by the distance equal to the radius. Use a pencil in one hole and a nail in the other to draw the circle. Then use the trammel as you would a compass to scribe the pentagon. Cut out the individual equilateral triangles and assemble into a pyramid with angle irons bent to accommodate the proper angle.

If you would like a base for your pyramid simply cut a square piece of cardboard or wood a few inches bigger than the base. The pyramid can be hinged to this base for access to the Pharaoh's Chamber.

You will get the most effect from the polarized reradiation of infrared rays off the sides of your pyramid by placing the objects to be acted upon about one-third the height of the pyramid from floor to apex (See Fig. 4-13).

Each of the four sides should point in the direction of the four cardinal points of the compass. You may use a compass or the north star for this orientation. Pyramidologists have told me that these devices must be oriented to the true north-south line. True north-south, of course, differs by several degrees from magnetic north-south. If you are a purist you can consult an almanac for your locality to determine the declination in your area and make the adjustments accordingly. My own theories involve alignment along the earth's lines of magnetic force so I prefer a compass alignment. For the same reason I like to keep my pyramid clear of all man-made electromagnetic energy and noise.

If you wish to sharpen or repair thin cutting surfaces you need to align the cutting edge along a north-south magnetic line. For other purposes—dehydrating foods for preserva-

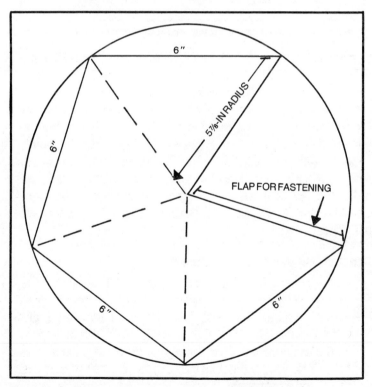

Fig. 4-12. Scribing a pentagon to construct a pyramid.

149

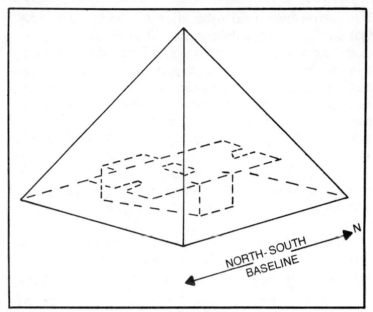

Fig. 4-13. Place objects one-third the height of the pyramid.

tion and salubrious effects on pets and people—you will have to experiment with alignment to see what works best. The only firm rule about things psychic is "what works works."

One thing that seem to work with pyramids of any size for any purpose is a supplemental input of infrared radiation via commercial heat lamp. Figure 4-14 illustrates this point. I have found the GE 250R40/10 heatlamp to be a rugged, safe, and long lived lamp for this purpose. The reradiated polarized radiation inside the pyramid appears to be more effective and far safer for long exposure than the direct rays of the heat lamp.

Constructing an Electronic Pyramid

The schematic diagram of Fig. 4-15 presents the electronic equivalent of the pyramid shape. Its geometry is electronic with a 555 timer IC driving an infrared Light Emitting Diode (D1). The light is polarized with an appropriate polarizing filter. Horizontal and diagonal polarization seem to work best, but get all three types of filter (vertical is the third) and experiment.

Parts

B1 - 9-volt battery

C1 - .33μF capacitor

D1 - infrared LED

IC1 - type 555 integrated circuit chip

P1 - 2 × 2″ polarizing filters, Edmund Scientific, Cat. #P41-168

R1 - 10K potentiometer

R2 - 1.2K resistor

R3 - 1K resistor

Misc. - small perfboard IC mounting socket, hardware for holding filter, solder, battery holder, etc.

Construction

Make it compact on a small square of perfboard with LED and filter holder on the underneath side so that the whole unit can be mounted in the top of a small pyramid, as shown in Fig. 4-16. Although the electronic pyramid was designed to operate by itself apart from any pyramid

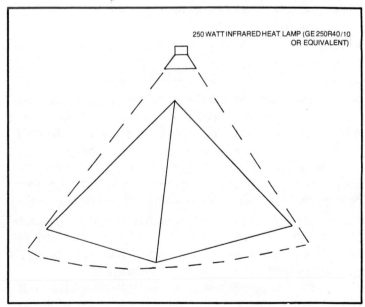

Fig. 4-14. Increase pyramid effect by placing ordinary pyramid in infrared heat lamp.

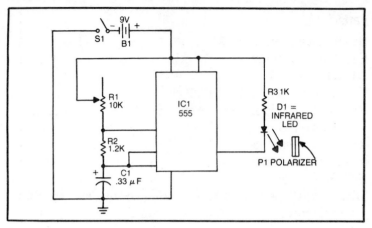

Fig. 4-15. Schematic for electronic pyramid.

structure—and it works well as a blade sharpener and dehydrator all on its own—you might want to mount one in a pyramid also to enhance the operation of the "natural" pyramid. Follow the usual precautions when wiring the IC and double check all your connections before turning on the power.

Once you have finished a pyramid, natural or electronic, or a combination of both, I suggest you throw a big party and christen it by some name. Have a pyramid "warming" by playing fun games and telling jokes and enjoying food and beverages. Let everybody participate in charging up the pyramid for your future activities. Any pyramid that has had this kind of send off will not fail or disappoint you. And don't be bashful about trying out far-out experiments with your pyramid, it is really quite an amazing device in spite of its deceptive simplicity. After all, historians tell us that the effort, expense, and national energy expended in the building of pyramids in ancient Egypt was every bit equivalent to the national effort we made to send men to the moon. If their pyramid building program was the analogue of our space exploration program what benefits must they have derived from their pyramids that are still unknown to us?

One of the benefits that we have derived from our pyramid experience is enhanced psychic abilities. Ruth, particularly, has found that by sitting in the Pharaoh's

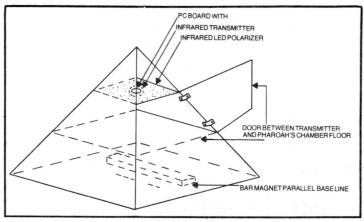

Fig. 4-16. Electronic pyramid placed inside ordinary pyramid.

Chamber of a person-sized pyramid her ability to distant view and precipitate clairvoyant experience is greatly enhanced.

Ruth's area of expertise and interest in parapsychology has centered around the detection and exploration of energy fields that have to do with the human body. She has been keeping our family healthy with no expenditure for medical bills or medicine of any kind for more than two years at this writing. By being alert to our energy fields we can see trouble coming and "ground" it before anyone gets sick—thus no "healing" as such is necessary—it is all preventative in nature, like the ancient Chinese practitioners who kept their clients healthy for which they were paid a fee. If one of their clients did get sick, treatment was on the house. If one of us should get sick we would, of course, not attempt to treat ourselves but go to the appropriate health specialist. But we know that treatment will not be on the house! And with the outlandishly high cost of medical treatment these days we find it pays just to stay well. So it will pay you big dividends to explore your energy fields and to get well aquainted with your aura and your acupressure points for these are the keys to staying well. You will also find that skill in dowsing will not only help you locate minerals like oil and water but will help you locate deficiencies in your diet before trouble shows up—to give you just a brief preview of coming attractions.

153

Chapter 5
The Human Field Effect

We are moving a bit farther out from the hands-on, solid-state world to investigate and play around with energy fields for a while. While most energy is quite respectable and afforded every curtesy offered to its alter ego, matter, there are some energy configurations that are still the Cinderellas of the investigative effort lanquishing in the ashes of neglect. And if there can be a Cinderella of Cinderellas, a sort of Cinderella to the Nth power, then the human energy field can in all likelihood claim that honor.

What human energy field? If you're asking that question urgently about now, don't worry: About 90 percent of us human beings have no idea that there is such a field—consciously, at least. And certainly very little, if anything, is ever taught about this field up to now. Only a few people, usually the ones who have a special gift or quirk of eye sight, which ever way you care to look at it, have been aware of the existence of the human energy field for some time.

We had an interesting example of this very phenomenon in our own experience. One night, after our first workshop on auras, we came home quite excited and stimulated by our new knowledge. In fact, we were flying so high that we couldn't stop talking about what we had seen, heard and experienced and our then 12-year old daughter, Melissa, was drafted to be the audience for an instant replay of the workshop.

Melissa, always polite, sat quietly for quite a while but the look of puzzlement on her face grew to such an extent that it penetrated our missionary fervor and we asked her if she had any questions.

"Just one thing," Melissa said hesitatingly, "You're not talking about that band of color around a person are you? That kind of shimmery, shiny light?"

We looked at each other in amazement. Then we assured Melissa, that yes, indeed, that was what we were talking about.

"But why do they have workshops about that?" Melissa said, still looking puzzled, "I thought everyone sees these bands all the time."

So it turned out that our daughter had seen auras all her life and had never thought it important enough to mention, since, as she said, she thought everyone else saw the same things as she.

Dr. Evelyn Monahan of Georgia State University suggests that our not seeing auras might be a case of functional blindness. After all, hardly any mother goes around telling her baby to look at the pretty blue aura around Auntie Jane or the yellow light around Reverend Jones. It has been proven that people often see selectively; that is they may be unaware of much detail on certain objects, or they may attend only to special features of others. Auras may be such a feature or detail that, because it is never mentioned or pointed out, is literally not registered. However, Dr. Monahan is quick to assure us, almost anybody can learn to see an aura within five to ten minutes.

As you may have noticed this leaves the question of what exactly is an aura? Or a corona, the more up-to-the-minute nomenclature.

Technically an aura is an energy field that surrounds a living entity, be it human, animal or vegetable. There are those who include mineral also, but that can lead to a debate as to what is living and at the moment we are not prepared to go into that (the next book maybe). Ancient scientists in India and China asserted that invisible energies circulate in and around the human body. This is the basic concept on which the healing system of acupuncture and acupressure is based. More about this in the next chapter.

Auras have been seen since the beginning of time by psychics and mystics and have been depicted in the halo surrounding the heads and sometimes the entire bodies of saints in paintings up through the Medieval era.

Science has paid very little attention to the aura. Here are a few exceptions. In the first decade of this century an English physician, Dr. Walter J. Kilner by name, who worked at St. Thomas Hospital in London, began some experiments to investigate the haze he perceived surrounding the human body. He hoped to correlate his findings with people's health and illnesses. In other words, he thought it would make a great diagnostic tool. In the course of time Dr. Kilner found just what he hoped for—as all of us do if we search diligently and narrow banded enough, and published his findings in two books, *Human Atmosphere* and *Human Aura*.

The aura, Dr. Kilner stated, surrounds the human body whether the person is asleep or awake, burning up in the midst of summer heat or freezing in artic weather. It can be seen by most people if the conditions are favorable. Furthermore, said Dr. Kilner, there are three auras not just one: a narrow transparent portion that looks like a dark band, just about a quarter of an inch wide, that follows the body all the way around, a denser band called the inner aura also quite even which follows the contours of the body and the outer aura which starts at the outer edge of the inner aura (where else?) and according to the good doctor is quite variable in size.

As is to be expected, Dr. Kilner used the aura in diagnosis of his patients. He was quite meticulous in noting down symptoms in the aura and in the patient and setting up elaborate correlations. Whether these would hold true for other people or whether most of these observations had a strong subjective, intuitive component is up for grabs. Dr. Kilner did assert that the aura—the outer one, does vary in size and conformation, and that last I can corroborate from my own limited experience.

Dr. Kilner, in a true missionary spirit (or did he want to get his of the fame and fortune envisioned?) wanted to make his discovery, this aid to diagnosis of disease, available to the rest of the medical profession. Unfortunately, not many of his colleagues, even the ones who were open minded enough to show interest, were able to see what Dr. Kilner saw.

Undaunted, the good doctor invented a system by which people could be trained to see auras. This included a very special screen, made out of glass and stained with dicyanine dye. With this device Dr. Kilner went on to train people in aura detection and diagnosis.

Today the Kilner system, or an outgrowth of the system, is still in use. The Metaphysical Research Group in Hastings, England have worked with Dr. Kilner's ideas, modified some and developed some goggles, naturally called Aura Goggles. These goggles with their filters dyed with pinacyanol are supposed to be good aura-viewing training devices—according to the MRG, that is. In scientific circles, this method is considered quite controversial.

Personally we don't recommend the goggles, but we might be prejudiced in favor of those systems that we worked with which suit us better. Personally that is. There is always that personal, individual factor that is most important in this kind of experimentation. What works great for me doesn't necessarily work great for you. Or vice versa. That's why we try to give you a choice of devices, so—if you would like to try the Kilner system, and it is interesting, you can obtain a set of aura goggles and filters from Clark Publishing Co. P. O. Box 671, Evanston, IL 60624. At least they were available through this source at the time of the writing. There are other sources, too. You might investigate your metaphysical, 'New Age', parapsychological or whatever other name it might be described by local book stores; in fact, do that anyway. It'll be an interesting experience if you've never been to one.

At this point, being an experimenter, I feel it's high time for you to have some experiences—like seeing an aura for yourself. So let's give it a try.

AURA VIEWING EXPERIMENT #1

What you need:

1) A room with plain walls, preferably in a light color. White, beige, light gray, any of these will be good, even a pale blue or green will do.

2) This room should be fairly dark, so a dimmer switch is great. Don't get it too dark though, you should still be able to distinquish the person's features—the one whose aura you are going to discover.

3) A person, anybody will do, but to begin with try someone whose hair is fairly smooth and close to his/her head. Leave the people sporting Afros for later. It's a bit more difficult.

4) If you have a movie screen handy you might want to use that instead of a wall. Just make sure that it is big enough to show the person to the waist.

Procedure:

1) Put your person in front of a blank wall or the screen.

2) Instruct the person to take a deep breath and make-believe the breath is going to go through the top of his head—a sort of Mount St. Helens effect.

3) You can omit this step if you feel it's "non-scientific". It's your feeling that counts. Actually it works. But each to his own taste.

4) Now dim the lights.

5) Station yourself where you get a head-on view of the person.

6) Now glance at the person's forehead and then let your eyes go slightly out of focus and look just to the side of the person's head.

7) What did you see?

What people usually perceive is a misty band or ball-like configuration either following the contours of the head and shoulders or, at times, flaring up from the top of the head—yes, that Mount St. Helens effect, again.

It is a good idea to try the experiment with two or more people. You'll probably find that the mist is there with all of them but that it may take different shapes or be larger or smaller on various persons. Also, you might see aura mist only on one side of the body. Dr. Kilner had dire predictions for such people but I have found in my research, both of other people's work and empirical, that this often has to do with personal idiosyncrasies—the subject's, not the viewer's, with what the person is thinking of and a host of other things all very innocent and foreboding nothing at all. In fact, some people seem to have a more prominent aura on one side of the body—whether that has to do with dominance of one hemisphere over the other, a curvature of the spine, or an imbalance I don't know. Why don't you investigate this? I have to write this book. But let me know, please.

So now you've seen your first aura. If you are like the rest of us you're already dubious that you've really seen anything at all. Don't worry about it. Look again. It's free.

AURA VIEWING EXPERIMENT # 2

What you need:

Same as for aura Experiment #1, plus a subject who doesn't mind following directions no matter how absurd they seem from a rational frame of mind. Nothing embarrassing though.

Procedure:

1) Again have the person stand in front of the wall or screen and dim the light.

2) Now instruct the person to go through the top of the head Mount-St. Helens breathing again.

3) Look for the aura at the top of the head.

4) Now ask the subject to repeat this type of breathing for three more exhalations.

5) See anything different? Any flares?

6) Now ask the subject to concentrate on his right hand which he has up in the air, Statue of Liberty fashion, except that instead of clutching a torch, he is showing the viewer his palm. Ask the person to take a deep breath and pretend to exhale it through said hand. (I know it sounds silly but do it anyway).

7) What did you see?

8) You don't believe it? Well, look away from the person for a moment, and ask the person to repeat the performance. Then look again.

9) So?

Well, in all likelihood you've seen something. But even if you haven't, don't give up and say the whole thing is a crock. I almost did. And think what would have happened if I had. You wouldn't be reading this chapter now, would you? Horrors. Anyway, if you have seen little, or are not convinced that you have seen anything at all you might want to practice with seeing your own aura. Yes—your very own. It is done thusly:

AURA VIEWING EXPERIMENT #3

What you need;

1) A room with a mirror opposite a plain wall or movie screen. Your bathroom will do nicely unless you have some of that art decco wallpaper in which case the movie screen set in the tub will do quite well.

2) Yourself.

Procedure:

1) Turn off the light in the room. Have the light source outside the room, but keep it light enough so you can see your own features in the mirror.

2) Now take a deep breath and do the Mount St. Helens bit.

3) As you look in the mirror don't look straight at your face but instead direct your attention just over your shoulder, right or left, it doesn't matter which. What do you see?

4) Take another breath like the one above, now look again.

5) You can practice for as long as you like but I found that a couple of minutes several times a day are much better than one longer session. At least for me.

Are you convinced there is such a thing as an aura now? Or at least that there is some kind of haze one can see if one puts one's mind to it? Or, even more provisional, some kind of haze seems to be visible at certain spots under specific conditions which seem to have some of the properties of the alleged aura?

Well, even if you've seen it you still don't know exactly what it is. Cheer up, the experts aren't sure either. Nicholas M. Regush, in his book "Exploring the Human Aura", presents the aura as a sort of bio-computer, a mind/body extension, which receives, transmits and processes information between the person and the outside world. The Oriental scientists and philosophers conceive of it as a subtle body (man having two bodies—the material or physical and the subtle) through which people are in touch with cosmic energies. Which, come to think of it, is pretty close to what Nicholas Regush says in his own tongue.

Dr. Boris Tarusov, Chairman of Biophysics at Moscow University talks about electromagnetic luminescence and uses highly sensitive photoelectric multipliers to explore it further. These multipliers are similar to those hush-hush devices used in best James Bond fashion as snooper scopes by the military and police. They can "see" in total darkness. Dr. Tarusov found that not only were light fluctuations present, but that they were not random. The breakthrough came when he was doing plant experiments (Yes, Virginia, plants have auras, too) and it was discovered that the fluctuations were closely related to the plants' metabolisms. And, to top it all, certain light patterns indicated particular conditions, such as too much water, fungus invasion or lack of fertilizer, *before* the plants showed any of the give-away symptoms.

In a curious way this repeats what the healers have been yakking about for ages, and I mean ages, that is that a person's aura will show signs of disease long before there are clinical symptoms. Curiouser and curiouser.

In the meantime, a colleaque of Dr. Tarusov, Dr. Victor Inyshin, and his team at the State University of Kazakhstan in Alma-Ata (if you think that sounds like outer Siberia you're right on target) have been exploring ultra-violet eminations coming from the eyes of humans and animals which he manages to capture on ultra-violet sensitive film. How this is related to the aura is not clear but there is some connection, obviously.

Dr. Harold S. Burr, professor of Anatomy at Yale and Dr. Lenard J. Ravitz, a psychiatrist are working with what they call the Life Field or L-field that they postulate to be of electromagnetic origin. Their experiments have been many and varied. They have used eggs to trace development in relations to the L-field, L-fields and the cicadian cycles, lunar cycles, and even solar storm cycles. In addition, they have used psychotic patients and studied the relationship of their L-fields to their psychoses. Studies were also conducted on diagnoses of malignancies through the L-field and lastly, the relationship of changes in the L-field and trance states.

Dr. John Pierrakos, Director of the Institute for Bioergetic Analysis in New York has other ideas. He has studied the energy fields of the human body simultaneously with his psychiatric practice. As a further boon, it is said that Doctor Pierrakos has some psychic ability. Or at least he admits to some. He believes, contrary to some of the scientists mentioned above, that the energy fields are tied up with the body's metabolism, heat, emotions and also with atmospheric conditions and other factors.

Most interestingly, Dr. Pierrakos describes this pulsating field as moving around the body. " . . . the field moves from the ground up on the inner side of the legs and thighs, up the trunk and outer side of the hands, forearms and arms. The two mainstreams meet and travel upward towards the neck and over the head. At the same time, there is movement at the inside of the lower and upper extremities toward the ground. As we can readily see there is a distinct relationship to Mike's convection currents here.

Researchers at the City University of London directly investigated what they termed convection currents around the human body. They saw the following: . . . starting at the soles of the feet the air layer moves slowly upward over the body. At the groin and under the armpits it reverses direction briefly. At the shoulders it spurts upward to

dissipate a feathery plume about five inches above the head."
Halos, anybody?

By now you are probably anxious to try out something else. And guess what, we have another project for you. This one is called the Schlieren System, a venerable German technique, that makes convection currents visible and gives the warm air around the body a shimmering appearance. By the way, the Schlieren system is also used to study airflow in supersonic wind tunnels so if you get bored with studying the aura, fascinating though it might be to me, you can always use the apparatus for an in-depth view of airflows and the like.

A professionally put together Schlieren System can be bought from Edund Scientific for around $150.00. The order number is #71,014. However, it's much more fun and a whole lot less expensive to make your own. So here we go.

Basically the Schlieren System consists of a strong light, a screen, some magnifying glasses and pinhole screens. As the light strikes the object viewed the heat currents cause the light to break up into bands of color which the optical arrangement—the pinhole screens and lenses, magnify onto the viewing screen. Simple, isn't it?

SCHLIEREN SYSTEM

What you need:

3 magnifying glasses, good sized, with steady handles; a 4 foot 1' × 4' board; 1' of ½" dowel; white poster board; aluminum foil; several wood blocks of equal size; a little wood putty; a #2 photoflood light (the kind used by photographers), or a "movie light", of the ultra-bright short-lived variety, set in a porcelain socket; a handy spring clip-on fixture to use with the above and a small movie screen if you have one. Note: you can use a high intensity light instead of the photo light.

Procedure:

1) Drill holes in three of your blocks large enough to contain the handles of your magnifying glasses.

2) Set the magnifying glasses into the blocks and, to hold them precisely vertical, fill in around the handles with a bit of wood putty. Let dry. See Fig. 5-1.

3) Cut out 2 squares of poster board 2 ×2 inches.

4) Cut out 4 squares of aluminum foil of the same dimensions.

5) Glue the aluminum foil to both sides of the posterboard.

6) Punch a tiny pinhole into the center of each piece of aluminum-foil cardboard.

7) Drill a hole in 2 more cubes.

8) Cut the dowel into two small pieces. Set one end into the block and steady with wood putty. Make a cut into the other end of the dowel so you can insert the cardboard. See Fig. 5-2.

9) Assemble your little screens making sure that the pinholes will be in line with the center of your magnifying glasses. See Fig. 5-3.

10) Lastly make a light shield around 8 × 8 inches from some more of the poster board. Glue 2 more blocks to the bottom of the posterboard so the screen will be self supporting. Or, if you are clear out of blocks, you can use a stray piece of wood along the bottom edge. Alternately, you can make a stand from some additional posterboard. See Figs. 5-4, 5-5, and 5-6. Punch a hole with ½ inch diameter in the center of the light shield.

11) If you want to make your Schlieren system permanent, which is a good idea, set it up on the board we dubbed optional and mark the position of each piece when it is just right.

Assembling the Schlieren System

1) Set up your viewing screen, or improvise a viewing screen with a sheet of white posterboard taped to a wall, about table level.

2) Your work table, counter or whatever else you are going to set your system on, should be about 6 inches away from the screen.

3) Your light source, that is your photoflood light or high intensity lamp, should be set up about 3½ feet away on the other end of your table or whatever. The light beam should fall into the center of the viewing screen.

4) Put one of the magnifying glasses in its holder close to the light source.

5) Set up the light shield 3½ inches from the magnifying glass. Make sure that the light is focused through the glass and the hole in the screen.

6) Next comes one of your foil screens; set it up 2 inches from the screen and line up the pin holes.

7) Magnifying glass #2 is next—a couple of inches down the line. Again make sure of the focus.

8) Magnifying glass #3 follows directly. Set it up 6 inches down from #2 and again check the focus.

9) Put the last foil screen an inch or so from magnifying glass #3.

10) If you are confused study the sketch. See Fig. 5-7.

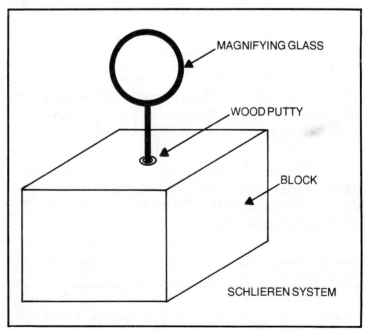

Fig. 5-1. Detail, Schlieren system.

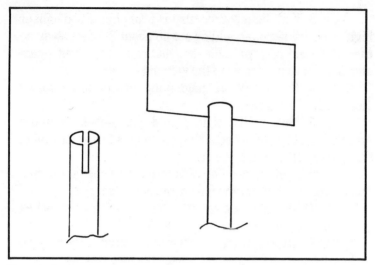

Fig. 5-2. Detail, Schlieren system.

Using Your Schlieren System

1) Place whatever you want to view between magnifying glass #2 and #3 and observe it on the screen. You might try a small candle or a flashlight and adjust the components until you have the best possible image. Lower the light level in the room.

2) At this point mark around each component on your board. When you get through with your viewing you can put up your components yet set them easily into place the next time.

3) If you put a heated object between the #2 and #3 magnifying glasses you'll see a beautiful rainbow effect. You may, until you get good at using the system, practice with objects you have pre-warmed.

4) Your next observation might be your own or somebody elses' hand. If you know of someone who can warm his hand at will, and there are more of these kind of people running around everyday thanks to bio-feedback training, by all means use him as a subject. Check the alignment carefully, adjust if necessary.

5) Now you're on your own—experiment with whatever you like, from plants to your cat's tail if you can get her to hold still.

6) If you have a rearview projection screen you can photograph the image you get from the other side.

7) If you are not so endowed, you can draw sketches which is easily done if you use posterboard for a screen and draw directly on it, tracing what you see, using crayons or pastels.

While the Schlieren system seems to be completely geared to convection currents, it was originally designed to detect flaws in glass (would you believe?). There are other ways to catch sight of body fields which may be a bit more than just convection currents.

An argument, long favored by people working with parapsychology, is that seeing auras is simply a matter of extending the visual function. Yet this argument has a definite weak point, namely if the aura is electro-magnetic in origin as most parapsychologists claim, these people who can see auras with the naked eye then also see literally in the dark since everything would seem to glow brightly. Fortunately in 1972 the seeing of auras was made respectable and

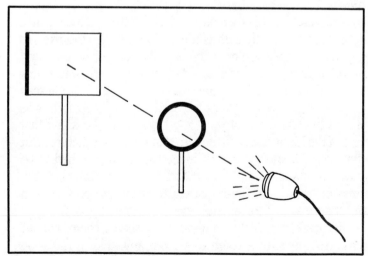

Fig. 5-3. Detail, Schlieren system.

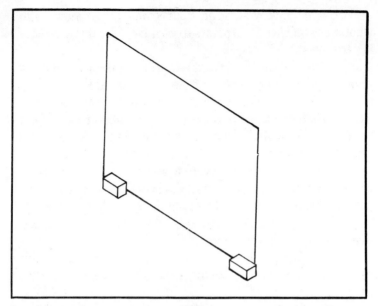

Fig. 5-4. Screen detail, Schlieren system.

possible without the inference of having to see infrared at all times.

It all started when Dr. Richard Dobrin, a radiation physicist at the New York University Medical Center, was told by his friend, that he, a well known and respected doctor, could see his own aura. Since he trusted his friend's integrity he was left with three options, either the friend's eyes were somehow different from other people's, the friend had hallucinations, or maybe, just maybe, there was a new energy field that nobody had found yet around the human body. It had to be new because, familiar as Dr. Dobrin was with radiations emitted by living organisms, he knew that none of the known ones fitted into that particular picture. But whatever the energy was, if indeed it existed, it had to be somewhere near the edge of the visible band. And since the emission was in all likelihood quite weak the only certain way of detecting the presence was a totally dark room.

By dark, Dr. Dobrin meant more than a room without light. He specified a room free from any kind of radiation which was luminescent. The sealing putty, for instance, that

Table 5-1. All about energy fields.

Name of field	Apparatus for detection	Description	Movement	Special info	Psychic perception
Electro-dynamic	Burr voltmeter	Energy fields around living organisms.		Patterns seem to control growth of seeds, embryos, healing of wounds. Registers cosmic effects on body. Registers changes in body during hypnosis	Energy fields Changes when state of consciousness changes
Convection currents of warm-air around body	Schlieren system	3" colored envelope of warm air. halo effect at head	From feet up over body. reverses at arm-pits & groin	Can be used in diagnosis of disease.	2" colored band moves from feet over body, surrounds head. Illness changes color & pattern
Ultrafaint luminescence	Supersensitive photomultipliers	Flashing light patterns emitted from body		Can be used to diagnose illness before physical symptoms appear.	Colored flares. Holes in patterns of energy before person or organism becomes clinically ill.
Force-field detection	Segeyer detector	Field can be detected at a distance from the body.	After death force fields of energy pulsing at distance from body.	Can be used to test for anxiety & stress	Wide energy field surrounding body. At death swirls of mist leave body.
Acu-point energy ki (shi)	Tobioscope bio-meter	Detects ki energy. Finds acu-points on skin. more conductivity of electricity	Ki energy flows through body along a 12 meridian network	Can be seen with Krilian photography	Energy flows and energy blockages in the body
Electro-magnetic fields	Gulyaev auragrams	Changes of energy around muscles		Diagonosis of Internal organs	Energy changes in internal organs
Electro-magnetic force field	Sophisticated bio-electronics set-ups	Charged fields (positive or negative in various areas)	Polarity changes	Altered states of consciousness, other chemicals, other fields change polarity. Visible on modified TV screen	Polarized energy fields. Polarity changes in altered states.

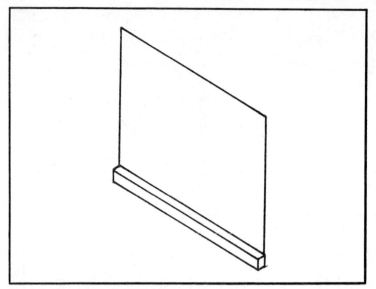

Fig. 5-5. Screen detail, Schlieren system.

was first thought to be the solution to fill in cracks and holes threw off a surprising amount of radiation. The same held true for clothing; certain fibers as well as dyes proved to have not only electrostatic discharges but often also a certain fluorescence.

Finally it was ready, and the doctor entered the room barechested. The door was sealed. The doctor took up his place in front of the photo-multiplier tube which detects very minute quantities of light and amplifies them to readable current. This device was hooked up to a chart recorder outside the room. Dr. Dobrin asked his friend to increase and decrease his body field, a capacity the friend had attested he possessed. The instructions were random; there was no pattern to them at all.

What Dr. Dobrin found was pretty amazing. Just as he had said, his friend did indeed emit a glow, a visible field of light. And, furthermore, this field could be increased up to 500 percent simply by his friend's volition.

So the aura was at last officially seen by scientists and they concluded that it was in the range between the blue and red portion of the visible spectrum. And when the scientists, as curious as you and I as to how the doctor managed to increase or decrease his luminous field, investigated, they found to their astonishment that it was all done with breathing excercises. Yes—just breathing. Maybe the yogis know what they are talking about after all.

Since it would be quite difficult to build your own "darkroom" we have come up with an electronic aura reader for you, which at least will help you read auras if not prove them.

THE ELECTRONIC AURA READER

What you need (see Fig. 5-8):

B1 - 9-volt battery
C1 - 0.1μF capacitor
C2 - 10μF electrolytic capacitor
C3 - 0.1μF capacitor
C4 - 22μF electrolytic capacitor
D1 through D1D - TLR-107 LEDs
IC1 - TL084
IC2 - LM386
IC3 - LM3915*
J1 - 2 wire polarized socket
P1 - 2 wire polarized plug
Q1 - phototransistor (Radio Shack 276-130)
R1 - 220K resistor
R2 - 1K resistor

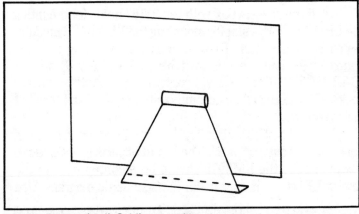

Fig. 5-6. Screen detail, Schlieren system.

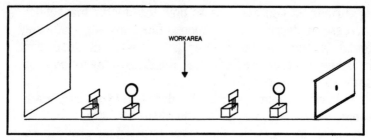

Fig. 5-7. Schlieren system set-up.

R3 - 10K resistor
R4 - 10K potentiometer
R5 - 10-ohm resistor
R6 - 1K resistor*
S1 - spst switch
S2 - spot switch*
Misc. - Perfboard; wire wrap; solder; battery holder; 6 ft. 2-wire, shielded cable connector; hardware; IC sockets; chassis box 3″ × 6″ × 2″ or larger; etc.

Construction:

The phototransistor should be soldered to the leads of the connecting cable and the plug soldered on the other end. Check very carefully to be sure that the polarity of the phototransistors is not reversed when plugged into the circuit. E must go to the common ground, while C goes to C1 and R1, the input of IC1.

Drill the chassis box with ten 3/16″ holes for mounting the LEDs, or with a slot for mounting the VU METE module, if you are using that. Drill the box for mounting the gain control (R4) and the two switches, S1 (OFF-ON) and S2 (BAR-DOT). The LEDs, control and phototransistor socket (J1) should all be accommodated on the front panel of the chassis box.

The bulk of the circuitry is assembled on a piece of perfboard about 4½″ × 2″. The layout of parts is not critical, however IC3, the LM3915 should be mounted next to the row of LEDs, as it appears in the schematic diagram. Use

---

*Radio Shack's LED VU meter module (Cat. No. 277-1099) may be substituted for all these parts. Use a separate 12-volt battery to power this module.

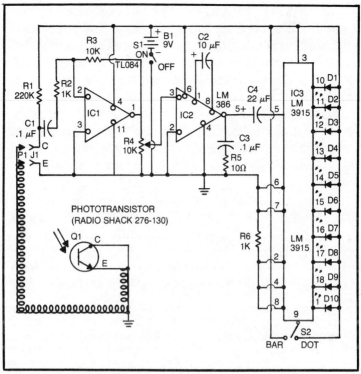

Fig. 5-8. Schematic diagram for Mike's electronic aura reader.

¼-watt resistors throughout and a mini PC pot for R4 and parts will not be crowded.

Pay close attention to the polarities of C2 and C4. Check and double check your wiring on the IC leads before you turn on the power.

How It Works:

The electronic aura reader is a very sensitive light amplifier that "sees" mostly in the infrared range. What the phototransistor sees is displayed by the ten LEDs as a moving dot or bar of visible light.

The phototransistor should be placed on the forehead first in the "third eye" position. The amplifier turned on and the gain adjusted (R4) so that only one LED is lighted (see Fig. 5-9). Now move the phototransistor over the skin of the entire body—from the top of the scalp to the soles of the feet.

Areas of high infrared radiation will be indicated by six or more LEDs that light to show energy "leaks" from the body, possibly foretelling a future illness. These areas need to have their acu-points worked on to "plug" the leaks and get the energy flowing properly *through* the body rather than *away* from it.

Incidentally, Dr. Glen W. McDonald of the U.S. Department of Health, Education and Welfare agrees that human bodies emit infrared. "If the eyes were structured to see this emission we would all have an incandescent glow," he states.

Another interesting bit of information substantiating the auras comes from Dr. James B. Carlton, who is of all things a research engineer in applied electrostatic technology. According to his research, most young children readily see auras around human beings, but as the children reach adolescense, this ability seems to fade out in all but a few individuals.

It would be easy to argue the point that this decrease of ability is a) a decrease in use and b) a culturally imposed

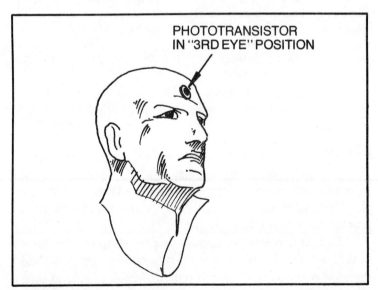

PHOTOTRANSISTOR IN "3RD EYE" POSITION

Fig. 5-9. "Third eye" position for adjusting aura reader to individual (see text p. 185).

atrophy. Since the ability to see auras is not useful to the individual in our society, is in fact, never mentioned or discussed as a common occurence, less attention would be paid to it until the very image would be erased from conscious recall. On the other hand, one could also suggest that during the early teen years the eyes undergo several changes. Some of these again are culturally imposed. The teen years are when children's eyes are more used to study fine print and less to observe what's going on around them—except on the tube, of course, and auras don't seem to transmit readily on TV.

Whatever the causes for losing the ability to see auras, the very fact that at one time or other we all were able to see them may account for another fact, one stated by Dr. Monahan (and others who have taught people to see auras) that most people can learn (or relearn?) to see auras within the space of 10 or 15 minutes.

An aspect that tends to be neglected in aura study is the fact that all living organisms from single cells on up emit an aura. It is held that so called inorganic substances also emit an aura and that can be justified by bringing in the matter of relative time frames. At the moment, as I've stated before, I don't feel like coping with this one. However, the matter of other living organisms, particularily plants is quite important here.

Plants emit an aura that can be studied much more easily than the aura around a person. Why? For one thing, plants don't wear clothing. Their outlines are clear and simple. Furthermore, plants are infinitely patient and don't mind being observed and studied. They don't have urgent appointments or need to complete chores or have an overwhelming desire to do something more entertaining.

When you want to study a plant's aura with your naked eye you go basically through the same procedure as I've outlined for learning to view the aura #1. The only difference is that instead of looking at a point just over the shoulder to the side of the head or over the top of the head, you will now look just to the side of the plant near the top or just over the top.

However, even more interesting, you can study the aura of a single leaf. For this you need a large leafed plant, a split-leafed philodendron for instance, or better yet a rubber plant or Fiddle-leaf Fig plant. What you do is select a leaf for study, preferably one that is nicely separated from its neighbors. Look straight at the leaf but let your eyes go out of focus slightly. The aura will appear around the leaf but also on the leaf itself, if it is the broad leafed variety. What you'll observe is the leaf surface getting slightly brighter and hazier at the same time.

Now, for the coup de grace: Seeing your own aura and that of your favorite plant at the same time.

AURA VIEWING EXPERIMENT #4

What you need:

The same set up you used for aura viewing experiment #3—that is a room that has a large mirror opposite a plain wall. You'll also need a plant you've experimented with before.

Procedure

1) Dim the light as before.

2) Set up the plant near you so you can see the plant and your reflection side by side in the mirror.

3) Make sure that the plant is close to you but not touching in any way.

4) If you have observed that your own aura tends to be more prominent on one side of your body; i.e., shoulder/head area, put the plant on that side.

5) Now go through the viewing technique you used for Aura Viewing #3.

6) Surprised? Sure, you saw two auras for the price of one.

7) Now if you really want a treat, think nice thoughts about your friend, the plant, while you go on watching the plant and your image. Think about how the two of you are connected through the oxygen/carbon-dioxide cycle. How as you breathe out, the plant breathes in and vice versa.

8) Now look again. Anything happen to the auras? I won't tell you what. See for yourself. It's more fun that way.

Aura watching and detecting is not just fun and games, however. If it were, why should such an august body as the Interdisciplinary Conference on the Voluntary Control of Internal States Awareness, sponsored by the Menninger Foundation and attended by eminent scientists from several foreign countries as well as the creme de la creme of the homegrown sort, be engaged in learning to detect auras?

The ready answer is that aura reading seems to have its most direct practical application in medical diagnosies work. Several rather prominent medical men have admitted to me that they do see auras and always have. And while they don't rely on this ability to make complete diagnosis, they do use the information they gain in this fashion as an important clue in ordering tests and other investigative procedures. "It's like narrowing down to a city block instead of studying the entire suburb," is the way one of them put it. "It helps zeroing in on the cause and starting treatment quickly."

Naturally, most of the good doctors prefer to remain nameless at this writing. The AMA as a whole still tends to take a dim view of such things. But there are exceptions, like Dr. Norman Shealy who publicly stated during the symposium right here in Austin that he not only saw auras but used the information in his practice.

Drs. Elmer and Alyce Greene at the Menninger Foundation, Topeka, Kansas, currently use a program to train people to extend their senses and develop aura-vision. The program was begun by Jack Schwarz, a highly trained and accomplished person- a scientific psychic so to speak. After becoming aware of his own unusual abilities and talents, Jack decided to make much of this knowledge available for general use and study. And while many psychics fear, or at least strongly dislike, modern technology and apparatus, Jack Schwarz perceives these things as opportunities to explore and verify paranormal skills. The program used by the Drs. Greene has been successful in training medical personnel to perceive energy fields around the body and to diagnose with them.

Schwarz has also developed an aura-vision training device which he calls by the rather overwhelming and memory defying name of "Integral Stimulating Intensity Stroboscope". The ISIS, as it is mercifully referred to in the in-circles, is an adaptation of an optometric instrument.

Anyway, the ISIS directly designed for auric vision training does its thing by stimulating the rods and cones in the eye, just as its progenitor did to encourage better vision. The device comes with special training charts and eye exercises which should be used in conjunction with it.

You can get information and/or the ISIS Aura-Vision Trainer Model 1204 by writing to Aletheia Products and Publishing Corp., 1015 SW Yamhill, Portland, Oregon 97205.

Chapter 6
Your Hidden Energy of Many Points

It would be nice to tell you that I have been into Ki or Chi energy for ages—at least back to Mr. Nixon's famous journey to China, which brought the news to the U.S. But in all honesty, I can't. Back then I was immersed in the Earth Mother bit. You know, the kids were clinging to my skirts, those long trailing vaguely ethnic ones, and I was busy baking bread, canning food, sewing clothes, and, in case I got bored, making my own dinnerware and those for other people on my trusty wheel in the back studio and firing them bright and shiny in the home-made kiln. When I heard talk about acupuncture, I remembered vaguely that it had to do with China. But on the whole, it felt more like something out of an old Charlie Chan movie than something that would have a tremendous effect not only on me but on the way a lot of people look at life.

Mike, on the other hand, was quite interested and even read the relevant bits and pieces while I tripped around doing my appointed tasks. I recall one story he read me out of *Newsweek* which related the experiences of two doctors, part of Mr. Nixon's entourage. The names escape me at the moment, but I do recall that these doctors were invited to visit several hospitals during their stay in China, the usual professional courtesy bit. There, to their amazement, they observed operations performed according to strict Western protocol, except for the use of anesthesia. The patients were wide awake, conversing with the doctors or studying little inspirational texts while the surgeons removed lungs, kidneys, and other major organs. And all that protected them from pain were some funny looking needles stuck here and there upon their bodies.

If this was bizarre, equally astonishing was the fact that after the patients were properly sewn up, they slid off the operating table, thanked the doctors politely and rode off on their wheeled carts sipping juice and munching goodies. The visiting doctors were properly amazed and the press, once they got hold of that tidbit, had a field day.

While waiting for Mike one day, I wandered into a lecture on acupressure and acupuncture. Since this was more interesting than sitting in the lobby, I listened skeptically to what was being said. The one bit of information that I retained was that if you ever had a toothache it would be a good thing to push a point between your thumb and first finger, which the lecturer called Hoku. I filed that under "useful information."

Only a few days later I had occasion to be in need of just such info. I developed a throbbing toothache on the weekend and, since we were new in town, had no dentist. Aspirins barely took the edge off the pain. And, I must admit, I'm a coward as far as toothaches are concerned. In desperation, I punched hoku as directed. Nothing happened—not right then. But one-quarter of an hour later, to my utter delight, I was free of pain. And while the pain did return after a few hours, a few more punches worked again and again. I not only survived the weekend in comfort, but also the following week in which the dentist waited for the abcess to subside before working on my poor tooth.

While, it took a toothache to make me aware of what the Chinese had known for 5000 years, I won't make you wait for one to find out all about acu-points and how they are used to manipulate energies within the body/mind system. In fact I'll start at the beginning and bring you all the way up to the present state of the art. And I'll include some experiments, too, so that when we get that bio-meter built, you'll not only be able to locate those elusive acu-points easily but will know how to use them. It takes quite a bit of study to become expert at this, though.

Basically, acupuncture is an old Chinese art and form of *preventitive* medicine. So firmly was the idea that disease could be prevented by acupuncture entrenched in the Chinese culture that people visited their physicians regularly four times per year and expected to be well. Not only that, but while they paid for these visits and any treatment that they received during them, the doctors worked free of charge if their patients got ill between times. How is that for faith in a method?

The theory behind the system—simplified, of course— is based on an energy system within the body, one that our western anatomical charts don't show. It has often been likened by Westerns to an internal circuitry through which energy flows. To be healthy and feel well, the energy needs to flow freely through the circuits of the body. Each part of the body has to have its sufficient share of this energy, and the energies in different parts of the body have to be balanced in relation to each other. In other words, the state of health means sufficient and equalized energies throughout the entire body/mind system.

Disease, on the other hand, indicates a major imbalance that can be illustrated by a simple garden variety irrigation system, such as you might have for your yard. The energies flow along certain pathways, or meridians. If there were insufficient energy flowing along one meridian, the glands associated with that particular internal circuit would have less energy input.

While this would lead to stunted growth in your garden, a similar condition in the body can lead to the stunted growth of antibodies and enzymes necessary to guard against the invasion of bacteria and viruses. So the altered energy pattern will lead, if it persists, inevitably to manifestations of disease on the physical level.

If, on the contrary, the flow of energy is balanced throughout the body most of the time, all organs and systems receive the energy they need to maintain themselves, make the necessary repair quickly and easily, and be immune to outside invaders (be they cold viruses or strep bacteria). This applies to allergents as well, because a balanced body will not be susceptible to outside irritants to the point of violent reaction but will rather protect itself by the proper dose of self-produced antihistamine.

How the ancient Chinese found out about this system is not known. There is a simplistic theory that states it all started with wounds inflicted by stones or sharpened flint. Supposedly the priests/doctors observed the curious effects some wounds had on other parts of the body. One instance, often sited is that a wound in a special part of the foot would relieve a headache or toothache.

The ancient Chinese were very bright. At the same time, let's afford them the courtesy of granting them more sophisticated means for arriving at truths that we Westerners, after all, didn't even know existed until a very few years ago. Obviously, the ancient Chinese had their own way of arriving at the meridian system.

Another theory, which is much more credible, is that some of the ancient masters experienced the flow of ki (or chi) in their own bodies, and from these experiences mapped the meridians. This is reasonable because through meditation or indeed acu-point stimulation itself, one can become conscious of the ki flow. Jiro Murai, a Japanese master who transmitted the ancient acu-point stimulation technique of Jin Shin to present day use, explained that he did it in just this way.

In any case, when the Yellow Emperor reigned in China some 5000 years ago, 800 acu-points had been discovered, each about one-tenth of an inch in size. Furthermore, the Chinese knew that if they activated these points with needles all sort of marvelous things started to happen to the body and mind. The Yellow Emperor was much taken with this method and raised it to the most important method of treatment. He further ordered " . . . That this method and knowledge be recorded and transmitted to future generations and its laws should be recorded so that it will be easy to practice it and difficult to forget it."

And so it was done. Treatises were written, and charts were drawn. During the Song Dynasty, Emperor Wei Te ordered that statues of men were to be cast in bronze. These statues were to contain all the acu-points. Chinese doctors had to locate these points, which were filled in with wax and the entire statue covered with rice paper. If a doctor missed, he didn't get licensed.

It wasn't until the first quarter of the 19th century that acupuncture came to Europe. At the Royal Infirmary in Edinburgh, it was used successfully for the first time in 1827. In the same year, it also surfaced at St. Thomas Hospital in London, equally successfully. However, it never achieved a great deal of acceptance and many derided it as the "pin cushion" therapy.

The French consul to China early in the 20th century, Soulie de Morant, was instrumental in bringing acupuncture to France. In 1928 he persuaded several French physicians to learn the art of acupuncture. By the middle 1960s, a dozen hospitals in Paris were using acupuncture as routine treatment in general medicine. It is a recognized method under the French National Health Service, and patients can claim a refund of part of the fee just as they can on other treatments if acupuncture has been recommended by their doctors.

The rest of Europe is also cognizant of acu-points and the methods of using them. German doctors order acupuncture or acupressure treatments routinely, and so do Swiss physicians and doctors in Central European countries.

Meanwhile, in the U.S.S.R., acupressure research and practice grew and flourished. Starting in the early 1950s, the U.S.S.R. had spent many a research Rubel and uncounted hours of investigative time on the ancient Chinese healing art.

In 1972 the June issue of *Zdorovye*, a Soviet health magazine, carried an article in which the then minister of public health, Dr. B.V. Petrovsky, stated that he had supervised the opening of special acupuncture facilities in large medical clinics in most major cities and industrial centers in the U.S.S.R. The same issue of the magazine carried data about acupuncture treatments compiled by the

Gorky Medical Institute for the past 15 years. It covered 1146 patients, who suffered from asthma, ulcers, high blood pressure, and colitis. Two out of three of these patients were reported cured while an additional 221 were considered to be markedly improved.

Since that time, acupuncture has become an accepted part of Soviet health care. It is less discussed now than it was, partially because of the China/Russia friction, and also because the very acceptance of the matter makes discussion much less important.

The story of acupuncture in the U.S., however, is strikingly different. Although acupuncture has been practiced here in the various Chinatowns across the country, it has been ignored by Westerners and written off as old country superstition. It was Mr. Nixon's journey to China and the events mentioned earlier that brought acupuncture into the limelight in this country; however, the acceptance here has been slow and the arguments vociferous. In fact the topic developed into one of a bitter controversy.

The first acupuncture clinic opened in New York, NY, only to be shut down by the New York Department of Education a few weeks later. Undaunted, the clinic and staff removed themselves from the inhospitable confines of New York and moved south to Washington, DC, where the climate was much less hostile and the laws more lenient. In California, the situation was even more muddled. While the California Medical Association at first encouraged the study of acupuncture, and the legislature voted in a law to permit acupuncturists to practice under the supervision of licensed physicians in research projects, an expansion of this provision was vetoed by the governor of California in 1972.

This is not to say that all medical people are against acupuncture; in fact, many physicians are eager to learn about Chinese medicine. Symposia in California, Florida, and Louisiana have drawn distinguished crowds. Even New York hosted a symposium for physicians and dentists in 1973. The U.S. National Institute of Health organized a committee on acupuncture in 1972. Within one year, the *Journal of the American Medical Association* not only acknowledged the existence of acupuncture but began to publish articles on the subject. Shortly thereafter some health insurance companies extended coverage for their clients for acupuncture treatments performed by a licensed physician.

THE BIOMETER FOR LOCATING ACU-POINTS

Now I will let you build your very own biometer so you can locate acu-points on your own (see Fig. 6-1).

What you'll need:

B1, B2, B3 - 9-volt batteries
C1 - 0.05 μF capacitor
C2 - 200 pF capacitor
D1, D2 - 1N4004 (or any silicon diode)
D3 - TLR - 107 LED
IC1 - integrated circuit 709C (Fairchild)
J1 - closed circuit jack
R1 - 75,000 ohm ½ watt resistor
R2 - 100,000 ohm potentiometer
R3, R4 - 1000 ohm ½-watt resistor
R5 - 1 megohm mini-potentiometer
R6 - 240,000 ohm ½-watt resistor
R7 - 1800 ohm ½-watt resistor
R8 - 382 ohm ½-watt resistor
R9 - 10,000 ohm ½-watt resistor
S1 - dpst switch
Misc. - eight pin to-5 socket (for IC1)
one pair "flexiprobes"
5-foot "flex" test leads (Radio Shack # 278-740)
3 battery clips
hook-up wire
wrapping wire
IC perfboard
project case
hardware
knobs, etc.

How to Build It

The acu-point detector/biometer is built on a perfboard cut to fit into one of Radio Shack's small project cases. The Null and sensitivity controls, as well as the LED, the jack for plugging in the test probe, and the on-off switch (S) are mounted on the front of the panel.

How It Works

The complete schematic for the Acu-point detector/ biometer is shown in Fig. 6-1. It is an adaptation of a circuit by Robert E. Devine (*Popular Electronics*, February, 1969), which Devine called a "Psych-Analyzer," to "check emotions and sensibilities by Galvanic skin resistance."

We built it and discovered that it made an excellent device for finding acu-points. We replaced the voltmeter of the Psych-Analyzer with an LED, which glows when the test probe touches an acu-point. The other lead of the test probe pair should be held in the subject's hand.

Normal skin resistance, as we mentioned before, is about 1 million ohms, but on acu-points the resistance drops to between 50,000 to 100,000 ohms. The null control, R2, is set so that the LED is dark when the probe is on an area of skin known to be a non-acu-point. The exact setting needs to be adjusted for each individual subject. The adjustment will balance the bridge consisting of R1, R2, and the subject's skin resistance. When an acu-point is touched, the balance of the bridge is upset and current flows through the integrated circuit, which is a dc amplifier, and the LED lights up. R5 will adjust the overall sensitivity of the device.

The test probe pair should be soldered to a plug that will fit a normally closed jack. Inserting the plug in this jack will energize the bridge circuit. Don't leave the probes plugged in when not in use, or you will run your bridge battery (B1) down, even with the off-on switch (S1) in off position.

THE TOBIOSCOPE ACU-POINT FINDER

For those of you who want to spend less time and still have fun finding acu-points accurately, we designed a simplified version of the acu-point finder, but one which will also be quite exact in detecting the presence, or absence of those elusive acu-points.

What you need:

    B1, B2 - 9-volt battery
    D1 - TLR-107 LED

IC1 - integrated circuit 741C
J1 - closed circuit jack
R1 - 75K resistor
R2 - 100K poteniometer
R3 - 50K potentiometer
R4 - 1K ½-watt resistor
S1 - spst switch
Misc. - eight pin socket for IC1
1 pair "flexiprobes"
5-foot "flexi" test leads (Radio Shack # 278-740)
2 battery clips
LC perfboard
hook-up wire
project case
hardware

Figure 6-2 is a complete schematic for a simplified device for locating acu-points. Construction and operation are similar to the Biometer/Acu-point detector.

So you have found those acu-points. Now what? Or more accurately, just what is it that you have found?

There are some indications that the meridian system of the body might be another circulatory system. The acu-points are those locations on the body where the meridians come close to the skin surface.

The acu-points themselves have been proven to have less electric resistance and higher electric potential than the surrounding skin. That is how our biometer can find them, of course. It has been proven that the bioelectric properties of these acu-points can be precisely measured and used for diagnostic purposes according to Dr. Louise Wensel, the author of *Acupuncture for Americans*.

In other words, while the normal skin resistance is about one million ohms, resistance on an acu-point registers a drop to 50,000 to 100,000 ohms. What's even more amazing is that Soviet work showed shunt paths in the body; that is, low resistance paths which connect to each of the acupuncture points. And they further discovered that if electrodes of different materials are connected to two acu-points—silver and nickel, let's say—a voltage of 50

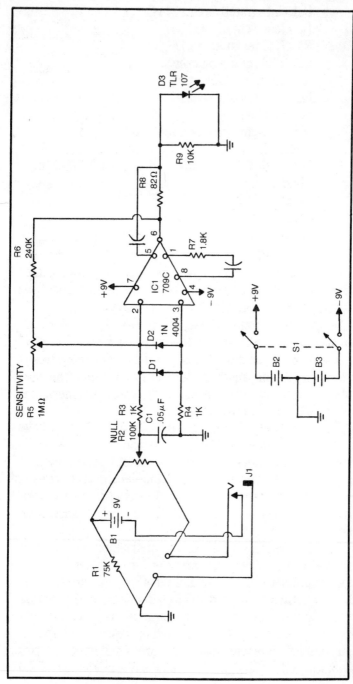

Fig. 6-1. Biometer, or acu-point detector, adapted from a circuit by Robert E. Devine (schematic).

millivolts between acu-points can be generated and a current of up to 10 microamperes drawn from those electrodes. If you were to connect a bunch of those electrodes in series, you might be able to get a volt from the body and run small electrical apparatus with it.

Korean professor, Kim Bong Han was the first to actually trace a meridian by different means. He injected radioactive phosphorous into an acu-point and found that it traveled primarily *along* that particular meridian, rather than laterally. In addition, he carefully monitored the other acu-points along that meridian and found a high concentration of radioactivity in each of them.

In a twin experiment, Professor Kim injected the same radioactive phosphorous into the ear vein. Only a small trace could be detected anywhere in the meridian system. By the same token, the radioactive phosphorous in the meridian system introduced via the acu-point did not appear in the blood vessels at all. This, of course, proved the independence of the meridian system from the vascular system.

Actually, Professor Kim divides the meridian system into four subsystems: the internal duct system free floating in the vascular and lymphatic vessels and containing a fluid or liquor; the intra-external duct system found on the surface of

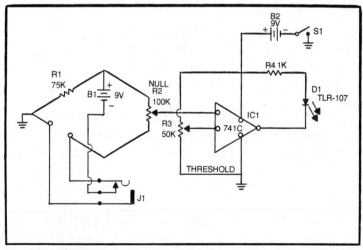

Fig. 6-2. Tobioscope circuit by Wolverton for locating acu-points.

189

the internal organs, which form a network completely independent of the vascular, lymphatic, and nervous systems; the external duct system running along side the outer surface of the walls of the vascular and lymphatic vessels (this system is the one most commonly tapped in acupuncture); the neural duct found in the central and peripheral nervous systems. And says the professor, all the systems are linked together and interlinked as well.

Furthermore, Professor Kim stipulates that we human beings are not the only creatures to boast meridian systems. After experimenting with all types of organisms he believes that a meridian system exists in all multicell structures, animal as well as vegetable.

While seeing has long been equated with believing, in working with the esoteric acu-points, one has to add the dimension of feeling or touch to be really convinced not only of their existence but their effectiveness. You've seen the resistance change every time you touched an acu-point with your biometer. Now you are going to *feel* what happens.

EXPERIMENT # 1

For our first attempt, we will use the point called Hoku, partially for sentimental reasons because it was this point—you might remember—that introduced me to the acu-points in the flesh so to speak.

1) Study Fig. 6-3, which is a schematic of a hand showing a meridian and the Hoku point marked x (appropriately, of course).

2) You may first locate this point with your trusty biometer.

3) If you like, you can even mark the spot with an x on your skin. It does not matter whether it is your right or left hand. These acu-points are completely unbiased and appear neatly bilaterally all over the body, with the exception of a few spots on the top of the head and down the midline of the body, front, and back.

4) With your other hand (using either your index or middle finger), exert pressure on the x in a true vertical direction.

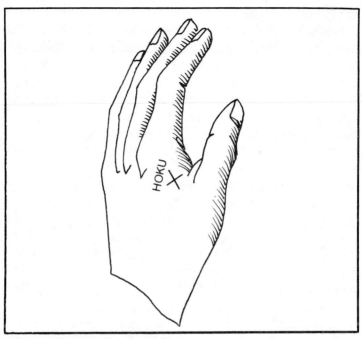

Fig. 6-3. The HOKU acu-point.

5) Support the hand that is receiving the pressure in your lap or on a table.

6) What happened? You probably felt pain. In most people, this spot will be quite tender.

7) Apply the same amount of pressure to a spot one-half inch away from the *x* in any direction.

8) What happened? In all likelihood, not much happened.

What you have observed first hand is that acu-points feel differently from other points. If you want to repeat the experiment on someone else, you will notice that the same thing happens. Also, if you have an educated sense of touch, you may be aware that the Hoku point feels different to your touch. Like other acu-points, it is a bit more solid or tense. Sometimes these points can feel like hard pinheads or a 1-inch wide circular area can feel hard if a point needs work.

What does it mean when I say a point, or to be more specific a meridian needs work? Dr. William A. Tiller,

Department of Material Science, Stanford University describes very graphically what appears to happen. While visiting in London, England, he consulted a doctor about an on-going indigestion problem. The doctor prescribed acupuncture treatments. In Dr. Tiller's own words "The doctor had a device wherein one electrode was held in one hand and the other electrode moved over the body. The electrodes were connected to each other through a special amplifier. Then, when she (the doctor) touched certain points on the skin, the needle would swing up-scale abruptly. This would detect the acupuncture points and the degree of reading on the meter indicated whether there was sufficient energy in that circuit or not. It is interesting that, when there was an imbalance in the circuitry and a needle was inserted in the appropriate point, there is almost a suction force holding the needle in the point until the necessary stimulation and energy transfer has occurred. If one tries to pull the needle out to soon, it does not pull out easily and the skin pulls up around the needle. One must exert a considerable force to remove a needle under this condition. However, when balance has occurred, the needles withdraw with no difficulty; in fact, they fairly leap out. Of course, this balance is often temporary and energy changes occur in many circuits for up to weeks after a treatment." And the indigestion problem was cured permanently.

Dr. Tiller very graphically described what happened when a meridian was stimulated with acupuncture needles. But the acu-point along any meridian can be stimulated by other means. The least effective method is chemical stimulation. Chinese practitioners often burn herbs over the site of the acupoints, a practice referred to as *moxibustion*. This, as well as direct stimulation of the points with various chemicals, seems to have the least results. Other means of stimulating the points are manual massage, electrical stimulation and laser stimulation. On the whole they all will work well if some are somewhat slower than others.

But while I've told you a lot about how it works, I've still begged the question of why it works. The truth is that nobody knows for absolutely certain, but here is the most used explanation.

According to the acupuncturists all the way back to the Yellow Emperor and beyond, the whole five thousand-year bit, an energy, called ki, chi and various other names according to locale of the person speaking, flows along specific pathways or meridians. These meridians connect the organs within the body with the acupoints on the surface of the body. (Soviet experiments have demonstrated that this energy does indeed take inner pathways and not travel on the surface of the body.) The ancient Chinese have further stated that this vital energy of many names is polarized into positive and negative, just like electricity. The Chinese call the positive polarization Yang, and the negative Yin. And they are adamant that this energy, positive or negative, is quite separate from the electrical energy also found in the body.

The vital energy can become blocked through various means since there is a constant interplay between the mind, the body and the environment, all three of which, according to the Chinese, are linked by that same vital energy. And to make it even more complicated, the positive and negative aspects of one's vital energy are in constant flux, affected by weather, seasonal changes, moon phases, and cosmic radiation, as well as by internal reactions such as moods, thoughts, emotions, and mental and physical trauma.

As Dr. Kim Bong Han explained in biochemical terms, the acupuncturist's keyboard of meridians plays a vital part in the smooth functioning of the organs of the body and so, of course affects the total well being of the individual. It seems, then that when acu-points are activated, the homeostasis of the body is directly helped. By removing blocks and balancing the flow of the vital energy, the body is helped to operate at the most efficient level and in turn is able to produce sufficient enzymes and antibodies to protect it from any cruising disease bacteria or virus.

So now you know—at least as much as most authorities. In medical circles, they are still arguing about this and that. Particularily the embarrassment of never having thought of a fourth circulatory system. And if the news hasn't come from the AMA, can it be real?

But whatever theory there is to be disputed and discussed, the fact remains that activating the points brings results which can be felt subjectively and observed objectively. And you don't have to hunt up an acupuncturist in your local phone directory to do this.

Along with the needles the acu-points have traditionally been also stimulated manually. Quite a few specialized systems, some Chinese, some Japanese have been evolved. Some of these have been translated into English, furnished with nice big charts and made available to us at our favorite bookstore. *Acupressure*, the term used to cover several of these systems, has been gaining steadily in popularity. Not as anxiously watched by the medical people since it is essentially a form of massage, it has grown in popularity all over this country. There are practitioners available to give treatment in many a health spa. Often acupressure is used by coaches and physical education teachers. And lastly, acupressure is ideal for the do-it-yourselfer.

But back to our experiments. We have found that the Hoku point feels different when pressed, than the skin around it feels. That holds true of all acu-points. You will find some are more tender than others just as some might be harder than others to the touch. But everywhere your trusty biometer tells you that you'll find an acu-point, you'll find that your skin and body have a different sensation from the one perceived quite close by.

Now to conduct an experiment that will really prove something to you. Select a time when you're either A) sluggish and tired as we get when we have attended one meeting too many in a day, B) have a headache, or C) have been on your feet all day and your legs ache. If you want to be the objective observer, then select a time when any or all of the above are happening to a friend, your spouse, or co-worker.

EXPERIMENT # 2

1) Use your biometer or tobioscope to locate your hoku point or the hoku point of the person who has the headache.

While you're at it, mark the one on the other hand, too.

2) If the headache is on the right side of the head, exert pressure on the hoku point on the right hand.

2) If the headache is on the left side, then press the left hoku.

3) If the headache is in the middle of the forehead or at the base of the skull use both hoku points together if you're applying the pressure to a friend, or one after another if you are doing it to yourself.

4) Press straight down using either your index finger or your middle finger. You may also use your thumb if you feel it's easier that way.

5) Maintain a steady pressure for at least 30 seconds. A minute is better.

6) As you press you'll find the tension in the spot, the hardness loosening up and becoming softer. If you are the recipient, either in a do-it-yourself experiment or by someone else applying pressure on your hoku, you'll become aware that the pain or discomfort will diminish and be replaced by a sensation of deep pressure which is rather pleasant, if a might strange.

7) Have the person stretch a couple of times and roll the head in a circle—first to the right, then the left.

8) Wait a while. Quite soon you'll notice that you feel fine or the person you were working on will cheerfully go back to work or do whatever it was that was interrupted by the headache.

9) After 15 minutes or so, ask about the headache. In many cases the answer will be, "What headache?"

The headache experiment is, of course parallel to the toothache experiment that originally started me on the path of investigating acu-points. Actually, any acute pain, like a slight injury or bruise, a bump on the head or elsewhere, can be easily controlled with good old hoku. Just remember to apply pressure to the same side as the pain.

Incidentally, you don't have to believe a word of what you've read so far to make it work. This has nothing to do with faith healing or even mind over matter. This is strictly a physical phenomenon.

I can even give you an example of how this worked for me. Not very long after my own toothache episode, I went to visit with my oldest daughter and found her up to the eyeballs in codeine and still suffering from what the dentist quaintly described as a "cold" in the tooth and surrounding bone.

While my daughter and I have a nice relationship most of the time, there are still occasions when she falls back into the "Oh Mother!" syndrome of her early teen-age years. Some of my less conventional ideas are sure to activate the "Oh Mother!" bit so I was reluctant to mention my experience to her. But since the poor girl was suffering and I held the key to her improvement, I finally punched her hoku while giving her a very terse account of why I did such a weird thing. As it turned out, she was too worn and weak to even whisper "Oh Mother!" and simply turned her head on the pillow, rolling her eyes heavenward at such nonsense.

I eventually settled myself with a book on the patio, but not for long. Because a scant 20 minutes later, my daughter appeared and suggested we take in a bit of shopping. I went along and neither of us mentioned hoku. Not until a couple of hours later when in an off-hand manner, she inquired just where that point was that I had pressed. The tooth was making itself felt again.

EXPERIMENT #3

Here's an experiment that proves you can keep your eyes open even under the most exhausting circumstances. This comes in handy whenever keeping your eyes open—and yourself alert—is necessary to avoid embarrassment or injury.

1) Sit back in your chair with your feet (both of them) squarely on the floor. If you've been clutching a briefcase, clipboard or purse, put it on the table or floor.

2) Put your hands in your lap. With your right thumb, dig deep into the middle of the palm of your left hand. Hold for one minute.

3) Reverse and dig your left thumb into your right palm.

4) Now pinch the base of each finger tightly. Hold each about 30 seconds.

5) Repeat with the other hand.

6) Now press with your thumb on the outer edge of your forearm at about 2-inch intervals all the way up to the elbow on one side.

7) Now continue on the other side back down to the wrist.

8) Do the same with the other arm.

9) Amazing, isn't it? Those eyes stay open all by themselves, and the old brain might even deliver up an idea or two.

I came across this bit a couple of years ago when I attended a two-week seminar that ran from eight o'clock in the morning until six at night. Add to that an hour of commuting at each end and you can see why I was a bit apprehensive about my capabilities to absorb the material delivered in the late afternoon.

Sure enough at about 10 o'clock the first morning, I felt the familiar dull drowsiness creep over me. My frantic efforts to stay awake were interrupted by the lecturer, who suggested we put aside our notebooks and proceeded to teach the routine I have just outlined for you. I was quickly

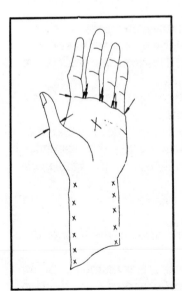

Fig. 6-4. Acu-point experiment No. 3.

awake again and able to absorb some more of the rather condensed and esoteric material presented.

The answer, of course, was the routine which the lecturer insisted we do every hour and half. That kept everyone alert and fresh, ready to learn for as many hours as necessary.

Incidentally, a year or so ago I found the source book for this exercise. It is included in a book on Shiatsu, one of the Japanese acupressure methods I mentioned earlier. (Our lecturer had passed the whole thing off as one of his own innovations.) This book is available in paperback and is a good introductory course in the gentle art of punching oneself and others. This brings us to the exercise involving tired legs and feet.

EXPERIMENT #4

This experiment is a bit more elaborate than the other experiments, so you'll need your biometer or tobiascope, and either one of the illustrations in this book.

1) With your biometer or tobioscope, locate a point which we call # 45 at the back of your, or your friend's leg. You'll find it right below the bulge of the calf. Mark it with a circle.

2) On the same leg, locate an acu-point on the outside of the foot just below the ankle bone. It will be a definite "ouch" spot and light up your LED nicely. This is named # 12. Mark it with an x.

3) Next look for a spot in the center at the back of your knee. This is # 31. Mark it with an x.

4) And lastly find a spot one-half way down the arch of your foot on the inside, still on the same leg. It is just under that bony rim in a little depression. This is # 10. Again mark it with an x.

5) Set your acu-point detector aside for this time. It has done its bit. Now do your thing.

6) Put your left thumb on the circle at the back of the calf, # 45 and press down. Hold.

7) With your other hand, using either thumb or middle finger press down on the x at the ankle marked # 12. Hold for at least 30 seconds, although a minute is better.

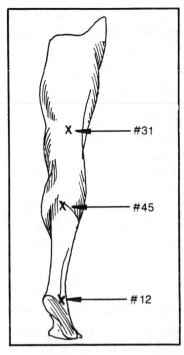

Fig. 6-5. Detail, locating acu-points.

8) Now move your right thumb or middle finger to the x, #31 in the back of the knee and press. Hold this.

9) With your left hand you're still keeping a thumb on #45, the circle just below the bulge of the calf in the back of the leg.

10) If your thumb is getting tired, change to another finger, but keep pressing down on that point.

11) Next switch your right hand to the x at the inside arch of your foot and hold for the required time. Still keep pressure on #45 with your left hand.

12) With your right hand, you are going to pinch your toes at the base—where the foot starts or the toes begin, whichever way you want to look at it—one by one and you're going to hold that pinch for 30 seconds each. Pinch from side to side, not front to back.

13) Your left hand should be still pressing down on #45, which by now shouldn't feel a thing and is nice and soft.

14) What do you feel—a tingling running up your legs or something moving upward or downward?

15) What you are feeling, whether you want to admit it or not, is the vital energy of many names becoming free to flow as it should.

I learned this series of manipulations in a workshop I attended recently. Yes, in case you're interested, I do attend workshops a lot, probably more than most. I am forever doing research on one thing or another and workshops are the best way I've found to check out the information I've acquired through books and other means.

The workshop was led by Iona Teeguarden, the one with the posters I mentioned earlier, and sponsored by the Nursing Association of Austin, TX. Iona teaches the Jin Shin Do System of acu-point manipulation. It takes a bit longer to learn, but it works absolutely beautifully. The greatest thing about it is that if you give someone else a pressure treatment according to this method, not only will they feel better but so will you.

Iona has written a book, *Acupressure Way of Health: Jin Shin Do*, which I heartily recommend. I recommend even more heartily that you try out what you read. One of the greatest things about the Jin Shin Do Teeguarden style is that she has simplified the system. Instead of having to worry about 800 odd acu-points, you're basically dealing only with 45—the most important ones. Furthermore, she has labeled these points 1 through 45 and put them neatly on a great big chart (the poster). So there you are doing it by the numbers. And with your wonderful biometer or tobioscope to help you locate these points precisely, you should become quite proficient in no time. And believe me, it comes in handy, particularly if you have kids.

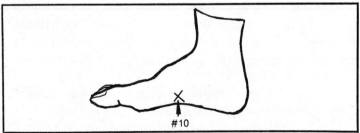

Fig. 6-6. Locating acu-point on foot, detail.

For instance, take what happened with my son David just before his birthday. He was kidding around with some of his friends—he's in sixth grade and you know how boys are at that age—when he somehow tripped and dislocated his knee. When I returned from one of my routine trips to the library, I found him bandaged practically from ankle to groin crying in the living room. The message from the hospital that he had just left was that Dave was to stay off his foot for several days, that he would have considerable pain and swelling, and that I was now $45 poorer.

"The birthday party," Dave moaned while clutching his knee.

"The birthday party!" I moaned while trying to imagine ways of keeping 10 boys happy and quiet at the same time. My mind balked at the prospect. I couldn't cope with that one. Dave simply had to be up and about by Saturday afternoon, a mere 42 hours away. I remembered Jin Shin Do and went to work immediately.

By the time Dave went to bed there was no additional swelling. In fact, what there had been had gone down a little and he was feeling very little pain. By morning there was no more swelling and David hobbled about cheerfully. He wanted to go to school, which he did after another bout of Jin Shin Do. When he came home, he was hurting a bit and there was a little puffiness, but another round of pressure fixed that.

By the time the birthday party began, David was no longer wearing bandages and chased and caroused around with his buddies as good as new.

One thing that I have not mentioned so far is that manipulating the acu-points cannot hurt anything. There are no aftereffects or side effects. Nobody is allergic to acu-point manipulation although the manipulation will *help* you with your allergies.

So use your tobioscope or your biometer or both if you like, and chart the points for yourself. It is a trip all in itself. Just think, dealing with an energy that was discovered 5000 years ago, but that we didn't know about, that many people don't believe exists, but that will light up your little LED brightly anyway.

Chapter 7
A Dowsing We Shall Go

Some of my best friends are dowsers. And they're the sober citizens who have their tidy abodes and drive sparklingly waxed, U.S. medium-sized cars. They're the kind who wear coats and ties when you invite them to supper.

I found out about one of these closet dowsers one day when our combined families went hiking on a fine spring day. Until that time I had been most careful not to mention any of my "unusual" ideas in their presence.

As we went trotting up the valley, nothing was further from my mind than anything parapsychological. I was admiring the wild flowers for which Texas is justly famous. Suddenly Glen, who was walking right in front of me, stopped and broke two forked branches off a small tree.

"Let's see if we can find some water," he said to his older son and handed him one of the branches. And off they went, father and son, each holding a forked branch in his outstretched arms. Naturally I trailed along right at their heels. Within a few minutes the branches started a curious dipping movement, and we all discovered a small spring in the side of the cliff.

In answer to the many questions that bubbled forth more abundantly than the spring water, Glen told us that he had been dowsing for water since he had been a small child in the Midwest. For some reason, water dowsing was a normal everyday sort of thing in that part of the country. If you needed a new well, you simply called a dowser to tell you where to dig. The dowser—clutching his forked stick—would walk back and forth until the stick dipped, and that was the place where your well was going to be. The art of dowsing, the finer points of technique and protocol, were learned by apprenticeship of a sort. Those interested to learn how to dowse followed the dowser on his appointed or not so appointed rounds and were instructed in the fine art of cutting a Y rod from certain trees; whittling it to the right dimensions if necessary; and, once the Y rod was held in the approved manner in the outstretched arms, to interpret its behavior so that the hidden water could be located quickly. That's how Glen had learned and then and there he offered to teach me. It was the best offer I'd had in quite some time so I pounced on it.

He handed me the forked stick cut from a sumac tree (dowsers usually have an affinity to a certain kind of wood and can't dowse with any other). He showed me how to grasp each end of the fork with the backs of each hand turned toward the ground and the ends of the Y rod parallel to it. My thumbs were tucked against the ends of the rod, while the rods rested between my third and fourth fingers. That grip gives maximum control (Fig. 7-1).

At first, holding the rod moderately tight, I had to practice tipping the rod forward and back until the rods felt natural in my hands. I could anticipate what Glen called the *toggle point* or point of no return, when the rods tipped down of their own weight. Next I was to ask the rods a question, such as "Where is some running water?" Last, I was to concentrate on the thought of trickling water while beginning my walk.

Feeling foolish and awkward, I trotted off between the trees, trying to keep my mind on visions of trickling sparkling water. Just when I was ready to drop the blasted rods on the ground and admit to utter failure in the water dowsing game, those rods in my hands seemed to take on a life of their own. They tipped down and toward the right.

"Turn to your right," called Glen who'd been watching from a few feet away.

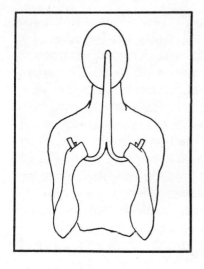

Fig. 7-1A. Holding a Y-rod in the search position.

I turned right and the rods went crazy. Their weight seemed to increase in geometric progression as they bobbed downward in fits. At last the tip pointed directly toward the ground and the rods returned to their original inanimate or at least only slightly animate state. But, as far as I could see, there was no water. The rod pointed at a bunch of rocks in a small clearing—very dry looking rocks, at that.

"Hey, that's not bad for a first try," Glenn commented when he reached the spot and pointed out that what I had found was what we call in Texas a *dry creek*. This is a creek that flows underground part of the year and only runs full on the surface during the rainy season.

I would like to be able to tell you that since that day in the woods I have dowsed up many a well and have helped to irrigate much of West Texas, but I can't. West Texas is as dry as ever, and I haven't even attempted to remedy the situation. Dowsing, somehow, isn't something that is easily done when you have a few minutes of spare time. At least not water dowsing when you, as we do, live in the city. Unless you enjoy dowsing for water mains and that just isn't my thing at all; however, that little experience had turned me on to the whole idea of dowsing and I have spent considerable time and effort finding out what other people have done with their dowsing instruments.

The first thing I found was that there were different kinds of dowsing rods, but most of them quite simple and easy to make. While the forked stick or Y rods are still most common and preferred by many for water dowsing, the L-rods are gaining steadily in popularity in dowsing circles.

L-rods are made of copper-coated steel of a gauge a little thicker than an ordinary coat hanger. In a pinch, however, you can make a pair of fair L-rods from some extra coat hangers. The wire is bent into an L shape at a right angle with the long portion, or pointer, measuring about 1 foot in length and the short ends, the handles, 5½ inches. The short ends are set into sleeves in which they can rotate freely. Fancy L-rods have special plastic sleeves (Fig. 7-2).

L-rods are a bit more sophisticated than Y-rods. They can be used to answer yes or no questions. I suppose you could do the same with the Y rods if you only expected one kind of response and took inaction as the other; that is, if you stipulated that *no* meant nothing happening to the rods, and yes would be indicated by the rods dipping. The L-rods, however, may turn up with two different yes positions, while they—just as the Y rods—indicate the negative by doing nothing at all. How is that for positive thinking—simply ignoring the negative all together.

In any case the L-rods will indicate a yes answer most commonly by flying apart and pointing in different directions. In some cases or for some people, the rods will turn inward and cross each other when they want to state the affirmative.

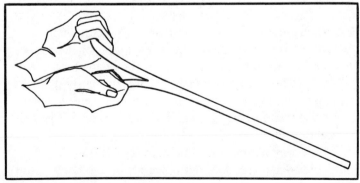

Fig. 7-1B. Y rod in "yes" position.

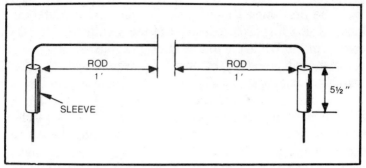

Fig. 7-2. Details of L-rods.

It would be interesting to speculate if the position has anything to do with the kind of question asked, that is if a qualified yes, or a yes that has some ambiguity attached would be more likely of the crossed variety. But I have no data along that line.

To use the L-rods, or dowser's angle as they are sometimes called, you hold them by the grips at waist level. The rods point down. This position is called the *search position*.

To get them to work for you ask them a question, just as we did when dowsing for water. You can then concentrate on the question, repeating it in your mind, or make your mind a blank. But don't think of something else, or let your mind flit ahead to a possible answer. While it's not easy to make one's mind a blank, the rods usually respond quickly enough so that you're faced with only a minute bit of blankness.

The L-rods can be worked singly also, mostly to indicate directions. You could ask a single L-rod "Where is north?" and the rod will swing into the north-south line.

Harvey Howells, in his book *Dowsing for Everyone*, describes how master dowser Gordon MacLean asked one of his L-rods to point to true north which it promptly did, and then inquired of his other rod to show him magnetic north. The second rod obligingly complied and formed a V formation with the other rod.

By the way if you're in a mood to try out dowsing in its simplest form and are clear out of L-rods or Y-rods, you can still have fun by using the coat hangers—the simple wire kind. Hold them one in each hand by the long side, with the hook pointing forward and the ends of the hooks down. In answering your questions, they should respond the same way as the L-rods; that is, *no* is no action, and *yes* can be either a flying apart or crossing of the coat hangers.

Whatever your instrument, in order to have success you have to relax and enjoy what you're doing. Don't worry about whether you can do it or not. Don't trouble your mind as to how it is done. Obviously, some kind of energy is at work, but it will work very well for you even if you don't identify it and call it by its correct name. In any case, it could be the energy of the many names and then you'd really have a problem picking out the correct one to use for this particular occasion. So go ahead and ask your questions and don't be too amazed at the answers (Fig. 7-3).

Another of our coat-and-tie friends is a geologist who works with oil companies. It wasn't until Mike inadvertently dropped a remark about designing an electronic dowsing rod that Jim, jumped out of the "closet" and confessed. It seems that good old Jim was using a dowsing rod on the sly every time he was hired as a consultant to a research and development department of a petroleum concern. In other words, Jim dowsed for oil and, according to him, has been rather successful in finding Texas gold.

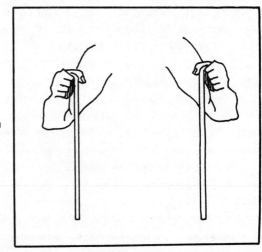

Fig. 7-3A. L rods in starting position.

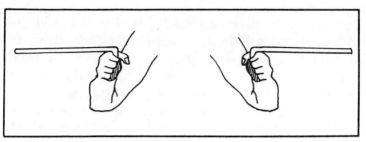
Fig. 7-3B. L rods say yes.

In fact, Jim is now in the throes of raising enough money to drill a well on some land he has on option. "I know I'll strike it rich," he told us the last time we saw him, a few weeks ago before he took off on round trip in his little Cessna to tie down the last of the needed backers. "I've refined my technique. I could tell you the barrels per minute," he claimed.

And he probably could at that; however, since the oil is many feet underground and since it takes many dollars to move the said oil up to the surface, and since we won't know if he is right or wrong until his gusher comes in, we'll have to wait for the proof. And Jim begs to remain surnameless until that glad day.

Jim is not the only professional person who uses dowsing, albeit sub rosa in his work. The lists of the American Society of Dowsers Inc. lists efficiency analysts, army officers, educators, judges and businessmen among their membership. The society is thriving and has chapters in more than fifteen states at this writing.

However, on the whole American dowsers are keeping their activites hidden from their colleagues in the professions. While it is an open secret that many oil and mineral development companies hire dowsers to locate sites, statements to the press as a rule categorically deny such things, and names of the dowsers involved are kept secret. Recently, since off-shore drilling became more important and more costly, dowsers have been kept busy locating the exact spots.

How is that done? How can a dowser detect oil under thousands of feet of seawater? Bascially, how does any dowsing take place? While the subject has suffered greatly from neglect and disbelief in the phenomenon in this country, the U.S.S.R. and Czechoslovakia have spent a lot of time and money to answer these questions.

Today dowsing is a legitimate field of study in the U.S.S.R. Major geology schools in Leningrad and Moscow have large research groups consisting of geologists, geophysicists, and physiologists hard at work studying dowsing. Dr. A.A. Ogilvy, when he was chairman of the Geology Department of Moscow State University, stated that dowsing will be used to solve problems and may supplant many contemporary geophysical methods. He also stressed that there was nothing mystical in the ability of man's body to react to underground water or minerals.

Interestingly enough, the Russian geologists and geophysicists do not study dowsers at work. They do the dowsing themselves and so can study the phenomenon first hand. Being experts in their fields, they can interpret the behavior of the dowsing rods in a more meaningful and precise fashion.

This all began when some years ago Professor G. Bogomolov, a famous Soviet water geologist, got hold of an old "wizard rod," as the Russians call it, and found to his utter amazement that he could determine the depth of underground streams and cables. Furthermore, he was somehow able to even specify the diameter of water pipes. Convinced that he was on to something exciting, he enlisted the help of two hydrology engineers, Drs. Tareev and Simonov, and began to run a large battery of tests. They

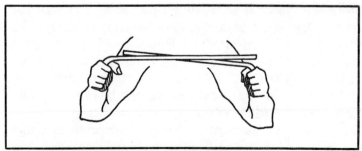

Fig. 7-3C. A different kind of yes with L-rods.

concluded that man indeed had the talent to detect substances deep underground, an ability that had to be understood and used to serve science. And despite the constrictions being imposed on everyone during that time, the Stalin era, they published their findings in a scientific journal, "The Journal of Electricity," in 1944.

The response to the article was mixed but it engendered a mass test. A hundred persons, some from the Red Army and others from the geological institute, were equipped with fresh Y-rods cut from the same shade tree and told to find water pipes, ground water, and electric cables. And, being used to doing what they were told, they did just that. The only difference was that for some people, the rod dipped, while for others, it rose straight up in the air. The scientists explained this quickly as a consistent phenomenon indicating the way current flowed in the cable or pipe.

Another thing the scientific commission did was to take the wizard out of the wizard rod, and the magic element out of dowsing. The dowsing rod was declared to be the simplest electrophysiological instrument because the wooden fork acquired supersensitivity to underground objects when held in human hands. And, when they measured the force that dipped or raised the tip of the rod, they found it ranged from 100 to 1000 grams per centimeter.

Also it was discovered that there seemed to be no shield that would keep out the energy that caused the rods to move. They tried rubber and steel plates, and even lead suits. Nothing worked. The only way the presence of water could be kept from the rod in a human hand was to run the water through a rubber hose. Another interesting fact was that after two or three days, the forked branch would lose its sensitivity (the branch, not the human being). If the person was equipped with a fresh branch, all was well and the dowsing activity proceeded as before. Also, if the branch was broken it lost its sensitivity and couldn't be restored to its former state no matter what was used to patch it up.

Many a test later, and the Russians are pretty thorough and have many "willing" subjects readily at hand, the scientists concluded that the dowsing rod can be used with striking success to locate underground electrical cables, water pipes, minerals (from gold through to lead), and, of course, water.

Today, dowsing is a respectable part of the Soviet repertoire of scientific techniques. It is now known by a nice new scientific name, the *biophysical effects method* or BPE, and the people practicing it are referred to as *operators* This makes it all neat, tidy, and completely unmystical.

Since we have been talking about our brethren in the U.S.S.R., I'll give you directions to build a Soviet-style dowsing rod, based on the one Sheila Ostrander and Lynn Schroeder describe in their book, *Psychic Discoveries Behind the Iron Curtain*.

YOUR BPE U-ROD # 1

What you need:
5 feet of Number 8 gauge wire,
Pliers and a yard stick

How to do it:

1) Bend the wire into a big loop.

2) Cross the ends over each other and straighten the ends into 3-inch handles (Fig. 7-4).

YOUR BPE U-ROD # 2

What you need:
Same as in "BPE #1."

How to do it:

1) Mark the center on your wire length.

2) Make an 8″ loop in the center of the wire.

3) Cross the ends over each other.

4) Bend them out horizontally 6 inches on each side.

5) Bend them down vertically for a foot on each side forming a U.

6) Bend out 3 inches on each end horizontally for handles.

7) The distance between the handles should be close to 2 feet (Fig. 7-5).

HOW TO USE YOUR GENUINE BPES

Hold the rod horizontally in your hands with your arms outstretched. Hold the handles loosely in your hands so that

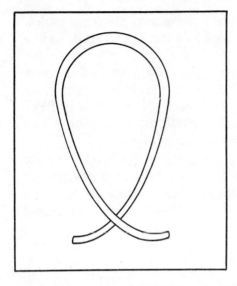

Fig. 7-4. BPE U rod No. 1.

they can move freely—similar to the sleeve on the L-rods. When you walk over underground water or some electric cables the rod will turn in a circle.

In Russia, automatic recording devices are attached to these rods, which graph, what went on and what gyrations the rod went through. In this way they seem to be able to estimate depth and size of underground water and mineral deposits. The relationship is between size and the number of rotations of the rods.

ELECTRONIC DOWSING ROD

What you need (Fig. 7-6):
B1 - 9v battery
C1-2.2 μF capacitor
C2 - 1 μF capacitor
C3 - 0.1 μF capacitor
IC1 - integrated circuit 567 Tone detector
LED - light-emitting diode TIR-107
R1 - 100K potentiometer
R2 - 1K ¼-watt resistor
on-off switch
length of copper wire No. 6
4×2×1 inch project case

PC board to fit
hook-up wire
solder
hardware

How to Do It

Bore a hole in each side of project box to accommodate the length of No. 6 copper wire (Fig. 7-7). Use rubber grommets in the holes. Make sure that enough wire protrudes on each side so that you can grip it firmly in both hands. Assemble the IC, resistor R2, and capacitors on the PC board. Drill holes for potentiometer shaft, LED, and off-on switch, and then mount them on the front of the project box. Slip the assembled PC board into slots in the project box and wire in the LED and the pot. Push copper dowsing rod (No. 6 copper wire) through the holes provided and solder a lead from the copper rod to Pin No. 3 of the 567 IC. Mount the battery holder and wire in last. Double check your wiring and insert the battery. You are now ready to dowse.

How It Works

The electronic dowsing rod is basically a tone detector capable of detecting "tones" in the frequency range from 0 -

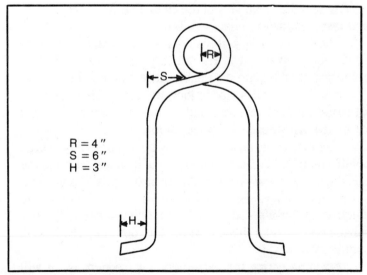

Fig. 7-5. BPE U rod No. 2.

213

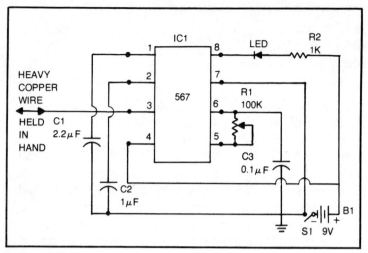

Fig. 7-6. Electronic dowsing rod.

0.01 Hz (less than 1 cycle per minute) to 500 KHz. The 567 chip contains a phase-locked loop. When the input frequency matches the center frequency of the chip, pin 8 goes low and allows the LED to glow.

The input frequency is the signal picked up by the dowser's body, fed to the 567 through pin 3. The potentiometer R1, sets the frequency of the chip. This frequency can be determine by the formula: $f = 1.1/RC$

The 567 can be adjusted to detect any input between the ELF band well below 1 Hz, all the way to the AM radio broadcast band—quite a valuable little chip for the serious dowser. The natural period or long-wave frequency of almost all materials and minerals fall in this spectrum. Of most interest will be those ELF waves below 10 Hz.

The electronic dowsing rod can be calibrated by using a pointer on R1 and making a notation of its position when the LED lights up. You will find water at one position setting, silver at another, and so forth. You can calibrate the electronic dowsing rod (EDR) by holding these and other substances in your hands while the dowsing road is in operation.

When detecting the extremely low frequencies, it will take the 567 a second or two to lock on, so give the device

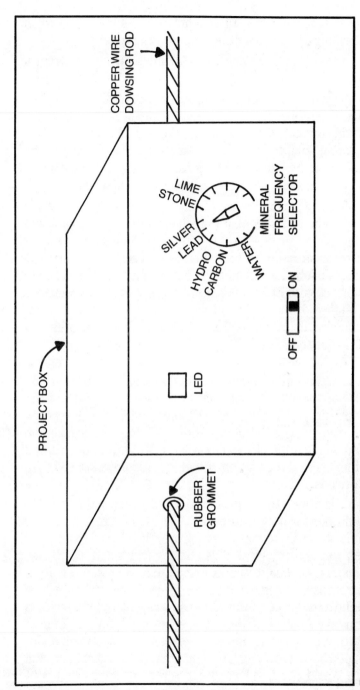

Fig. 7-7. Front view of electronic dowser.

COPPER WIRE DOWSING ROD

PROJECT BOX

LIMESTONE

SILVER LEAD

HYDRO CARBON

WATER

MINERAL FREQUENCY SELECTOR

OFF

ON

LED

RUBBER GROMMET

time to respond. Don't be in a hurry. Take your time when calibrating or using your electronic dowsing rod.

All substances, organic and inorganic, give off ELF waves. And most substances have one certain ELF wavelength that is one particular substance's signature. The human body, because of its many miles of nerve fiber, is a natural antenna for picking up these ELF waves. When operating devices like the dowsing rods or a pendulum, the muscles of the hands and fingers tend to go into resonance with these signals when they gain sufficient strength.

Thus, a pendulum, when lengthened to swing in a period equal to the ELF frequency of silver, will stop swinging and go into a circular motion at the frequency being detected and felt most strongly by the body. So it can be said that the muscles operate a pendulum or a dowsing rod in response to resonance with ELF waves. And in this case of the electronic dowsing rod, the body can work in conjunction with electronic circuits to respond more sensitively—accurately, as well as dependably.

Before we leave you to your dowsing, let me remind you not to wear leather gloves while dowsing. The leather will "kill" or "insulate" that energy the Russians dubbed the "biophysical effects" and which I like to think of as the energy with many names. If you insist on covering your hands, you might wear cotton gloves or even rubber gloves, but never a leather pair. (When using the electronic dowsing rod, use bare hands.)

The Soviet Union is not the only country in the world to use dowsers and their rods. The British have invented a rod that is so sensitive that it can apparently be used to pinpoint sites for archeological digs. The government of British Columbia, Canada, commissioned the famous dowser, Evelyn Penrose, to come and dowse for minerals and oil, which she did most successfully. Penrose was equally successful in her native Australia, where she spent much time helping to locate the immense mineral deposits in the then undeveloped bush. Dowsing has been going on in Czechoslovakia since World War I, at least as far as records are concerned. I am sure that the origin of dowsing in that country is in the dim dark past.

The Czecks use their dowsing rods not only for finding water, but they also have in war time located ammunition, food, and enemy encampments with dowsing. Particularly during World War II, the underground (hiding out in the Bohemian countryside) made good use of its trusty dowsing rods to avoid German traps and track the enemy when the occasion arose.

The Germans themselves have used dowsing rods to find water and are at present engaged in research about the nature of the dowsing phenomenon. The Dutch and Swiss, the Hungarians and the French—east, west, north, and south—the dowsing rod is being used and investigated all over Europe.

Back home in the U.S. the dowsing rod was used in semi-secrecy in Vietnam to discover mine fields. And, even though the powers that be do not like the fact made public, Vernon L. Cameron, one of the best known dowsers in America, asserts that L-rods are in daily use by almost every water and pipe line outfit in the country.

If you think that you know all about dowsing now and can move on to other subjects, you are in for a surprise. While dowsing rods are commonly used, another method of dowsing is even more popular and has been developed to a point where this rather esoteric seeming art can be safely called a *science*. This device is the *pendulum* and the person almost solely responsible for the current high development of the technique of pendulum dowsing is a Britisher named T.C. Lethbridge. Before we go into Mr. Lethbridge's innovations and discoveries, however, let's take a look at the simple, garden variety pendulum and what can be done with it.

Basically, a pendulum is a string or wire with a weight at one end (Figs. 7-8 through 7-11). It really doesn't seem to matter too much whether that ball is a lovely Bohemian crystal on a fine gold chain or an ordinary string plumb line with a weight at the end.

217

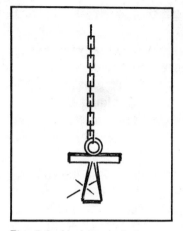

Fig. 7-8. Ahnk and chain pendulum.

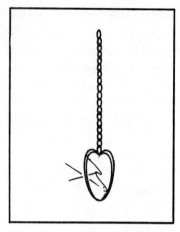

Fig. 7-9. Locket and chain pendulum.

A pendulum that might be suitable for you is one described by J. H. Howell as his favorite. That pendulum has a three-quarter-inch electronic capacitor fastened to a 12-inch fine metal chain by an eye bolt, whose point is allowed to protrude through the other end and make a needle-like stylus which gives tremendous precision (Fig. 7-12). Whatever kind of pendulum you select—and we have a surprise one for you later on—the pendulum has to be tuned to you before you can expect it to do any real work for you.

A pendulum has six basic modes: it can swing sideways, diagonally, back and forth, clockwise, and counterclockwise,

Fig. 7-10. Bead and string pendulum.

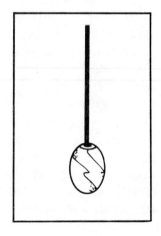

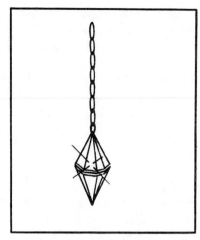

Fig. 7-11. Deluxe Pendulum: crystal on chain.

and it can rest. The first thing to do is find out what length of chain or string is right for you. To do this hold the string or chain in your hand, steady your elbow on a table, and experiment by letting the chain slide through your fingers and slowly lengthening the distance between the bob or weight of the pendulum and the ends of your finger. Some people like to work with as short a length as 3 inches; others prefer a much longer string. And, of course, Mr. Lethbridge has a whole lot of very specific instructions for his experiments, but we'll get to that later.

Once you have adjusted the length and your elbow is still propped up on the table and your fingers and hand are as still as possible, ask the pendulum a question to which you

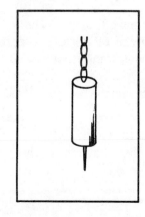

Fig. 7-12. Capacitor pendulum.

know the answer is yes, something as penetrating as "Is my name Ruth?" or "Is this table round?" Observe closely what happens. You have started with a completely still pendulum. Within 10 seconds or so after you've asked your yes-assured question, you'll begin to see movement in the pendulum. It will go into one of its five other modes of behavior, but which one it will be is up for grabs; that seems to be strictly a personal matter.

Let's say for argument's sake that the pendulum has begun to swing back and forth. That would indicate that back and forth is affirmative in your case, but before you accept this as a fact, try a few more certain yes-assured questions. If the pendulum continues to answer them with the same back and forth swing, you may now ask a question to which you know the answer is a resounding no, such as "Is today Sunday?" when you have just returned from a long hard day at the office on Monday. Or, pointing at your dog, "Is that my cat?"

You should now get a different response from your pendulum, most likely a side-to-side motion, or a diagonal one. Continue to ask the pendulum some more of those leading no-assured questions to make sure that you get the same response every time. Make certain that the pendulum is completely at rest between answers. You can do that by simply telling the pendulum to "stop" or "rest." It will follow that command, begin to slow down immediately, and be at complete rest within seconds.

Next, mix up the questions, but stick to those with known answers. Check each time to see if the pendulum is giving the correct response; that is, the response it has made consistently before. After another six responses, you are home free. Your pendulum is properly tuned to answer yes and no to your questions.

What you and your pendulum are going to discuss is between the two of you. Some of us have a lot of questions; others have only a limited amount. When you run down on the inquirer's end, you might want to shift your investigation of the possibilities of the pendulum to other spheres.

For one, you can use your pendulum just as you would your divining or dowser's rod to locate water, metals, and minerals. You can also use it with good success to locate lost objects. You'll find when you put your pendulum to this use that the motion of the pendulum will be a circular one, either clockwise or counterclockwise when you have "struck oil." Incidentally, as before, keep your mind on what it is you want the pendulum to locate. Particularily with a lost article, try to picture it as clearly as possible; it will help immensely.

The pendulum has been used to locate land mines, enemy ammunition depots, and troop convoys, as well as deposits of minerals and water. This is usually done by *map dowsing*. When you want to try your hand at map dowsing spread out a map on the table (with as large a scale as possible) and then slowly move your hand across the map, keeping your elbow propped up on the table and your hand holding the pendulum still. At the same time, keep in mind what you're dowsing for. When you get to a place where the substance is found, your pendulum will begin to rotate. To check this out, you might try it with your map covered with some newspaper or a tablecloth. Mark the points where the pendulum gyrated with a pin in the paper or cloth. If you try dowsing for water to begin with, your pins will coincide with lakes or rivers on the map, depending on whether you instructed the pendulum to find large bodies of water or running streams. Always be specific when you ask your pendulum the leading question, such as "Where is a *large* reservoir?" or "Where is the nearest above-ground stream of water?" The pendulum is quite literal in its answers, so don't confuse it and yourself with ambiguities.

Before we go on to more complicated uses for the pendulum, you might like to try some simple experiments in dowsing *for time*. In other words, you can find out what time it is without resorting to the usual means of telling time, such as clocks or watches which clutter our lives, as well as the radio, TV and even the oldest means of telling time, the sun.

In Europe, children have been practicing a simple form of time dowsing for generations. Nobody knows from what antiquity the idea came. It is much like the children's games that seem to be transmitted by osmosis from one generation to the next.

You must remember that in Europe, when I grew up, watches were not for children. If you were lucky, you got a gold watch for your confirmation present from your godmother or father. But even when you did possess such a timepiece, you wouldn't have dreamed of wearing it out to play—or even to school. Those watches were strictly for Sundays and state occasions. There were, to be sure, clocks on the many church steeples, but unless you happened to be at the right place when you wanted to know what time it was, these were of little use. You could also listen to those ubiquitous bells from those same steeples, but they were confusing because different bells rang at different intervals and in different patterns and it was often hard to tell whether it was half past ten, twelve o'clock, or maybe a quarter past eleven. And the bells also rang for funerals, weddings, at the beginning and close of mass, and many other occasions, which made telling time by the bells even more risky. Time dowsing with our own hands was easy, accurate, and could be used wherever we happened to be: skiing in the Vienna woods, hiking, sledding, and even out on the meadows playing soccer.

EUROPEAN CHILDREN'S DOWSING FOR TIME METHOD

Hold out your left hand (if you're right handed, and vice versa for lefties) palm up. The palm is your clock face. The base of your middle finger is 12, the point just opposite it at the bottom edge of your palm, just beyond the thumb is 6. The extension of the fold between your thumb and index finger is 9 and just across from it at the little finger side of your palm is 3 (Fig. 7-13). In order to tell time, you have to go through three steps: ask the question, dowse for the hour, and dowse for the minutes.

The questions were asked in a ritual rhyme: *Meine gute Uhr Du bist, sag mir doch wie spaet es ist*. In English, my good dear clock are you; tell me the time correct and true. While you ask the question concentrate on your palm and move the index finger of your other hand around the palm in a clockwise direction.

Stop the movement when it feels right and note the position of the index finger. This will be your hour reading. Repeat the tracing procedure and again stop where it feels right. That will be the minute reading.

A good time to try out this way of telling time is when you first wake up in the morning on a weekend and have no idea what time it is. Even better, is to try it when you wake in the middle of the night. You can then check it against the clock. It takes a little practice, but it works beautifully once you get the hang of it.

The method can also be used to "set your alarm." Trace the hours and minutes in your hand. Only this time stop at the place you want the hands to be when you wake up (Fig. 7-14). Again, with a little practice, you'll be able to wake up on your own at just the time you decided.

Another old method of time dowsing involves a pendulum. This time you hold the pendulum so that the bob is inside a tumbler (Fig. 7-15).

Again concentrate and ask your question in prose or rhyme (whichever feels better to you). The pendulum will begin to gyrate inside the tumbler and strike against the glass the required number of times to give the reading for the

Fig. 7-13. Palm clock face.

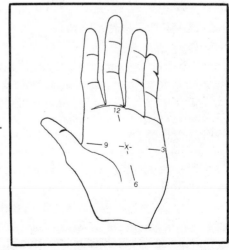

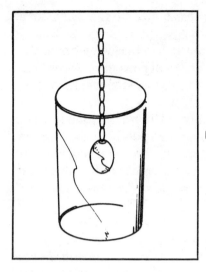

Fig. 7-14. Detail of time dowsing.

hour. Sometimes it will give a gentle tap for the half hour. Of course, if you like, you can ask the question twice, once for the hour and once for the fraction of the hour. Don't ask for minutes, you might get worn out waiting for the 45 or so taps.

It's time to concentrate on the work of the great old man in the field, the aforementioned T.C. Lethbridge, author, lecturer at Cambridge England, archeologist, scientist, and one of the most unusual and creative men of recent times. Let's begin by contructing a pendulum to his rather simple specifications.

THE LETHBRIDGE PENDULUM

What you need:

A small ball or bead of wood, about 1″ in diameter.

2 yards or so of linen thread (Number 10 cotton will do, too, but don't substitute nylon or polyester thread, it doesn't work well)

1 short end of dowel about the thickness of a pencil and 3 inches in length

1 wooden match or other small peg to fit the hole in the bead.

How-To Do It

Peg the thread into the ball with the matchstick. Make sure it is in good tight. Wrap the other end of the thread around the center of the dowel or pencil.

With this simple device, Mr. Lethbridge made some rather amazing discoveries. The only additional objects he used were a steel measuring tape, a notebook, and pen. You will need them also. The real difference between the Lethbridge pendulum and other pendulums is the length of the thread, commonly seven inches or less.

The short pendulum will answer your yes and no questions and it will also, according to Lethridge, tell you in advance if a certain food will suit you. To do this, you swing the pendulum very gently between you and the food. If the pendulum begins to swing in a circle, you better skip that dish. It seems to be an old French custom. The French have been avid pendulum users for quite some time—and rather openly so, too.

The problem with the short pendulum is that when you want a bit more sophisticated information you have to make up samples of what they wish to find. These samples are called *witnesses* and are often a nuisance to obtain. Without them, you're out of luck. With the long pendulum, however you can dispense with witnesses or samples all together. As long as you have your trusty steel measuring tape and your notebook with the requisite numbers, you are in business. The Lethbridge method of dowsing is based on *rate*. Rate, an old term, means the length of thread from the top of the ball or bob of the pendulum to the bottom point from which it is suspended.

To use the Lethbridge pendulum, you must find out the rate for different things. Let's say you want to dowse for silver. You will find out the rate for silver once and for all. No

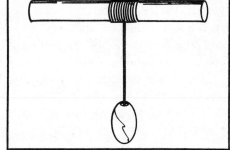

Fig. 7-15. The Lethbridge pendulum.

need to get near another silver object once you have the rate number in your notebook. Here's how you find the rate for silver.

Place a silver spoon or silver object on the floor. Hold the pendulum by the windlass (the dowel wrapped with thread) between your thumb and forefinger above the spoon. Very slowly begin to unwrap the thread. At the same time, keep the bob of the pendulum swinging very slightly back and forth. At a certain length, the oscillation (back and forth movement) will interrupt or slow down. At about another half inch farther, the pendulum will begin to gyrate into a circular motion. This will be the rate for silver. Mr. Lethbridge found it to be 22 inches.

Silver is not the only thing that has a rate of 22 inches; Lead does, and so do calcium, sodium, and the color gray. Yes, colors have rates, too. Also, some quite abstract ideas do too. So you will need more to identify silver accurately than just the rate. And while it took Lethbridge a long time to figure out just how to pin down that elusive second factor, you can have the information right now. The answer was simple and elegant as most great discoveries are. The qualifying factor to the rate is the number of gyrations. Isn't that beautiful?

This is the way it works. At 22 inches the pendulum stops to move back and forth and begins to gyrate over the silver spoon. It doesn't just keep on gyrating, though. It gyrates exactly 22 times and then sedately resumes a back and forth swing. So the pendulum code you'll write down for silver is 22:22.

If you have an unknown substance and the pendulum begins to gyrate at 22 inches, you might find out that you have calcium if the pendulum gyrates 30 times, which you would note down as 22:30. Or you might come up with 22:7 notation, which will turn out to be the color gray.

One of the most exciting discoveries in Lethbridge's research is that the pendulum, by using his method, will deal with abstract ideas, as well as with concrete one. Lethbridge explains it this way. "Every thought, whether concrete or abstract, appears to have a series of coordinates which enables one's superconscious to isolate it instantly. They seem to be like a much more extensive telephone directory, and we have only found the first pages of it. . . . In fact, the pendulum is dealing with thought forms and not with the kinds of things you can measure in a laboratory. It is the idea in one's mind of a pin beneath the ground which it will demonstrate for you and not the solid metal object as we believe it to be in ordinary life. You can dig up the pin, and it will be hidden exactly where the pendulum said it was, but it was the mental impression which was shown to you in the code."

And so Lethbridge has found the code for love to be 20:20 and anger, cold, black, north, sleep, and death in the 40 range.

Here is an ELF electronic pendulum (Fig. 7-16).

THE ELF ELECTRONIC PENDULUM

What you need:

B1, B2, B3, B4 - 9-volt batteries

C1 - 0.1 μF capacitors

C2 - 2200 pF capacitors

C3C4 - 0.01 μF capacitors

IC1 - 3160 integrated circuit op amp (National Semiconductor)

IC2 - LM331 integrated circuit V/F (National Semiconductor)

IC3 - 741C integrated circuit op amp (Radio Shack)

J1 - jack for single test lead

J2 - jack for two wire electrode leads

Mi - 0-1 mA meter

(All resistors ½-watt 5 percent tolerance)

R1 - 75K resistor

R2, R3 - 100K potentiometer

R4 - 90K resistor

R5 - 10K resistor

R6 - 100K potentiometer

R7 - 4.71 resistor

R8 - 10K resistor

R9 - 9.09K resistor

R10 - 2K potentiometer

R11 - 5K potentiometer
R12 - 10K resistor
R13, R14 - 100K resistor
R15 - 1 megohm potentiometer
R16 - 100K resistor
R17 - 5K potentiometer
R18 - 10K resistor
S1, S2, S3, - spst switches
Electrode set (as suggested in Chapter 3)
one test lead with plug
battery clips
project case and PC board to fit
wrapping wire
hardware

How To Do It

Construction is straightforward. Observe the usual precautions when handling and wiring the ICs. The LM331 chip incorporates CMOS circuitry; therefore, CMOS handling precautions *must* be observed to avoid permanent damage. (See the Appendix on MOS and CMOS handling precautions.)

Mount the meter (M1) and all "tuning" controls and switches on the front panel where you can operate them. Check, double check, and triple check your wiring before turning on the power to the circuit. Make sure that there is a good ground connection at G. A good earth ground is absolutely essential for operating the ELF electronic pendulum.

How It Works

The bridge circuit in connection with battery B3 (Fig. 7-16) delivers a small voltage to op amp IC1 when it is unbalanced by the adjustment of R2 and R3. The 3160, used as an integrator, drives the LM331 voltage/frequency connector. The voltage to frequency conversion is perfectly linear from 0 to 9 volts, producing a frequency range of from 0 to 9 kHz at the output (pin 3) of the LM331.

We are interested in the very low voltage to frequency conversion of microvolts and milivolts to produce frequency

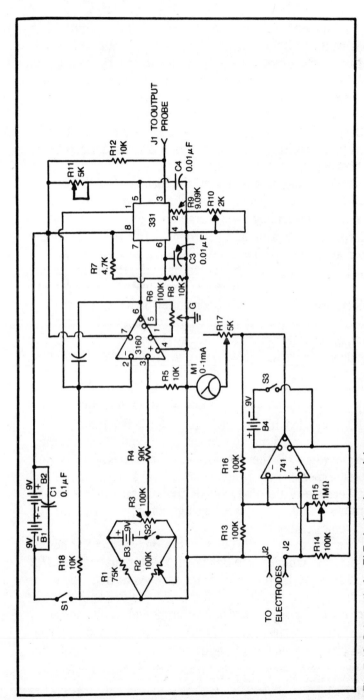

Fig. 7-16. Schematic for ELF electronic pendulum.

229

outputs below 1 Hz, on as low as the IC will operate. The probe containing this output signal is held in one hand of the operator, who serves as a receiver for the ELF waves given off by bodies of water and mineral deposits, each with its own resonant frequency. By fine tuning the frequency of the V:F connector at R2 and R3 (R3 serves as a fine tuning or "bandspread" control), signals may be superimposed so that when in phase, they will double their amplitude, and when out of phase, they will cancel.

This situation will upset the balance of the bridge amplifier (IC3) and cause a wild swing of the meter. Thus, if the subject is standing over a large body of water, such as an underground stream, and receiving ELF waves from the water at its natural frequency of—say, 60 cpm (cycles per minute)—when the V:F converter is tuned to that frequency *or one of its harmonics*, (which is more likely) the meter will deflect, provided that it has been nulled by R15.

R17 can be used to put the null reading in the middle of the meter scale so that both in-phase and out-of-phase signals can be read. R11 can be used to calibrate the device with a voltmeter connected to the input and a frequency meter connected to the output. Adjust R11 until you get a 9-kHz output with exactly 9 volts input. R10 is the trimmer for R11, and R6 will trim the input for extra fine tuning.

Keep in mind that the human body (with its many miles of nerve fibers) is the only known efficient receiver of ELF waves, especially for frequencies below 1 Hz. You will find that because of the body's sensitivity, you can use all the trimming, nulling, and balancing controls built into the electronic pendulum.

But once the electronics of the device and the human subject are trimmed and balanced, the tuning controls (R2 and R3) can be calibrated to give you deflections at frequencies or harmonics that correspond to water, silver, gold, lead, petroleum, and most other mineral substances.

Each substance has its own ELF *signature* which can be recognized by bringing body-mind and electronics into resonance with that signature. These frequencies correspond to Lethbridge's rates.

As you have undoubtedly noticed, the electronic pendulum works on the same principle as Lethbridge's pendulum. The relationship between the thing dowsed for and the dowser is simply described in different terms and from different frames of reference.

So what are you going to do with all those pendulums that you now have in your possession? Well, if you read Lethbridge as we strongly recommend you should, you will be kept busy with ideas.

Here are just a few samples of the kind of discoveries that can be made with a pendulum:

☐ You can find mineral deposits of any kind.
☐ You can dowse for water.
☐ You can dowse for oil and gas.
☐ You can find artifacts of archeological importance.
☐ You can dowse for gem stones.
☐ You can dowse for lost articles.
☐ You can dowse for missing persons.
☐ You can dowse for absent pets.
☐ You can test food to see if it is fresh.
☐ You can test your own reaction to different foods.
☐ You can test food supplements and see which ones you need.
☐ You can study map dowsing and find out where mineral deposits are in far away places.
☐ You can map dowse your way from one place to another.
☐ You can find out what your plants need to grow profusely.

What is really fascinating when you get tired of doing all of these is dowsing for relationships, or ecological dowsing. This, to me, is probably the greatest contribution that Lethbridge has made.

He found that grass, for instance, has a pendulum rate of 16. This same grass, in the natural course of events (when it isn't used to adorn your front lawn but grows naturally on a field or meadow, will be eaten and expelled in the course of time and digestion as manure. This manure will also have the rate of 16, and so will the scarab beetle family which feed on and spend their entire existence in manure.

This relationship—the sharing of a given rate—seems to hold true for predators and their prey, as well as their vegetarian brothers and their food supply. And there are other more mysterious connections that will give you food for thought for many a long winter evening—and hours and hours of dowsing practice.

For instance, Lethbridge states that the 29-inch length of the pendulum is shared by the concept, female; gold; yellow; and the concept, danger. Now how do you relate these bits and pieces to make an ecological whole? Lethbridge himself speculated that the relationship might be an explanation of the affinity between females and gold. There is yellow in the gold and there might be danger. Lethbridge, on the other hand, being male brings the danger back to the female and quotes Kipling's " . . . and the female of the species is more deadly than the male." Also he brings up the fact that plants that have yellow blooms are quite often poisonous.

You see how it goes? It's practically endless, like that huge telephone directory Lethbridge likened it to earlier. During his lifetime, Lethbridge charted a few hundred rates. According to his estimates, there must be thousands, if not millions. Where he had discovered two of the coordinates, he felt there must be dozens more to find.

And if you are a bit awed, as we all are when faced with such tremendous opportunities for discovery and learning and can't quite find a good starting point, I have one for you. According to Lethbridge, you can figure out a person's *psi* count. This is generally found at 9½ inches. And here is the way you can tell just how much potential a person has brought into this world in the psi arena: A person whose pendulum gyrations at 9½ inches are less than 10 will have some difficulty in learning to use a pendulum or divining rod, and probably any other of the psi skills. But—and here is the great news—with repeated experiments with either the pendulum or a dowsing rod, the gyration number will steadily increase.

Chapter 8
Kirlian Photography

Although researchers and experimenters in America have
been paying attention to electrophotography, now known as
Kirlian photography, only since the early to middle 1970s, it
is not new. Nikola Tesla (the great genius who gave us
alternating current and the power grid) invented the first
high-frequency spark generator (the Tesla coil) around the
turn of the century and undoubtedly made some photographs.
One of his contemporaries, Yakov Yokdo, displayed such
photographs at the fifth photographic exhibition in Russia in
1898. In the early 1900s, several Czechs and one American
(F.E. Nipher) published monoliths on electrophotography.
From about 1940 to 1970, Semyon and Valentine Kirlian
invented a wide range of devices that take up much space in
the annals of the Soviet patent office with which to make
spark generator-induced photographs for research and experimentation in such diverse areas as dentistry, botany, and
holography. It was the Kirlians that developed the technology of electrophotography to a high art-science.

The publication in 1970 by Sheila Ostrander and Lynn
Schroeder of their best selling book. *Psychic Discoveries
Behind the Iron Curtain,* brought interest in the Kirlian
technology of electrophotography to America. Soon scientists from Stanford, UCLA, the University of New Mexico,
and the Newark College of Engineering, to mention just a

few, were experimenting and publishing in the field. The editors of *Popular Photography* magazine coined the term technology-art-science for Kirlian photography and commented, " . . . the imaginative possibilities are terrific." Even the medical journal, *The Osteopathic Physician,* devoted the entire October, 1972 edition "to this exciting new phenomenon."

As we said, there was really nothing new about it, except in America we had simply been overlooking more than 20 years of developments in Soviet photography of electric fields surrounding living things. It is still a frontier field, even in the Soviet Union, especially as it applies to the field of parapsychology where most American research has been concentrated.

You can delve deeply into this technology-art-science whether you have little or great interest in or knowledge about electronics. I will pass along the Ostrander and Schroeder Beauty Shop Special for those with little or no knowledge of electronics and the dc Kirlian device designed by Robert Martin for those who will want to build their own with up-to-date electronics. I have built and used both and the range of experimentation possible with either one is unlimited. If you'd like to design your own, from scratch, what is needed is a good basic square wave oscillator working in the 120-Hz to the 1-MHz range, with discharge voltages from 50 kV to 200 kV.

Figure 8-1 will give you a schematic for a good square wave oscillator using a 566 IC for voltage control of the frequency. Pin 3 will provide the square wave output (pin 4 gives a triangular wave output, which is not desired). The oscillator is very stable over a tremendously wide range of frequencies. R1 and C1 control the center frequency over which R2 controls either side. It is the voltage at pin 5 that determines the frequency. Output voltage does not fall to zero, but varies from six to about 12 volts up and down the square. This oscillator triggers a high-voltage source, usually with SCR control of a large capacitor.

I suggest you build and operate both the Beauty Shop and Martin versions before you start designing on your own.

Actually, any high-frequency spark generator can simply be used with its glass electrode to make Kirlian photographs without any adaptation at all. If you place a piece of film in a light-tight envelope and hold it against your skin, or other photographic subject, and touch the glass electrode to it you will get an electrophotograph. This can be done in the daylight but the film, of course will have to be developed in the dark. You can also wire the spark generator to an exposure plate in a box, with a light-tight lid to be closed for daylight work. Edmund Scientific sells a Tesla coil for about $100 (cat. #70,301) that can be used in this way with no further fuss or bother. However, you will get far better photographic results with this Beauty Shop Special.

THE OSTRANDER-SCHROEDER
KIRLIAN PHOTOGRAPHY DEVICE

Your local beauty-supply company can supply a Tesla coil of excellent quality for under $50. It is a simple, plug-in

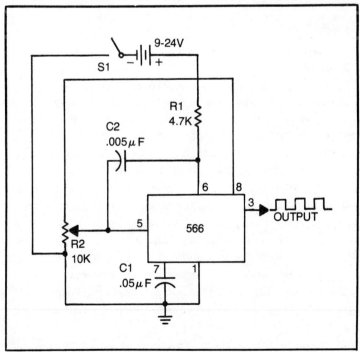

Fig. 8-1. Voltage-controlled square wave oscillator.

coil in an angular molded bottle-shaped handle used by barbers and beauticians for facial, scalp, and skin treatments. Although the unit delivers extremely high voltage, it puts out extremely low amperage and is quite safe to use. There are apparently no other hazards associated with being exposed to these high-frequency currents since the Kirlians exposed themselves daily for over 20 years and both lived quite long. I would suggest good ventilation of your working area since the device does give off ozone. Parts, other than the coil can be purchased for just a few dollars.

Parts

High-frequency spark treatment coil with one glass electrode*, 3-in × 6-in copper-clad board, single-sided (Radio Shack #276-1586), extension cord with built-in off-on switch, Misc.—6 feet copper bell wire, 4 alligator clips, electricians tape, rubber eraser, small wooden box 6-in. × 13-in. (cigar box perfect).

Construction

Cut a 2-inch length of bell wire and remove one-half inch of insulation from each end. Solder one end of the wire to the copper side of the copper-clad board, or tape it down firmly with electrician's tape. Drill a small hole in the exact center of the box lid and thread the wire through it so that the copper-clad board goes *copper side down* on top of the lid. Tape the board securely into place with electrician's tape on all four sides. Drill a small hole in one end of the box.

Cut about 2 feet of bell wire and remove a bit of insulation from each end. Attach an alligator clip to one end. Wind the wire around the screw in the clip in the direction the screw turns. Thread the other end of the wire through the hole in the side of the box and run it to the high-frequency unit, which can stay in its cardboard box. Make neat holes for access to the voltage control knob and cord. Push the end of the wire through the rubber eraser allowing about one-half

---

*Available from Illinois R.S. Company, 865 North Sangamon Street, Chicago, Illinois 60622. Ask for High-Frequency Unit No. 10 with the No. 1 General Electrode.

inch of bare wire to protrude on the other end of the eraser. This makes a plug that will fit snugly into the socket of the high-frequency unit. Be sure to push in the plug tightly so that the bare copper wire makes good contact with the metal of the socket. You can pull this plug anytime you wish to use the unit with its glass electrode. Then replace it after use. Now clip the alligator clip at the other end of the wire to the 2-inch length of wire taped to the copper-clad board on the box lid. Plug the high-frequency unit into the extension cord, as the hook-up diagram in Fig. 8-2 shows.

Put the remaining two alligator clips on each end of the remainder of the bell wire to make a grounding wire. Some objects photograph better if grounded, but when photographing people, do not let them come into contact with a real ground. Other subjects can be grounded to a cold water pipe, or to any large metal object if no water pipes are handy. The grounding of the Tesla coil is taken care of through the power cord so be sure your extension cord is three-way with a grounded plug on one end.

Almost any kind of film that is convenient to use will give you satisfactory pictures. I find flat sheets of film easiest to use and have tried and can recommend all of the following:

Kodak Tri-x-pan #4164
Kodak Ortho #4154
Kodak Ektacolor S6101
Kodak Ektachrome 6115
(All of the above are available 4″ × 5″ or 3¼″ × 2¼″.)
Kodachrome X, 35mm, ASA 64
Ektachrome X, 35mm, ASA 64
(Above two are available 20 exposures on one roll.)

Polaroid color pack #108, if you have a polaroid camera or developing unit.

My preference, far and away, for sharpest pictures is Kodachrome II, ASA 25. Use exposure times of from ½ to 2 seconds with this film. I find the short exposure times give the best definition (clearest pictures).

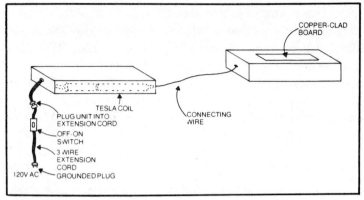

Fig. 8-2. "Beauty Shop" Kirlian photography device.

THE ROBERT MARTIN KIRLIAN PHOTOGRAPHY DEVICE

I like this design better than any of the American-designed Kirlian devices for several reasons. It is capable of good and very consistent results. It is portable. And it is a dc device, battery-operated, which eliminates the hazards of ac operation. Even though amperages are extremely low, they can still be hazardous under some conditions, when connected to ac power lines.

The schematic in Fig. 8-3 presents details of a device that uses one 6-volt lantern battery and one 22.5-volt transistor radio battery. Pulse rate and output voltage are variable. R5 controls the pulse rate, or frequency, and S3 the output voltage. Output voltage is highest when discharging through capacitor C4.

How the Circuit Works

An inverter, using two ordinary germanium pnp power transistors takes 6 volts dc from the lantern battery and converts it to 117 volts ac, then rectifies the output and feeds the *pulsed* dc to a discharge capacitor. This capacitor discharges through an auto ignition coil to provide the high-voltage spark current to the photographic film. T1 is a standard step-down transformer connected in reverse. The power transistors (Q1, Q2) alternately switch on and off, providing the pulsating voltage to the backward-connected transformer.

238

An oscillator utilizing a unijunction transistor (Q3) triggers a silicon-controlled rectifier (SCR1), which acts as a one-way switch that closes only when the trigger pulse from the oscillator fires it. This provides a discharge path for the capacitor (C2, C3, or C4), which has been charged by the inverter. The primary coil of the ignition transformer (T2) is in this path inducing a high voltage in the secondary, which is fed to the exposure plate, a layer of metal foil with a dielectric material on top. The exposure plate and the object to be photographed (usually grounded) make up the final discharge capacitor.

Parts

B1 - 6-volt lantern battery
B2 - 22.5-volt transistor radio battery
C1 - 2 μF capacitor
C2 - .25 μF 600-volt capacitor
C3 - .5 μF 600-volt capacitor
C4 - 1 μF 600-volt capacitor

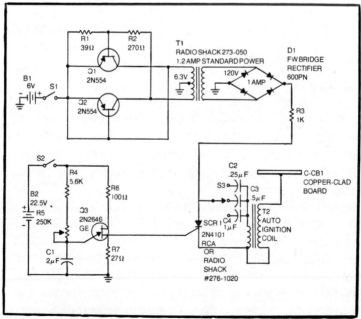

Fig. 8-3. R. Martin Kirlian photography device.

C-CB1 - 6×8" copper-clad board, single sided (Radio Shack #276-1587) exposure plate

D1 - Full-wave bridge rectifier, 600 PN, 1-amp.

Q1, Q2 - 2N554 power transistors

Q3 - 2N2646 unijunction transistor

R1 - 39-ohm resistor ½-watt

R2 - 270-ohm resistor ½-watt

R3 - 1K resistor ½-watt

R4 - 5.6K resistor ½-watt

R5 - 250K potentiometer

R6 - 100-ohm resistor ½-watt

R7 - 27-ohm resistor ½-watt

SCR1 - 6-amp SCR, GE 2N4101 RCA, or Radio Shack #276-1020

S1, S2 - spst switches

S3 - sp-three-position rotary switch, heavy duty

T1 - 1.2-amp standard power transformer, Radio Shack 273-050 or equivalent

T2 - auto ignition coil, any good one will work

Misc. - ground clamp, metal box to enclose electronics, cigar or other wooden or cardboard box to house discharge plate and photographic stage, aluminum for shielding oscillator circuit, hook-up wire and wrapping wire, hardware, solder, battery holders, etc.

Construction

Placement of parts is not critical but the oscillator circuit should be isolated from the inverter and high-voltage discharge section. Mount parts on an IC perfboard with the board bracketed to the metal cabinet. Place controls for R5 and S3 (frequency and voltage controls) on the front panel, along with S1 and S2. S1 is your exposure switch, and I have replaced my original toggle switch with a normally-open momentary switch. You need to find this switch in the dark, so it helps to put a strip of luminous tape next to it. You might also want to consider a foot-operated exposure switch to free your hands while working in the dark. And for the best of all worlds, a photographic timer capable of timing fractions of seconds up to a minute will allow you to bring your exposures under precise control.

A lead needs to be provided to the exposure plate, which is a copper-clad unperforated laminated board. The board is just a little larger than most cigar box lids and so can replace the lid, with the remainder of the cigar box furnishing support for the photographic stage, which is the bakelite surface of the board. Solder a short length of wire to the copper laminate and use an alligator clip to connect the auto ignition coil to the exposure plate.

Grounding

Grounding of the device and objects to be photographed is an important consideration in Kirlian photography. The device itself should be grounded to the metal box as indicated in the schematic diagram (Fig. 8-3), and the box should then be connected to an infinite sink of electrons. A cold-water pipe is the best of all grounds for this particular device. If one is not available, use some large metal object, or bury several feet of bare bell wire in damp earth. Objects being photographed need to be grounded and can be effectively grounded by taping or clipping a wire from the object to the metal box. Do not, however ground people! *When photographing people or their parts do not allow them to come into contact with a real ground.*

HOW TO MAKE THE PHOTOGRAPHS

You will be working in the dark when you make your Kirlian photographs, so you will need to have your objects to be photographed, film, and other supplies handy and know right where they are so you can locate them in the dark.

It is advisable to do your own developing right there in the darkroom so that you can make test runs using several settings of frequency and voltage. Always start with low voltage and high frequency and then test the higher voltages and lower frequencies.

If you are not a hobby photographer-developer already, I suggest you start with one of the photo kits available at any camera store and at most discount and department stores where cameras are sold.

Set your timer, if you are using one, before you turn off the lights. If you are not using a timer, be sure you know where your timing switch is and can find it in the dark.

Put your film *emulsion side up* on the dielectric surface of the exposure plate and place the object to be photographed on top of the film emulsion. Ground the object if it is *not* a person or a pet. If it is a human or a pet hand or paw, press down *lightly* on the exposure plate. Just make a firm connection with the photographic film.

Turn on the device for anywhere from one-half to five seconds, depending on your test results. Low voltages and slow-speed film will require longer exposure times than high voltages and high-speed film. Following exposure, your film must either be developed or placed in a light-tight envelope for development at a later time.

How to Photograph in Daylight

It is possible to make Kirlian photographs in daylight if you can't get a darkroom in which to work. The best way to work in daylight is to make use of a photographer's black film changing bag. You will need to have your exposure plate box inside the bag, along with your film, *and* objects to be photographed. You make your exposures inside the bag, of course in total darkness, since the bag can be made light-tight after your hands have been inserted. This is a good way to work with Polaroid film, especially if you then have a Polaroid camera handy in which to develop the film when you bring it out of the bag. This is also a good way to demonstrate Kirlian photography to a large group of people.

You can also work in the daylight by having each piece of your film wrapped in a black, light-tight envelope. Use the envelopes sold for this purpose at camera and photographic supply stores. You must use a dark room (or black changing bag) to load your envelopes with film. Be sure to remember, or mark on the envelope, which side is the emulsion side. Put the emulsion side up when you lay the envelope on the exposure plate and put the object on top of it (on the emulsion side of the envelope).

The envelope method of daylight photography can also be used to photograph different areas of the body and in instances where you cannot get your object on your exposure plate. Place the film envelope (always emulsion side *up*) over the area you wish to photograph. If it is an object, don't forget to ground it. If it is a person, just be sure the film envelope is firmly attached with an elastic band. You will now need to take your beauty shop high-voltage unit out of its box and pull the plug that connects it to the exposure plate. Insert the glass electrode that came with the unit instead. Now touch the film envelope with the glass electrode while making your exposure. If you are using the Martin or other high-voltage device, you can make a special connector to fit into the glass electrode onto which you can secure the high-voltage lead with an alligator clip. Using this method, you can wrap a large piece of film (in a black envelope) around an object of most any shape and make several exposures by touching the electrode to various areas of the film envelope. Each place your electrode touches the film will be exposed. This can be especially useful when exploring acupressure points on the body.

MAKING KIRLIAN SLIDE SHOWS AND MOVIES

The simplest setup for making a movie featuring Kirlian photography is to set up your exposure plate between two take-up reels and wind the film onto one of the take-up reels after exposing the film one frame at a time. Space your exposures as evenly as you can by winding it evenly onto the take up reel. You can keep your device on continually or run it intermittently for different effects. Be sure you do not exceed the recommended "on" time for your particular high-frequency device, however. Another technique that is effective in this simple setup is to use your glass electrode and touch it to the object once to make each frame of the movie. You may use eight, super-eight, 16 mm or 35 mm film for these movies. Slides can be made in a similar manner, with the 35 mm film being wound out of one cassette into another across the exposure plate. You can purchase an empty cassette and winder key at almost any camera store. It takes several turns of the key to advance the film one frame. Be sure to experiment with this so that you will know how many turns to make in the dark for each frame you wish to expose. A flat cardboard holder is a handy device to keep your film flat against the exposure plate when using these methods. You may need some tiny weights on the holder. For an interesting effect, try using tiny permanent magnets as weights to hold the film flat and move them around from frame to frame and see how the electric discharge tends to follow the fields of force.

If you send your 35 mm slide film out to be developed, be sure to mark it, *Do Not Mount,* so that the film will be returned to you uncut. That way you can clip each individual exposure from the roll and mount them in slide mounts with just the composition you want.

Your movie or slide show can be sent to a processing lab or taken down to your local television station for dubbing onto videotape if you like that method of presentation. Your local TV station might well do the dubbing for you in exchange for an interview with you about your work in Kirlian photography. I find it does tend to make you an instant celebrity.

Whether or not you derive any notoriety out of your new technology-science-art form, even the simple beauty shop Kirlian apparatus will set you out on a fascinating journey into a whole new world of energy patterns. By studying *electrograms* of your own finger tips under different conditions of tension and relaxation, and in the various states of consciousness you drop into, and by correlating your experience with various psychic effects, you will learn much about yourself at the very least and perhaps even develop a new form of artistic expression for yourself. And, if you are of an inventive turn of mind, perhaps you would like to continue experimentation where the Kirlians left off into the hundreds of possible applications of using high-frequency electricity as a photographic medium. One day, you might even discover just what it is we are really photographing.

It has been theorized by some, including Rodney Ross of the Foundation for Gifted and Creative Children, Warwick, Rhode Island, that Kirlian photographs are pictures of light emitted by the ionization of air due to cold electron emissions from the persons, pets, or objects being photo-

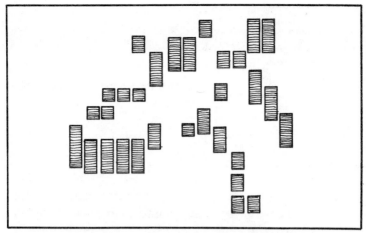

Fig. 8-4. Ivy leaf one minute after cut (Kodak infrared film).

graphed. Most investigators and experimenters see a connection between the human aura and the field we see in the Kirlian photograph. My own idea is that the Kirlian photograph is a true psychic event in that what we see is the end of

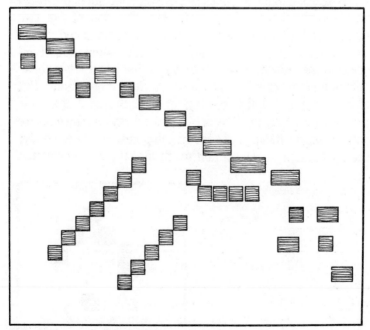

Fig. 8-5. Living African Violet leaf.

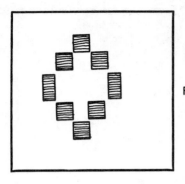

Fig. 8-6. Fake finger corona at 91°F.

a chain of events begun by the flow of thermal energy in the body or object. We have already identified thermal energy as the primary "psychic" energy, and a psychic event as the end of a chain of mundane events begun by the movement of thermal energy. I believe that the meridians mapped out by the ancient Chinese are pathways of subtle heat flow through the body (or any other object) and that the high conductivity areas along these meridians, which they identified intuitively as acu-points, are areas where the thermocouple effect between the heat flow and the juxtaposition of the two dissimilar metals, sodium and potassium, balanced within every living cell, creates an electrical potential that increases the emission of electrons at that point. It is these "electron fountains" we see in our Kirlian photographs. But since the output of the fountains is the end result of a chain reaction involving the flow of thermal energy and the delicate and necessary balance of sodium and potassium in the body, the photograph must contain much meaningful information

Fig. 8-7. Live finger corona at 91°F.

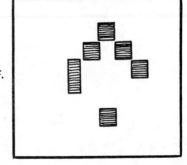

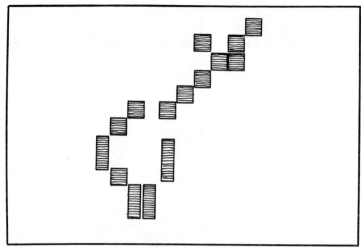

Fig. 8-8. Finger pad "sending" energy to sick plant leaf.

about the state of the health of the organism being photographed. In the case of objects not living, these patterns of heat flow still exist and the thermocouple effect can produce varying electrical potentials and any juncture where dissimi-

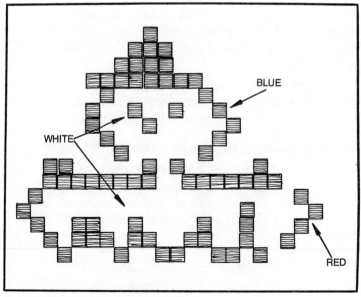

BLUE

WHITE

RED

Fig. 8-9. Freshly picked tomato.

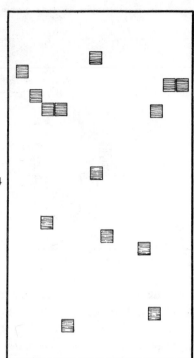

Fig. 8-10. Lettuce leaf picked 24 hours earlier.

lar metals might appear in the form of alloys or impurities. Similarly, the Kirlian photograph of such an object would contain much information about the condition or integrity of the object.

To read this information out of a Kirlian photograph, however, one must use the frames of reference of the ancient Chinese as expressed in their ideas about the flow and

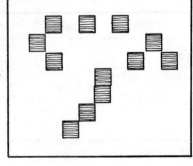

Fig. 8-11. Finger pad of mediator.

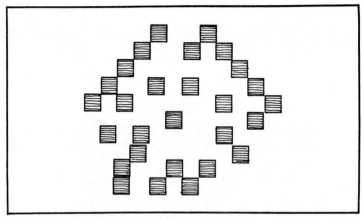

Fig. 8-12. Healthy geranium leaf, living plant.

balance of what they called "Yin" and "Yang," rather than the frames of reference of Western medicine and engineering science. I have speculated that Yin and Yang are very real but extremely subtle flows of thermal energy that behave in exactly the ways the Chinese said they did. Kirlian photography is one way to make visible some of the end results of this behavior. Properly interpreted, our electrograms most probably represent marvelous diagnostic and engineering tools. So far, there is only the bare discernible scratch of the surface on the applications of Kirlian photography as a technology, an art, or a science. Here are some ideas for application just within the confines of parapsychology.

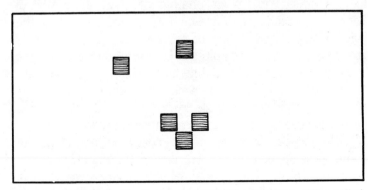

Fig. 8-13. Same leaf as in Fig. 8-12, dying 36 hours after being pulled from plant.

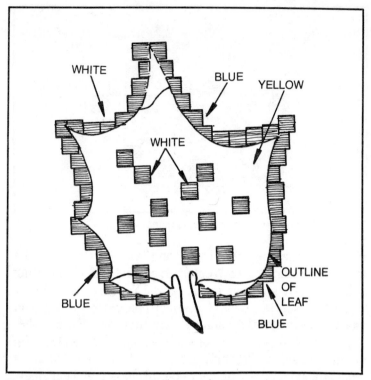

Fig. 8-14. Energy patterns persist after part of leaf has been trimmed away (dotted lines).

ACUPUNCTURE AND ACUPRESSURE

Researchers in the U.S., Japan, and the U.S.S.R., have found evidence in Kirlian photographs that some kind of energy is exchanged between healer and patient in the "laying on of hands" type of psychic healing. Light flares around the acupuncture points of the healer dim down during and right after treatment, while those of the patient flare up. Energy patterns shown on Kirlian photographs are interpreted to indicate that the energy flow of the patient becomes more balanced and that of the healer more unbalanced.

Do we see a lot of electrical energy discharging off the points of acupuncture needles during treatment? What is happening at the other end of the needle where it is contacting the skin? Does something similar happen when *pressure*, instead of a needle, is used at an acupuncture point?

How does the pressure feed back and affect the thermal flow in the area? Is there evidence through a possible thermocouple effect of an energy flow becoming unblocked? What kind of pictures does one get when using infrared-sensitive film for the electrogram? Is what is being photographed the result of the ionization of air due to cold electron emission, or is it some kind of interference pattern, or "beat frequency" pattern resulting from the direct interaction between the electrons being emitted and the high-voltage, high-frequency field? What would be the implications either way? Do all objects have subtle energy flows that break into invisible energy "fountains" analogous to the meridian/acupuncture point system in humans and animals? If so, how does this energy flow relate to the qualities and integrity of the material?

LEARNING BY LOOKING FOR BEAUTY

Take pictures of everything you can think of including fingertips, sprouted seeds, insects, jewelry, coins, plant

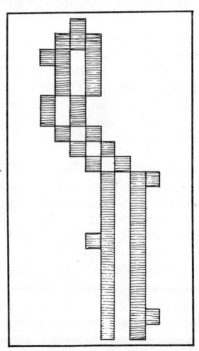

Fig. 8-15. Tail of one of my daughter's cats.

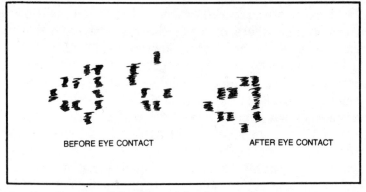

BEFORE EYE CONTACT · AFTER EYE CONTACT

Fig. 8-16. The case of the disappearing finger pad.

leaves, and look at the picture as a work of art, as a beautiful picture. Take pictures of your finger pads while you are listening to music you like, then music you do not like, then listening to noise. Which makes the most beautiful picture? Take pictures of your friends' fingertips and correlate them with their professions. Does a banker have more beautiful flairs than a musician? Does a teacher of children create a more beautiful pattern than a teacher of adults—a college professor, for example? Does a surgeon take a more beautiful picture than a psychic healer?

Plant leaves are often among the most beautiful of Kirlian photographic effects; on color film, many look like lighted Christmas trees. Which one of your favorite trees sparks your emotions most when saying "cheese" for the Kirlian camera?

LOOKING FOR PSI EFFECTS FROM YOUR PLANTS

If you have been experimenting with plants as suggested by our projects in Chapter 2, you will want to see what Kirlian photography reveals about the effects taking place when those plants are responding to human thoughts. Be very gentle with your living plant leaves when you photograph them. Bring your exposure plate to leaf height on the plant and then use a *light* piece of glass to hold the leaf flat against the plate. If the plant is rooted in a pot there is no need for grounding the plant directly. Grounding the pot if it is earthenware or metal may give a clearer picture.

Both the time of day and the phases of the moon seem to have some consistent effects on the photographic image. The electrical field of the earth changes at 4 A.M. and at 7 P.M. Universal coordinated time. Add one hour per 15 degrees longitude east of Greenwich, England and subtract one hour per 15 degrees west of Greenwich for the time in your locality when these field changes take place.

Photograph healthy and diseased leaves and notice what happens to the energy fields. Try "healing" a plant leaf that looks in need of it and see if some of your energy is actually transfered to the plant. We have healed plants this way and have a photographic record of the transfer of energy. Once the energy level in a sick plant reaches a certain point, the plant seems to take over and begins to heal itself. It does appear that people can give their energy to plants and that plants can reciprocate. While doing a "plant meditation" the plant brightens quite perceptibly, indicating a release of a higher level of whatever energy it is that our photographs track.

The death of brine shrimp can be tracked on Kirlian photographs of plants, as can a response to a show of blood if someone pricks their finger near the leaf of certain plants. Bean sprouts are readily available fresh from any supermarket or can be easily grown at home and they make marvelous subjects for Kirlian photography. They are highly energetic

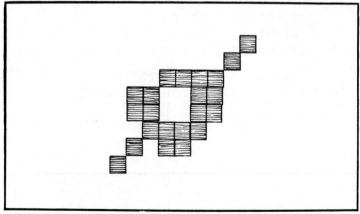

Fig. 8-17. Finger pad after considerable consumption of alcohol.

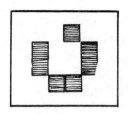

Fig. 8-18. Same finger pad as Fig. 8-17, the morning after.

and quite reactive to thoughts and energy transfers going on around them.

Music seems capable of transfering energy to plants and people if this is your interpretation of the fact that your plant's leaves and your own finger pads will glow more brightly after listening to music that you enjoy. Plants will react differently to different kinds of music, so apparently they do better with music they "enjoy" also! Try harp music, and especially some music of the glass harp (which was once considered to have hypnotic powers) if you would like to get amazing results.

KIRLIAN PHOTOGRAPHY AS A DIET WATCHER

Just as the pendulum can tell you a lot about what foods are good for you, possibly because of its resonance response to ELF waves eminating from you and the food, so electrograms made by the Kirlian method can disclose many hidden factors relating to the food you eat. How fast does the energy pattern fade from a head of lettuce between the time it is picked and the time it gets to your salad plate? How fast does the energy content of other ingredients of a salad fade? What are the energy patterns around meat, raw and cooked? How much "live" food and how much "dead food" are you

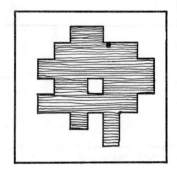

Fig. 8-19. Soybean before sprouting.

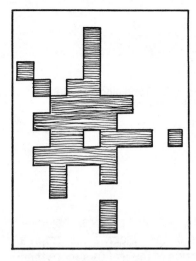

Fig. 8-20. Soybean after sprouting.

consuming? What happens to the flair of your finger pads after a vegetarian meal, or after a meal of meat and potatoes? Does the mood of the cook make a difference? Can you detect energy being transferred from the salad maker to the salad? If one makes a salad in anger, how do the salad ingredients react to that?

PATTERNS OF LIFE AND THE KIRLIAN EFFECT

Read the work of Dr. Harold Burr of Yale University (*The Electric Patterns of Life,* especially) and then see if you can discover and photograph the electrical patterns that

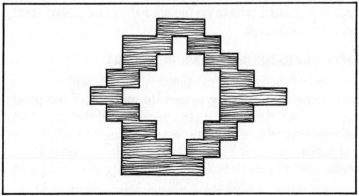

Fig. 8-21. Elbow before tennis match.

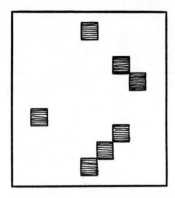

Fig. 8-22. Same elbow as in Fig. 8-21 in pain after tennis match.

appear to exist independently of the physical object—perhaps sustaining the pattern of the object. Photograph a living leaf. Then cut away a portion of the leaf (not more than 10 percent or you will damage the plant) and photograph the leaf again. Does the electrical pattern of the missing part remain in the electrogram? Try the same experiment with a just picked leaf and then an old one that has been preserved in the pages of a book for several days.

PHOTOGRAPHING INSECTS AND OTHER SMALL ANIMALS

A group of Kirlian photography researchers at the University of New Mexico has had good luck photographing a wide variety of small animals, including salamanders, cockroaches, and race runners. But you first refrigerate the creatures to slow them down. The cooling does not seem to have any harmful effects on the animal; it just makes them easier to photograph.

A MYSTERY OF THE DISAPPEARING CORONAS

One of the most consistent results you will get from your Kirlian photography is also, to me, one of the great mysteries of the medium. I can't help but feel that exploring this mystery can turn up some very useful information. It was first suggested to me by the research of Thelma Moss at the Center for the Health Sciences, University of California at Los Angeles. It sounds crazy and impossible so all I can tell you to do is *try it*.

Photograph the finger pads of two people standing close together but having no eye contact. You will likely get a nice corona from each of the person's fingers. Now, have your subjects make eye contact and stare at one another until you feel they have established really strong eye contact. Take another photograph of their two finger pads. In all probability *one and only one* of the finger pads will be visible on the second photograph. One of the person's coronas will simply have disappeared! Why? Maybe you can tell me—and Thelma Moss.

In her book, *The Electric Body* (St. Martin's Press, New York, 1979), Dr. Moss tells of other mysterious disappearances that seem to have a great deal to do with the emotional interactions between people. In some "family portraits," where finger tips of family members are photographed on one piece of film, one family member's corona will not photograph at all. Yet the same person photographed alone or with a non-family member will show a normal bright corona.

These experiments are easy to duplicate and well worth pursuing because of the interesting questions they raise, and the implications these questions have on the study of parapsychology. To help you know what to look for, I have made a number of drawings of the *patterns* turned up in Kirlian photography because I believe it is the pattern that is significant (Figs. 8-4 through 8-24). I have found it very useful to trace off these patterns onto graph paper and to

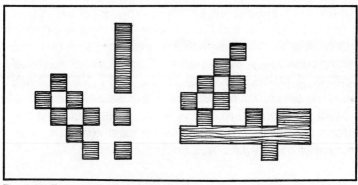

Fig. 8-23. Two rose buds side-by-side.

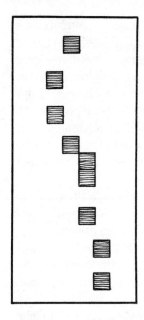

Fig. 8-24. Acupuncture points (acu-points) along stomach meridian.

classify and study them. Be sure to make notations about color, if your photographs have been made in color, and any other data that would be *pattern significant*. After all, information has been defined (in information theory, at least) as *a pattern transferred*. It is from patterns that we can get useful information even if we do not know exactly what it is we are photographing.

One final suggestion. You can fill a rubber glove finger with water at body temperature (98.6°F) and make a photograph of the tip, as if photographing a human finger. You will get a brilliant, large corona—a perfect one. You may do this a 100 times, and the corona will always be perfect, with none of the blotches, bubbles, gaps, and squiggles one always gets from a living finger. This means, to me, that there is a process at work in the living tissue which *modulates* the corona produced by warm water (living tissue is about 98 percent luke warm water, right?) and that the *patterns* produced by that modulation must contain a lot of information about what is going on inside a person.

Chapter 9
Stalking The Wild UFO

To anyone who has shuffled through several hundred Kirlian photographs and then glanced up to observe a passing UFO, the resemblance is striking—so striking, in fact, that one is tempted to ask if perhaps the UFO is "in substance" the sudden eruption of an electron fountain ionizing the surrounding air into colored patterns. Perhaps that does have something to do with the phenomena, but like the many fictions created for the U.S. Air Force by Dr. J. Allen Hynek before his "conversion," it would not explain anything about this widely reported phenomenon.

Since I am going to offer what has to be the most extraordinary explanation ever proposed for this event, I should probably state for the record that I have had encounters with UFOs on two occasions. I state this right off because I believe that no one should write about UFOs if they have not had personal experience with these apparitions of our technological age.

The writings of those who would speculate on what it is we poor misguided observers encounter, when we have our encounters, are like the writings of a victorian spinster who has never been kissed writing about what it is like to have a love affair. No matter how learned the lady might be, no matter that she might have a degree in sexology from Harvard, she is still going to come off spouting nonsense when she tries to be knowledgeable about something that simply has to be experienced to be *known about*.

There are signs and symptoms, which I will get to later. I will also tell you how to build a piece of electronic hardware that is guaranteed not to respond at all to the planet Venus, or temperature inversions, or even any type of passing aircraft being flown by us or the Russians. But first, I must tell you what I believe UFOs are and give you a brief but necessary lesson in "time reversibility" as it is understood in the current textbooks on electromagnetic theory.*

As I have mentioned in the introduction to this book and elsewhere, some physicists believe that the basis for quantum theory and the basis for understanding paranormal phenomena are related. If you read the journals, you will notice that there is a continuing dialogue about how to interpret properly the effect of consciousness (an observer) on experimental measurement. There is also considerable interest among physicists about the implications of our current ideas about the ordering in time and space brought on by recent evidence for what David Bohm calls "quantum interconnectedness of distant parts of quantum systems of macroscopic dimensions." This, of course has to do with Bell's theorem, which I remind you states that "no theory of reality compatible with quantum theory can require spatially separated events to be independent." In other words, if reality is anything like what quantum theory says it must be, then all events distant in either or both space and time must be interconnected in ways that seem contrary to ordinary experience. E.H. Walker and O. Costa de Beauregard have independently come up with the idea that there is a coupling between consciousness and environment, and that the nonlocality principle allows this coupling to overcome the usual barriers of space and time.

With that background, we come to the *Coup de Grace*. A solution to the equations in electromagnetic theory permits the reversibility in time of the usual cause and effect

*J.A. Stratton, Electromagnetic Theory, New York: McGraw-Hill, 1941

relationship; i.e., it is allowed that *an effect may preceed its cause!*

Discussing this allowed reversal of cause and effect in relation to precognition in the March, 1976 *Proceedings of the IEEE*, physicists Harold E. Puthoff and Russell Targ comment:

> In addition to the familiar retarded potential solutions $f(t-r/c)$, it is well known that the equations of, for example, the electromagnetic field admit of advanced potential solutions $f(t+r/c)$—solutions that would appear to imply a reversal of cause and effect. Such solutions are conventionally discarded as not corresponding to any observable physical event. One is cautioned, however, by statements such as that of Stratton in his basic text on electromagnetic theory.
>
> "The reader has doubtlessly noted that the choice of the function $f(t-r/c)$ is highly arbitrary, since the field equation admits also a solution $f(t+r/c)$. This function leads obviously to an advanced/time, implying that the field can be observed before it has been generated by the source. The familiar chain of course and effect is thus reversed and this alternative solution might be discarded as logically inconceivable. However, the application of "logical" causality principles offers very insecure footing in matters such as these and we shall do better to restrict the theory to retarded action solely on the grounds that this solution alone conforms to the present physical data."
>
> Such caution is justified by the example in the early 1920s of Dirac's development of the mathematical description of the relativistic electron that also yielded a pair of solutions, one of which was discarded as inapplicable until the discovery of the positron in 1932.
>
> In an analysis by O. Costa de Beauregard, an argument is put forward that advanced potentials constitute a convergence toward 'finality' in a manner symmetrical to the divergence of retarded potentials as a result of causality. Such phenomena are generally unobservable, however, on the gross macroscropic scale for statistical reasons. This is codified in the thermodynamic concept that for an isolated system entropy (disorder) on the average increases. It is just

this requirement of isolation, however, that has been weakened by the observer problem in quantum theory, and O. Costa de Beauregard argues that the finality principle is maximally operative in just those situations where the intrusion of consciousness as an ordering phenomenon results in a significant local reversal of entropy increase.

So, okay, it took me two years to cut through the jargon and get at what all the excitement is about, but when I finally did I realized that the reason the cause of the UFO phenomenon is so illusive is that their cause has not yet happened! What we are observing are effects whose cause is in the future—advanced potential solutions to the electromagnetic field equation. UFO are explained by the usually discarded solution $f(t+r/c)$!

That, of course, raises the intriguing question of what is the most probable *future cause* of the *present* UFO effect? I got the answer to that question during my own close encounter with a UFO on a desert in Northern Mexico on a night in early August, 1962. I did not know I had the answer at the time, however, since that was before I had heard about the advanced potential solution to the electromagnetic field equation. At the time I was as puzzled and shocked and shook as anybody else does when they have what I call a genuine encounter with a real UFO.

Perhaps I should explain. I had actually waited 10 years for my first encounter with a UFO event. In the early 1950s, I was employed as a script writer at Reid H. Ray Film Industries in St. Paul, Minnesota. We had contracts with the U.S. Air Force to write training films about jet engines and aircraft electronics. Those of us on the writing staff had a lot of contact with officers at Wright-Patterson Air Force Base, where *Project Blue Book* had been set up to investigate the then increasing scare over reported sightings of what were being called *unidentified flying objects*, or UFOs for short. While my film work had nothing at all to do with *Project Blue Book* and UFOs, I did have an opportunity to talk informally with Air Force officers who were involved in investigating reports at that time. The information was classified, of course, and although I had clearance to have access to classified information, my clearance was for information relating to jet engines and electronics, not UFOs. Those who did have access to the information gave none of it away, but I knew from the way they talked about what could be talked about that only a small percentage of what they investigated worried them, but that little bit worried them a great deal! I also knew that it was not just kooks who were reporting strange encounters to the Air Force, but that veteran pilots and seasoned police officers had reported strange flying objects that the Air Force knew were not its own, and had reasonable assurance from intelligence reports were not being flown by any other nation. I was intrigued, to say the least, and became an inveterate sky watcher, stalking the wild UFO.

When we moved to Indiana and started our own film business, we would often drive the back roads home at night from our business encounters of a writing kind and turn the lights off, especially on moonlit nights and search the skies. It was by now the late 1950s, and I had decided that the entities behind the UFO events must be friendly since they could have taken the combined air forces of the world and conquered us by this time if they had been hostile—if they existed at all.

We saw many things in the sky, often hoping one would turn out to be a "real" UFO, but none did. Always it was some object that had every business being in the sky. At this time I had no idea that I could have any influence on encountering a UFO, believing firmly in the doctrine of Einstein separability and the fact that observed phenomena were caused by some physical reality whose existence was independent of human observation. I also, at that time, held the unquestioned basic assumption that inductive reasoning was a valid mode of reasoning and could be applied freely so that legitimate conclusions could be drawn from consistent observations.

I kept observing consistently. Nothing happened until that night in the summer of 1962. I was in Mexico without my family, sitting with strangers on the patio of a small ranch south of Saltillo. It was about 10 P.M., and I was sky watching (not so much for UFOs—I'd about given up on them by then), but because the clear air at 6,000 feet made stars visible I could never have seen in Indiana. Also, the more southerly lattitude made the Mexico sky quite different from the Indiana one. My years of sky watching had made me something of an amateur astronomer. I was looking at Polaris—the north star—and admiring how bright it was, when I noticed another "star" very close to Polaris in a place where no star of visible magnitude was supposed to be. It then appeared to grow brighter and my thought was that this was a *live* nova—something else I had long hoped to discover during my binocular searches of the milky way. But this was not a very likely place in the sky for a nova. The "star" began to move away from the north star toward the east, growing quite bright by this time and apparently moving quite rapidly. Someone's retrograde satellite? Suddenly it stopped dead in its tracks and hung there, pulsating slightly east of the sprawling figure of Orion, as if about to make a plunge for his sword. It was then that I decided I could not identify this flying object and so for the time being, at least, it was the UFO I had been hoping to encounter. I called the attention of the group on the patio to what, I said, as casually as I could manage, "might just be a UFO." I asked them to keep an eye on the object and if it moved again to try to observe just how and where. On the pretext of getting a better view, I excused myself from the group and headed for my car, which was parked in a driveway a few yards away. I was remembering what I had learned from the close encounter with the *Blue Book Project* many years before. The thing that had impressed me most about the unexplainable encounters that was the electrical and magnetic activity that seemed to be a constant when the "real" thing was encountered. I had a compass in my car, and I wanted to see if it was being affected in any way. It had not moved from its earlier position indicating that my car was parked in a southerly direction. I looked up to the sky and saw the object moving again. Dropping lower now, it moved slowly and quite deliberately around the southern part of the sky, traveling west, skirting the top of a mountain which I could not see but well knew was directly south of the ranch about two miles distant in the direction my car was pointed. Suddenly it halted, reversed its course and swooped very low back toward us. It was now so low that had it been beyond the mountain it would have disappeared behind it. Instantly, everything seemed to take on a luminous glow and I could see a windmill about 200 yards from me quite well. I could also now just make out the outlines of the mountain and see that the object was passing between the windmill and the mountain—several hundred yards but not more than 10,000 feet away from where we stood. I glanced back at the compass in my car. It was spinning now—actually oscillating back and forth. I quickly fished out my car keys and tried to start the engine. It refused to start, although the starter motor turned the engine over numerous times. The glowing object was moving quite rapidly again, rose up into the sky, heading south toward the mountain, and very quickly disappeared behind it. I cranked my car engine once more and it started instantly.

My friends back on the patio had observed pretty much the same thing I had, and no one seemed particularly impressed by the show; in fact one of them said that it appeared to be a bit of St. Elmo's Fire, similar to what he had seen at sea once. I would probably have agreed and forgotten the incident rather quickly had it not been for the strange events that followed.

Shortly after the "visitation" we all retired, and I fell asleep thinking that I really had, finally, seen my first UFO. I decided not to buy St. Elmo for that night's flying object.

I was awakened with the distinct impression that someone had called my name. I jumped out of bed and dressed very quickly and slipped out the front door expecting to see someone on the porch, but no one was there. Surprising myself with very deliberate action, I walked down the steps and out toward the desert in the general direction of the mountain. I remember wondering why I was doing this and where I was going and thinking that it felt like I was responding to a post hypnotic suggestion, which was absurd because up to that time many people had tried, including experienced psychiatrists, and I was declared to be "unhyp-notizable." I decided that perhaps I had had a false awakening and was simply dreaming all this—a lucid dream triggered off by the excitment of experiencing my first UFO event. Then I became aware that although it was a dark night with no moon, I was able to see the ground around me quite well—as if a great full moon had suddenly appeared. I looked up into the sky for the first time since I had left the porch of my casa and saw one of the most beautiful and awe inspiring sights I had ever seen. If there will ever be such a thing as a spaceship made entirely of light, it might look something like what was hovering above me. It was no St. Elmo's Fire I can tell you. Nor was it anything else made of hardware. It was the stuff made in man's dreams, perhaps, but not in his waking world—at least not yet. It was quite plainly an apparition—a technological ghost, if you please—or perhaps a holographic image of staggering proportions. At that moment I was not so much concerned about what it was as with what this strange apparition and I were doing rendezvousing out here on this now haunted desert.

It was then that I became aware of ideas flooding into my consciousness—ideas like, yes, this was a UFO alright (what else?) but it was not a spaceship come to call from some far distant galaxy, but somehow an incident from our own future time, some kind of time travel—a ship of light made by those not yet born. I seemed to be getting ideas about cosmology—about how the universe pulsated through time in such a way that one could travel to the past by traveling toward the future, through all the linear time there is, pass a time pole and be traveling up from the beginning of time. The old Columbus trick of getting to the east by sailing west, applied to time.

I could write volumes about the revelations that seemed to pour into my mind from that beautiful "ghost of Christmas future" that hovered over me for I don't have any idea how long. At this point, any further details of the incident, though apropos, would take us far afield from this book of para-psychology projects, so I simply want to make the point that the ideas about time did not seem to make much sense on that particular occasion since I was unaware of the solution of the equation that allows for advanced potentials. Had I known that it is not forbidden, in this physical world, for effects to precede causes, I might have realized then and there that this was just such an event and that its cause would be found sometime perhaps in the next century.

If you stop to think about the fact that our technology may just develop to the point where time travel is possible, practical, and economical. I think that it is almost certain that with the further developments that can be made using quantum theory applied to the idea of non-separateness, at least in human consciousness, our progeny will (are?) make these expeditions with "hardware" of light and consciousness. I have concluded therefore that the UFOs are the advanced potential events of future archaeological expeditions—our own and also perhaps those of countless other advanced technologies around the galaxy. The intrusion of the observing consciousness creates what we observe as a UFO event.

My encounter on the desert in Mexico appears to have been an exchange of information. I am a journalist and science writer who has witnessed a lot of history between the 1940s and the 1960s and who has been exposed to the details of many of our historic technological achievements. Perhaps a lot of this first hand information was extracted from my mind during that encounter and I experienced an inflow of information that was in the consciousness of some of those 22nd century scientists involved. Who knows? Perhaps I am even written up in some scientific journal a couple hundred years from now!

One thing was certain. I confirmed that night what others who have encountered the UFO event have consistently confirmed; that is, the event is accompanied by a very intense magnetic field. In my second encounter out in the desert that night I felt the pulsations much more strongly than I had once felt them when touring a facility for extracting aluminum from sea water. This requires intense magnetic fields which one can feel, and I recognized the sensations. And, as a memento from that first encounter earlier in the evening, I was never able to properly *box* the compass in my car after its exposure to what was obviously a very strong magnetic field.

It is this field that is the basis for our design of a UFO detector communicator. Having examined thousands of sightings and events by people I would judge to be reliable observer-witnesses, such as airline and Air Force pilots, research scientists and police officers, and having experienced the event myself, I conclude that two things are always present: light in the visible spectrum and an electromagnetic field of considerable intensity, though both vary over quite a wide dynamic range. The magnetic field is such that the UFO which appears to be moving in our space over time can be detected up to several miles away. By feeding back a light signal that can be controlled by the movement of the UFO some kind of communication or signaling becomes possible.

HOW TO BUILD A UFO DETECTOR/COMMUNICATOR

Figure 9-1 shows a schematic for the UFO detector, and Fig. 9-2 shows the signaling part of the device. An audio transformer makes a very convenient pick-up coil to detect the high-intensity magnetic field of a flying object. The voltage induced in the transformer is amplified by the quad op amp TL084C, with all four of its amplifiers connected in series. The amplified output voltage is fed into the input of a 9400 voltage to frequency converter. The output of the 9400 drives a speaker and also operates an infrared LED. The pitch of the sound produced by a passing UFO event gives you an indication of its distance from the detector. The rapidity with which the sound rises or falls in pitch gives some indication of the velocity of the event. The lower the frequency is, the farther away the event is. The higher the frequency is, the closer the event is. A rising pitch indicates that the event is moving toward your detector. A falling pitch indicates that it is moving away from the detector. If the changing pitch suddenly ceases, that would be an indication that the event was hovering.

The communicating portion of the device operates as soon as an event comes within range of the detector. A signal

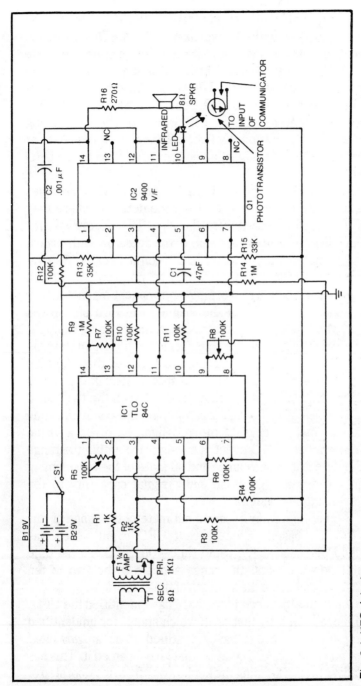

Fig. 9-1. UFO detector.

269

at the output pin (No. 14) of the 9400 V/F (IC2) activates the LED in series with the speaker. The LED activates a phototransistor which works through an amplifier and tone decoder to operate a relay which will shift a blue spotlight to red. Thus movement of the UFO event into and out of range of the detector will shift the light from blue to red. UFO event movement, then, can become the triggering mechanism for shifting the lights. This gives a two-state or binary capability for signaling or communicating to the UFO event.

The use of the infrared remote control system enables one to locate the lights apart from the detector where they can be seen or sensed from the sky. The phototransistor should be located in or very near to the detector, with coaxial cable connecting the detector to the communicator. Separation up to 400 or 500 feet should be no problem. Return signals can be sent by sweeping a permanent magnet across the transformer. Moving the magnet will turn on the red light, while holding the magnet stationary, or sweeping it away from the area of the transformer will turn on the blue light. The red light, which is much brighter than the blue light, since it is a short life photo spot, also makes possible an amplitude or intensity difference between the two visual states which give further capability to the communicating system. And, or course, the red light on gives a visual indication that a UFO event is taking place within the range of the detector, just as an on and off state of the tone coming from the speaker gives an audio signal capability to the communications system.

I do not have any accurate estimate of the range of this device, but based on one recent UFO event which was tracked on radar at the same time—one of those multiple simultaneous events, the range appears to be two to ten miles, depending on the strength of the event field.

Incidentally, since I feel that I have identified the UFO, I no longer call it by that term which stands for unidentified flying object. Since I have identified it as an *advanced potential event,* or APE, that is what I have named it. This has the advantage of keeping the kooks away from my doorstep of

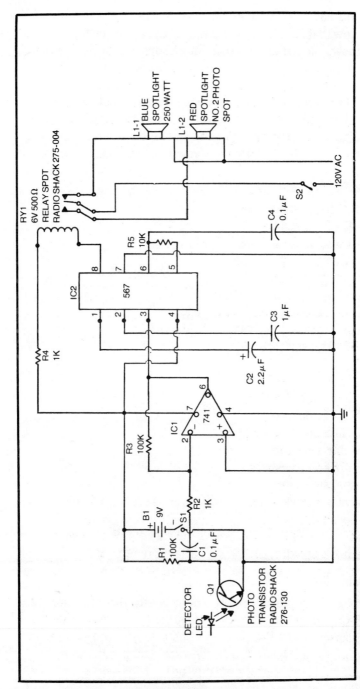

Fig. 9-2. UFO communicator.

271

which I had a goodly number when I was "tracking UFOs." But now that I am tracking APEs, I attract physicists, serious parapsychologists, and other interesting and helpful people like that. But UFO or APE, the pursuit of these events (and they are much more event-type processes like tornadoes or magnetic storms than flying objects) and speculations about what they may mean, as well as the effort to communicate on oscillating waves through time, make for a very addictive electronic hobby. Here is what you will need to get started.

Parts For The Detector

B1, B2 - 9-volt batteries
C1 - 47 pF capacitor
C2 - 0.001 μF capacitor
F1 - ¼-amp fast acting fuse
IC1 - integrated curcuit TL084C
IC2 - integrated circuit 9400
LED - infrared light emitting diode
Q1 - phototransistor, Radio Shack 276-130
R1, R2 - 1K resistors
R3, R4, R5, R6, R7, R8 - 100K resistors
R9 - 1 megohm resistor
R10, R11, R12 - 100K resistors
R13 - 35K resistor
R14 - 1 megohm resistor
R15 - 33K resistor
R16 - 270-ohm resistor
S1 - spst switch
T1 - audio transformer with 8-ohm secondary/1,000-ohm primary
Misc. - project box, PC board, IC sockets, 8-ohm speaker, hook-up wire, hardware, battery holders, etc.

Construction

Cut a printed circuit (PC) board that fits into a 7×4×2-inch project box and mount the IC sockets, resistors and capacitors in the positions indicated by the schematic diagram (Fig. 9-1)). Carefully wire all the resistors and capacitors to the appropriate pins on the IC sockets.

Mount the LED and phototransistor only a couple of inches apart and wire the phototransistor to a coaxial cable connector at the back of the box. Mount the speaker (Radio Shack 4-inch multi-purpose #40-1197 is a good choice) and off-on switch on the front panel and drill some holes to let the sound out. Mount the audio transformer on top of the box. Be sure to remove any shielding the transformer might have around it. Tie the secondary leads together and connect the primary to the input of the TL084C chip through R1 and R2. Mount the battery holders and hook-up the battery clips, speaker LED and transformer after sliding the PC board into place in the box. Check and double check all IC pin connections. Turn the batteries on and test by sweeping a permanent magnet past the transformer. If the circuits are working properly, you will get a rapid rise and fall in pitch from the speaker, along with a glow from the LED. Now for the communicator you will need:

Parts

B1 - 9-volt battery
C1 - 0.1 μF capacitor
C2 - 2.2 μF capacitor polarized electrolytic
C3 - 1 μF capacitor
C4 - 0.1 μF capacitor
IC1 - 741 op amp integrated circuit
IC2 - 567 tone decoder integrated circuit
LI1 - 250 watt outdoor type blue spotlight
LI2 - No. 2 photo spotlight with red filter
R1 - 100K resistor
R2 - 1K resistor
R3 - 100K resistor
R4 - 1K resistor
R5 - 10K resistor
Ry1 - spdt 6-volt 500-ohm relay. Radio Shack #275-004
S1 S2 - spst switches
Misc. - coax polyfoam RG-59/U cable, coax connectors, 120-volt light sockets, 120-volt power cord and plug, project box PC board to fit hardware etc.

Construction

Weatherproof your project box by painting it with epoxy paint. Mount the coax cable connector at back of box and the two off-on switches on the front. Mount sockets for spotlights side by side on top of box along with filter holder for the photospot. A matching 7×4×2-inch project box will give you plenty of room. Cut a PC board to fit. Mount the IC sockets and hook-up the resistors and capacitors following the schematic in Fig. 9-2. Mount and hook up the relay. Then the 120-volt light sockets. Mount the battery holder and hook up the battery clip. After double checking everything hook up the coax cable to the detector and turn the communicator on. The relay should be hooked up so that in the non-energized position the blue spotlight is on. Test by sweeping by the transformer on the detector unit with a permanent magnet. The No. 2 photospot should flash on as you make each pass. Install the red filter on the photospot and you are ready for action.

WHERE THE ACTION IS

No matter where you live in the world you will sooner or later detect one of the UFO or APEvents close by. At a recent symposium to study the relationship between UFO and psychic events Dr. J. Allen Hynek, the worlds leading serious scientific investigator of UFO asked, "What can and can't we believe? We can still only theorize. What do we know about thunder storms or tornadoes?" Dr. Hynek continued. "Nature hasn't changed much. Nothing much is different. We have plenty of cases to study. We have reports on 23,972 sightings—37 percent by single persons; 42 percent by two or more. This means 63 percent of the sightings were made by two or more witnesses, a sizable number for purposes of verification.

We are getting more and more 'contact cases,' and cases where humanoids have been sighted moving in and out of UFOs on the ground; more abduction cases difficult to disprove. But it all still defies acceptable explanation."

Dr. Hynek called for a show of hands from everyone in the audience of about one thousand who had seen what they thought to be a UFO. A large percentage of hands went up. Then Dr. Hynek asked; "Let's see the hands from those of you who reported what you saw to the police?" No one raised a hand!

"There you are," Hynek concluded, "think of the large number of unreported sightings because most of you have been intimidated. You don't want to be ridiculed or accused of being off your rocker. Our investigating office has a *hot line*—800-621-7725—in Evanston, Illinois. Call us next time you have a sighting!"

Dr. Hynek's organization publishes a newsletter you might be interested in reading for current information on UFO activity. I will suggest that it is most helpful to have a friend who operates aircraft radar in your locality. Radar often tracks these events but operators are not supposed to admit to it.

If the UFO phenomenon is, as I have suggested, an event whose "cause" is in the future, it may be that the cases Dr. Hynek referred to as "contact cases," and cases where humanoids have been sighted moving in and out of UFOs on the ground are the same order of psychic event as apparitions and hauntings. Indeed there is a striking similarity between the way psychic investigators have described the appearance and movement of ghostly apparitions moving about haunted houses and the way people describe the appearance and movement of "humanoids" and the so-called little green men. They all appear, if one takes the observations to be sincere, to be somehow holographic projections of consciousness. The result, perhaps of observer intrusion on our own space and time. Could it be that the classic ghostly apparitions are retarded potentials described in electromagnetic theory and the UFO are advanced potentials? Ghosts of Christmas past and Christmas future? We can only answer these questions by using our consciousness and our electronics working together in somewhat the way I imagined I might be working one day in the future as a journalist gathering the latest news from the other side of our galaxy. Here is the *Afterword* from my book, "And now . . the News" (Gulf Publishing Company, 1977):

THIS BROADCAST JOURNALIST IS CELEBRATING HIS 79TH
BIRTHDAY TODAY ON ONE OF THE SPACE OUTPOSTS BY
REPORTING ON THE PSYCHIC PROBE OF A CREW OF DEEP
SPACE COSMONAUTS. USING AN OSCILLATING WAVE
THROUGH TIME THE COSMONAUTS ARE COMMUNICAT-
ING WITH AN ANCIENT REALITY SITUATED ON THE FAR
SIDE OF THE GALAXY. THE ENCOUNTER IS PRODUCING A
HOLOGRAPHIC IMAGE AT THE INTERFACE OF OUR TWO
REALITIES. THIS USED TO BE CALLED A UFO BEFORE
SUCH THINGS WERE UNDERSTOOD. THIS REPORT CAN BE

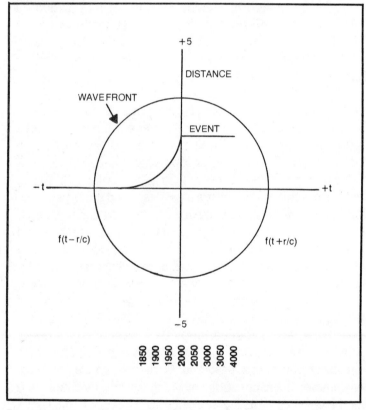

Fig. 9-3. Precursor wave in minus time before an event. Information in a
future event is carried into the past as a traveling-wave interferogram or
time varying hologram. This extends interaction time which can be quite
independent of the spatial distance between the event and the observer
(Graph represents usually discarded equation in electro-dynamics) (t-r/
c).

VIEWED ON CHANNEL 83 OF YOUR LITTLE BOX, OR IF YOU ARE INTO D.D.V. (DIRECT DISTANT VIEWING) PUT THE RIGHT HEMISPHERE OF YQUR BRAIN INTO ALPHA-THETA AT 7 HERTZ, DEEP MEDITATION. MY NEURO-TRANSDUCER COORDINATES ARE AVAILABLE ON YOUR MICROCOMPUTER INFORMATION SYSTEM. AND NOW, FROM THE FAR SIDE OF OUR GALAXY HERE IS THE LATEST NEWS...

The good news is illustrated in Fig. 9-3, which shows how information in a future event is carried into the past as a traveling wave interferogram or time-varying hologram. This extends the interaction time which can be quite independent of the spatial distance between the event and the observer.

This also implies that you can bring these events to consciousness by making the effort to sensitize your own consciousness to these time-varying holograms enabling you to "see" into the future and to exchange information with the perpetrators of future events.

Could it be that ghosts, apparitions, and hauntings are the same kind of events in + time? I.E. retarded potentials from a past event perceived as a time varying hologram with information carried into the future as a traveling-wave interference pattern? Chapter 10, next on the agenda, will explore this idea and present some electronic projects that can be built for its exploration.

Chapter 10
Stalking The Wild and Ghostly Voices

Friedrich Jugenson, a multi-talented documentary film producer, painter and musician, walked out into the country near his villa in Sweden on a summer day in 1959 and tape recorded a few bird songs. A few hours later when he was playing back the bird calls he was astounded to hear a quiet male voice discoursing (in Norwegian) on the subject of nocturnal bird songs. Thinking that his tape recorder was picking up a radio broadcast by one of those electronic flukes that often happens he investigated all the radio programming in northern Europe at that time and found that no one was broadcasting any kind of program in Norwegian about the songs of nocturnal birds. Intrigued, Jugenson began running his tape recorder "wide open" recording nothing but ambient sound and hoping to hear the voice again, or get some clue to explain this voice that seemed to be knowledgeable about nocturnal bird calls. What he got was apparently more than he bargained for. He heard nothing while taping, but on playback he heard voices that addressed him by name and conveyed personal information to him. To top it all off many of the voices claimed to be among his deceased relatives and friends!

In 1964 Jurgenson published a book in Sweden, sold with a record of many of his recordings, and in 1967, a second book, published in German as well as Swedish, *Sprechfunk mit Verstorbenen*, (*Radio-Link with the Beyond*) sent thousands of people in Europe to their tape recorders to try to record ghostly voices of their own. Many of them succeeded, and even the Vatican got into the act with the position that there was nothing in the teaching of the Church that was against the voice phenomena and that " . . . scientifically it has yet to be established that we are really dealing with voices from the dead. What we are faced with is a phenomenon; we need accept no more and can accept no less." That quote was in an official statement issued by Father Pistone, Superior of the Society of St. Paul in England. I find it to be the most sensible statement about the mysterious voices that I have heard.

THE VOICES OF AMERICA

The most accessible research available to those of us who speak only English (Ruth got the drop on me in this area since she speaks and reads German fluently) is in the book *Breakthrough,** by Dr. Konstantin Raudive (pronounced ROH-dee-vay) a multi-lingual psychologist who studied with Dr. Carl Jung.

In *Breakthrough*, in English, Raudive tells about his meeting with Jurgenson in Sweden in 1965 and gives transcripts of some of his early recordings and then tells in detail about his later work with physicist Alex Schneider and various electronic and recording engineers and expert technicians. One of these, Rolf Schaffranke, who was then a Senior Research Engineer with NASA (National Aeronautics and Space Administration), visited with Raudive in 1969 and reported, ". . . The existence of the phenomenon can be considered established with the statements of some three hundred independent observers who have listened to demonstration tapes and taken part in one or more of the sessions..."

Another American, Dr. Karlis Osis, Director of Research for the American Society for Psychical Research, traveled to Europe to inspect Raudive's equipment and work first hand. Osis is a Latvian and accomplished linguist, as is Raudive. He reported that he could hear twenty-six out of

---

*Breakthrough, by Konstantin Raudive, Taplinger Publishing Co. New York, 1971.

thirty voice texts clearly, but some he would not interpret as Raudive did.

We heard our first "paranormal" voices at a symposium in St. Louis, Missouri in the summer of 1976, brought from California by the wife of the late William Welch of the Southern California Society for Psychical Research. Welch was convinced that the voices were communications from a plane of life beyond death but when he had made his own presentations he never pressed this point of view. He always let his tapes speak for themselves. His wife continued in that tradition and so we were able to listen to the recorded voices without anyone shoving an interpretation at us. It was a convincing demonstration and we came away with record-ings of the voices to study and duplicate, which we promptly did. I don't believe, however, that I would have been able to detect or even hear the voices we recorded had I not listened to the recordings of Bill Welch over and over so as to train my ear for these really "out of this world" voices. I definitely do recommend that you get a copy of a recording of these voices and accustom your ear to their unusual rhythm, speed, pitch, and intensity. The Welch voices are available from the EPS Research Foundation, Suite 1630, Union National Plaza, Little Rock, Arkansas 72201. A recording made by Raudive, the *Breakthrough Record*, which includes samples of how the voices sound according to the different recording methods, is available from Vista Productions , 64a Lansdowne Road , London, WII 2LR England. The catalogue number is VMS 100. You will need to send about $6 American for the record and for speedy airmail service on return.

Keep in mind that the voices you are trying to receive are usually quite weak, in spite of conventional efforts to amplify the signal. A conditioning process seems to have to take place, too. Seemingly one has to learn to hear the voices, so it helps to devote a regular time each day to listening to your voice tapes. One half hour is enough time to spend on it. Longer sessions can be very tiring.

We have never heard of anyone who has been successful hearing much on a speaker—especially a hi-fi setup. The amplification of background noise seems to drown out the weak voice signals. A good headset, on the other hand helps to separate noise from signal and is absolutely essential to hearing the voices. Once you have made an interpretation of what a voice is saying and have located it on the tape, you can then often hear it on a speaker. If you have a family or share your living quarters with others, you will find that headphones are essential to preserve harmony since the high level noise one must listen through can become quite annoying to those not turned on to stalking these wild and ghostly voices. There is also what I call the *audio mirage* effect, which comes from prolonged listening to the *white noise* of a tape playback machine with its volume all the way up. One tends to hear things that are not recorded on the tape. These illusory voices, however, cannot be repeated on playback, or re-recorded, nor do they present a pattern on an oscilloscope, as the "real" voices do. When you have succeeded in recording these voices *something* is recorded on your tape which you can verify electronically. What it is that you have recorded is, of course, open to subjective interpretation. Voice print analysis has shown them to be voices— that much is objective—but what the voice is saying often is interpreted by different people as being a different phrase or word.

A reel-to-reel tape recorder, if it is a solid-state device, is ideal for recording the voices. We have used an old open-reel stereo and a new cassette recorder with equal effectiveness. The open-reel deck machine with good treble and bass attenuation has advantages for playback, however.

The older vacuum-tube recorders do not seem to work at all because of the noise and hum levels. I also suspect that in addition to being quieter, the transistor and solid-state recorders may somehow be making use of an as yet undiscovered property of solid-state devices that facilitates the recording of these voices. If your recorder has an automatic level control, be sure to switch it off when trying to record paranormal voices.

RECORDING TECHNIQUES AND METHODS

Some of the initial methods of recording were suggested by the voices themselves; others have come from both European and American recording experts. Here is a sample.

Microphone Recording

Far and away the simplest method is to use your tape recorder in just the way you would use it for any self-respecting earthly voice. Use a remote microphone far enough away from the recording machine so that it does not pick up the noise of the recorder. Use all the gain your machine will give you and place the microphone in a quiet place where it is not likely to pick up people talking or street noise. Sit some distance away from your microphone but where you can see the counter on your tape recorder. Make an identification announcement giving date, time and location of recording and other people who are present if you are not alone. *Then ask for the voice to speak to you.* Expect that they will. Your own consciousness seems to play a vital role in the recording of the voices so don't try to be "objective" about this. After you have asked the voices to speak keep perfectly quiet for a short period of time. Do not wait too long, since playback time will be much, much longer than recording time. Also the voices usually appear immediately after something is said.

Keep a log of everything that was said on the tape by yourself or others attending the recording session, and of any extraneous noises that were heard. We find that three minute recording sessions are best, with announcements being made every minute asking for voices. Record at the fastest speed your recorder will tape because you may wish to play back at a slower speed to locate voices. Sometimes this helps and sometimes it doesn't. One thing that does seem to help, however, is a good preamp ahead of the recorder if it has a good signal to noise ratio. Figure 10-1 is a good one, when used with a low impedance microphone. In fact, any 8-ohm speaker makes a good microphone for use in this method of recording, but be sure you use an audio coupling transformer between the speaker and the input of the chip. (See Fig. 10-2.) One-fourth of a TL084C quad op amp is used because of its low noise characteristics.

Parts

B1 - 9-volt battery

IC - ¼ of TL084C integrated circuit op amp

R1,R2 - 1K, ¼-watt resistors

R3,R4 - 100K, ¼-watt resistors

S1 - off-on switch, spst

T1 - audio transformer, 8-ohm secondary, 1,000-ohm primary, center tapped. Radio Shack 273-1380 or equivalent.

Misc. - 8-ohm speaker and cable, plug to fit input of tape recorder, hardware, hook-up wire, etc.

Construction

Use of the Realistic Minimus-0.5 mini speaker (Radio Shack #40-1995) is recommended as a microphone for this pre-amp hookup. It comes in a nice enclosure only a little more than 6×4×4-inches. The pre-amp is built on a tiny PC board just a little larger than the TL084 socket, and fastened to the inside of the speaker enclosure with a metal bracket. A battery holder is similarly mounted and a length of shielded microphone cable soldered to the output pin (No. 1) of the IC, with a plug soldered to the other end for plugging in to your tape recorder. If you should wish more gain you can use up to four of these amplifiers in series. Figure 10-3 gives you the pin connections for each of the amplifiers in the TL084 chip.

BROADCAST RECORDING

Raudive was always a great advocate of radio recordings because his voices seemed to prefer this method of getting through to us. Use a spot on the FM band or on one of the short wave bands that is not likely to have a signal coming in. Turn the volume on the radio receiver up to the point where you can just hear the "white noise". You will of course need a headphone outlet on your radio so that it can be plugged into your tape recorder, but if you do not, or wish to experiment with a combination of radio-microphone recording, simply place your radio speaker near your microphone.

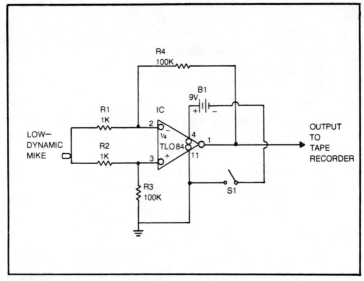

Fig. 10-1. Low-noise hi-grain pre-amp for microphone method of recording voices.

Empty TV channels are also very useful for broadcast recording either direct or via speaker-microphone. Some experimenters have had excellent results using the UHF channels.

CRYSTAL SET RECORDING

This is probably the most popular and widely used method of recording voices and it seems to attract a greater quantity of voices than any other. Figure 10-4 is the basic diode circuit suggested by European experimenters and one that we have had a lot of success with.

Parts

CH1 - 2.5 mH RF choke coil
D1 - 1N191 type diode
R1 - 100K ¼-watt resistor
Misc. - small telescoping antenna, ground wire and clamp, 2×2×1-inch chassis box, PC board with push-in terminals, shielded cable with plug to fit tape recorder in use, hook-up wire, etc.

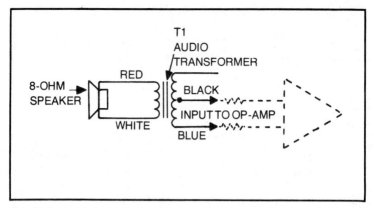

Fig. 10-2. Use 8-ohm speaker as microphone.

Construction

Breadboard the choke coil, diode and resistor with push-in terminals and mount inside metal chassis box. Drill the top of box and mount the telescoping antenna through rubber grommets so that it is insulated from box which needs to be grounded. If no external ground is handy, ground it to the chassis of the tape recorder. Use the *minium* length on the antenna—as little as four inches of antenna is desirable.

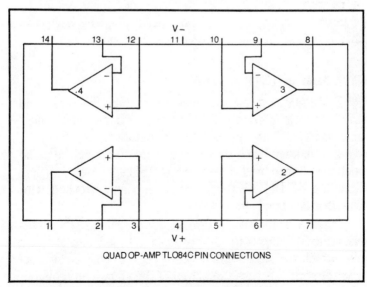

Fig. 10-3. Pin connections for quad op-amp TL084C.

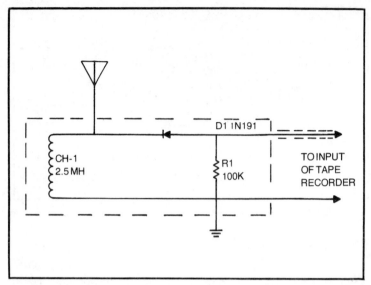

Fig. 10-4. Diode device recommended by European technicians for receiving paranormal voices.

For diode recording, it is recommended that tape recorder volume or gain control be turned up to maximum. According to Dr. Raudive's recording the diode recorded voices are the ones that can be recognized most readily by the untrained ear. Some of our clearest voices have also come by way of the diode receiver just described.

NOISE-GENERATION RECORDING

By far our best results, however, as far as frequency and variety of voices are the ones recorded using our "color" noise sources. The voices and the many sound effects we have gotten sound as if they are put together from the noise spectrum offered by the generators. This approach was first suggested by Dr. Alex Schneider who long worked with Raudive in Switzerland.

In our version (Fig. 10-5) an S2688/MM5837N noise-generating IC chip is used to produce a broadband of white noise which we then break up into "colors" with a resistor-capacitor combo across the output of the chip. The resistor-capacitor combo is variable so that one can run through the noise spectrum from pink to blue. The noise quality produced is very uniform and easy for the "voices" to use. It is produced by a 17-bit shift register which is clocked by an internal oscillator. A voltage regulated power supply is used since voltage variations and especially spikes bother complex logic circuits like the one inside the S2688/MM5837N.

Parts

B1 - 1A full- wave bridge rectifier (Radio Shack #276-1161)
C1, C2, C3 - 1000 μF 35 volt electrolytic capacitors
C4 - 0.33 μF capacitor
C5 - 0.1 μF capacitor
C6 - .01 μF capacitor
C7 - .047 μF capacitor
C8 - 0.1 μF capacitor
C9 - .22 μF capacitor
IC1 - 7815 voltage regulator (15-volts)
IC2 - S2688/MM5837N noise generating integrated circuit
R1 - 10K-ohm potentiometer
S1 - spst power switch
S2 - 4-position, single pole rotary switch
T1 - 18 volt CT 2A power transformer (Radio Shack 273-1515)
Misc. - IC sockets for ICs and B1, PC board and slope-front metal cabinet approx 7×5×2-inches, knobs, hardware, hook-up wire, solder, etc.

Construction

Drill the slope-front metal panel for an off-on switch at the bottom left of the one-inch front panel and two holes in the rear two-inch panel for the power cord and output cable. Drill the sloping front for the four-pole rotary switch and potentiometer. Mount the IC sockets on a PC board and carefully wire in all capacitors and the potentiometer. Mount and wire in the power transformer, being careful to insulate connections to the primary of the power transformer and the off-on switch. Be sure to use adequate heat sinking on the 7815 voltage regulator. It has a thermal shutdown circuit which turns off the regulator if the heat sink is too small. The

Radio Shack Universal heat sink #276-1361 is more than adequate. Figure 10-6 shows where to attach the heat sink on the 7815. Check and double check all IC and B1 connections before turning on power.

When operating the noise generator, switching in the different capacitors with S2 will give a different "color" or quality noise to work with. The setting on the potentiometer will then "shade" this color noise for a wide variety of raw material for the "voices" to work with.

You can use the noise generator alone, plugged directly into the tape recorder. Adjust the noise level so that it is audible but not excessively loud. Record for 30 to 60 seconds with the color and shade controls in one position. Then change the settings for a different quality of noise for the next 30- to 60-second recording period. Don't forget to ask the voices to speak to you each time and thank them for having spoken at the end of the recording period. Although you may feel silly talking to your equipment, this personal, concerned and involved method of voice recording gives far better results than just turning on the equipment and letting it run. Once you can learn to speak freely and naturally to the voices creating the effects, personifying them, your response will be excellent. Don't be bashful about asking questions, just be sure to leave time between for answers. And by all means respond to any voices and statements you hear.

The noise generator seems to work best when used in conjunction with the diode voice receiver, connecting the two devices in parallel and feeding the combined output to the tape recorder, as shown in Fig. 10-7.

PLAYING BACK THE VOICES

You will need a lot of time and patience on the playback of your tapes and remember that you have to educate your ear and your mind to tune these voices in. Your first trials are most likely to reveal nothing. Keep trying and play your tapes back over and over and over again. The voices are very quick and sharp and usually quite rhythmic. At first you may hear only something that sounds like a puff of air, or a hiss, or a whirring sound. As you play it back over and over it

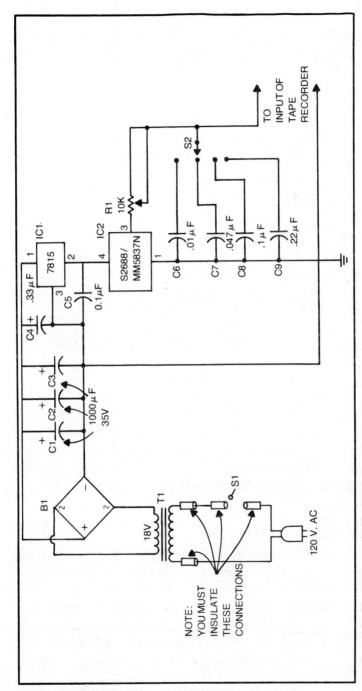

Fig. 10-5. Noise generator for broadband color for use by voices.

289

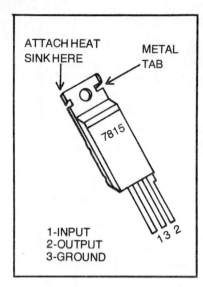

Fig. 10-6. Where to attach heat sink on 7815 IC.

ATTACH HEAT SINK HERE

METAL TAB

7815

1-INPUT
2-OUTPUT
3-GROUND

becomes clearer, and seemingly as your ear becomes accustomed to this particular sound, suddenly a voice is there saying something. More and more playbacks will tend to verify and "fix" what is said. It is somewhat like developing a picture in the darkroom, really. As you agitate your paper in the developer an image slowly comes through but it is *visible* before it is *recognizable* . As soon as it becomes as clear and distinct as you would like it, you plop it in the fixing solution to make the image permanent. "Developing" the voices on tape is very much like that. You have to run your tape back and forth a number of times without hearing anything. It is almost as if the process of repeatedly going back and forth is what brings in the sound. Then you hear something but it is not at all clearly defined. Back and forth many more times, like agitating your picture in developer and the sound takes form—becomes a word or a phrase or, sometimes a sound of some kind recognizable to you. Once you have understood it, it still seems necessary to run the tape back and forth to fix and verify what has been heard.

You will find that you will need to work for at least an hour on playback of every five minutes of recording. But the voices will develop for you if you persist. If you have had recording sessions daily for at least one week and have heard nothing on playback it is almost certain that you are missing your voices, or failing to "develop" them by persistent over and over playback. Instead of going on, trying to record more and more tape, it would be better to go back over the tapes you have already recorded—spend a whole week listening to the tapes you have already recorded. In my experience it is the playback and the listening part that seems to be far more important than the methods and techniques of recording. I have also found that repeated re-recording of the voices *improves* the quality and clarity whereas normal vice recordings tend to lose quality and clarity with repeated re-recording!

Be sure to experiment with any crazy thing that comes to mind for this phenomenom is truly wild and ghostly. I have not felt so much that the voices are *from* the dead but many may well be voices *of* the dead. The difference is that I can play a recording of one of Bing Crosby's songs and I will be hearing a voice *of* someone who is dead. But Bing is not serenading me from beyond the grave. I am listening to his voice as he once, in living real time, expressed with it. By the same token I might pick up Bing Crosby's voice on my

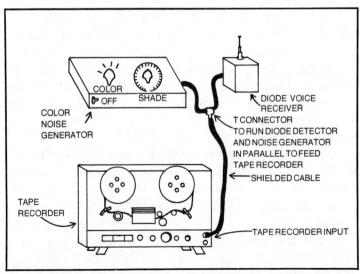

Fig. 10-7. Hookup using noise generator and diode receiver in parallel.

tapes, and it would not necessarily mean that he was trying to communicate with me from somewhere in the next incarnation or next life. I might be picking up something he once said while alive and well and living in this same space-time I occupy—something that somehow got "recorded" or maybe just remained as a retarded potential traveling wave interferogram that I recreated on tape by the process of projecting my consciousness into whatever electro-magnetic matrix is the carrier or preserver of such traveling waves.

The voices that I have heard and myself recorded (or developed?) sound more like audio apparitions—analogs of the classic holographic ghost that does not do anything much but put in a very repetitive appearance doing some insignificant thing over and over again. And while it may well be possible to exchange information, or carry on a conversation as many researchers apparently have, I think it would be somehow sending that information back in time with the reply coming forward in time, following a traveling wave front and somehow making an interference pattern on tape which can be developed into an audible "image." Figure 10-8 might illustrate such a process, which would be the mirror image of the process illustrated in Fig. 9-3, where future events send precursor waves back in time preceding the event. In the retarded potential diagram (Fig. 10-8), the amplitude of the wave would diminish with the passing of time so that the farther away in time one was from the event the less likely it would be that one could pick it up. This is born out by the record of the voices recorded by everyone from Jurgenson to Welsh—nothing they recorded and no one they recorded went back in time very far. Raudive's voices went back to the turn of the century but that was about the limit. I have heard no one come forth from ancient history. As our recording equipment and our developing techniques improve perhaps we can bring up the weaker voices of more ancient times. The curve probably never diminishes to zero so perhaps everything we have ever said is hanging around for all time just waiting for a technology that can make the words audible again. If that is the case, I hope that I will have said a few things in my lifetime worth someones efforts to

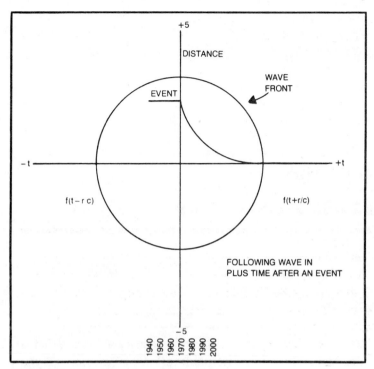

Fig. 10-8. Following wave in plus time after an event f(t+r/c).

reconstitute on tape or on hologramic discs, which are probably coming next. Meanwhile, I hope my words in this book have turned you on to the wonderful world of parapsychology and its potential for an almost endless variety of electronic projects leading to fascinating experimentation that constantly expands our human potential.

Appendix
Basics of Electronics

By learning to read schematic diagrams by becoming familiar with the symbols in Figure A-1 you can build any of the devices presented in this book even if you have never before done anything electronic. Schematic diagrams show you exactly what part to use where, and exactly how to interconnect parts, even indicating polarity of leads if that is important. The information that follows is honestly all you need to be knowledgeable about electronic circuits. The introduction of integrated circuits, which are simply complex micro-mini circuits on a little chip of silicon, has simplified the building of sophisticated devices tremendously. Having integrated circuits to use is like having prepackaged "TV dinners" and a microwave oven. Anyone can serve up an interesting, good tasting, and nourishing meal (within the limits of the necessary preservatives, of course!) the prepackaged microwave way. It is the same with integrated circuits. Anyone can serve up an audio device that sounds like a steam Calliope and plays the Star Spangled Banner every morning at sunrise just by knowing what pins of what IC (integrated circuit) to connect to a few resistors and capacitors.

There is a catch, of course, just as there is a catch to passing yourself off as a terrific cook when your secret is prepackaging—the catch is that *you must observe all operating instructions and directions to the letter of the law!*

You need this advice even if you are an "old timer" like me. I started building crystal sets and one and two tube vacuum tube radio sets when I was in high school, lo those many centuries ago. I was a ham radio operator during my youth and built all of my own equipment. I have written many a technical electronic instruction book and many films on how to repair everything from soup evaporators to nut smashers and guess what! When I first started building with ICs you wouldn't believe the vast numbers I ruined with all that overconfidence! And I did not realize that there is a profound difference between ICs and other kinds of electronic parts. It is as profound as the difference between a microwave oven and a brick kiln. That is why you will find me saying

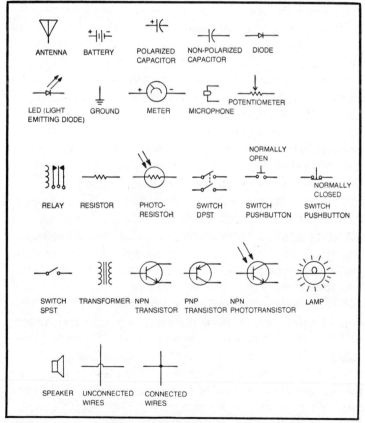

Fig. A-1. Schematic symbols used in this book.

throughout this book, "check, and double check, and triple check your wiring. Then check it again."

Reversed polarity, too much supply voltage, feeding or taking away too much current—excessive sourcing or sinking—can utterly destroy an integrated circuit chip. Be especially careful to pay close attention to which pins are the pins through which you channel your power supply—even if your power supply is only a little old 4-volt battery. Makes no difference. Only 4 volts with your pluses and minuses reversed can knock out your best octave synthesizer. This is not only expensive but also often heart-breaking when you are about to turn on and operate your electronic wonder after tedious hours of blood sweat and tears.

Most ICs are packaged in what are called Dual In-line Packages (DIPs for short). DIPs are packaged for 8, 14, or 16 pin ICs. You will always find a notch or circle near pin number 1. Turn the IC right side up and pin 1 will always be on your lower left. (See Fig. A-2.) The numbers go from left to right at the bottom of the chip, then from right to left across the top of the chip. Pin 4 is opposite pin 5 on an 8 pin chip, pin 7 across from pin 8 on a 14 pin chip and pin 8 across from pin 9 on a 16 pin chip.

All ICs may not have a date code on them but when they do the first two digits give you the year and the second two the week of that year that the chip was manufactured. Thus the one in the illustration was manufactured in the 52nd week of 1980. You may sometimes find the part number under the date code or other strange numbers which need not be of concern to you. Always read any instructions that come with your IC very carefully and do exactly what they tell you even if you were the guy who invented the chip.

There is a special family of ICs designated MOS/CMOS which simply contain more functions per chip than other kinds of chips, but they are very easy to use. They consume little power and operate over a low voltage range (3- to 15-volt range). You can power most MOS/CMOS ICs from two penlight cells connected in series for a total of 3 volts (each cell puts out 1.5-volts) but they will perform much better if you power them with a 9- to 12-volt supply. Figure

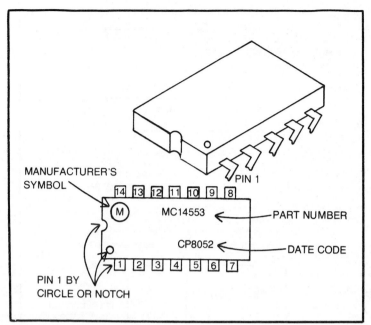

Fig. A-2. Layout of IC chips.

A-3 shows various combinations of batteries you can use and also shows how to connect them in series or in parallel. Series connected batteries give you an additive effect on voltage, while the amount of current delivered remains the same as for one single battery. Parallel connected batteries give you an additive effect on the current delivered but the voltage remains the same as if you were using one battery.

MOS/CMOS integrated circuits will not take more input voltage than they are rated for, so please do not exceed. Never, never connect an input signal to a CMOS circuit when the power is turned off.

All unused inputs on the chip *must* be connected to the pin designated V_{DD} (+) or V_{ss} (GND.). If you do not do this your chip will consume excessive amounts of current (running batteries down in a hurry) and behavior will likely be quite erratic.

Observe all handling precautions meticulously. Any kind of static electric discharge (like when you walk across a thick carpet and touch a metal doorknob) will ruin the chip, so

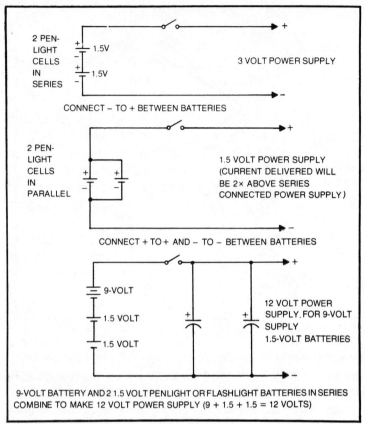

Fig. A-3. Power supplies for ICs.

never store MOS ICs in nonconductive plastic trays, bags or foam. Always place MOS ICs *pins down* on an aluminum foil sheet or tray when they are not in a circuit or stored in conductive foam. This will prevent the build up of static electricity and insure that the chip will not be destroyed by a static discharge.

When soldering MOS chips it is advisable to use a battery powered soldering iron rather than one powered from the ac power lines.

Questions to ask yourself when you have to go CMOS troubleshooting:

Is the IC running hot? If so, make sure the output is not overloaded and ask the questions 2 and 3, below.

Do all inputs go *somewhere?* They must.

Are all IC pins inserted into the board or socket?

Have you forgotten a connection somewhere?

Look at the CMOS operating requirements. Does the circuit obey *all* of them?

When circuit building I do recommend that you build your circuits on a breadboard with spring clip or other firm but temporary means of making connections. Find all the bugs and work them out. Then make your permanent version complete with neatly soldered joints and connections.

Radio Shack supplies modular breadboard sockets and experimenter's PC boards that are ideal for building your initial version (Cat. Nos. 276-170, 174, 175, etc.).

When you are debugged and ready for your permanent version use regular PC boards and universal PC boards depending on the complexity of your project. Big boards can always be cut into smaller boards with a handy saw.

A wire-wrapping tool is a real good investment for IC projects. Use wrapping IC sockets inserted in your PC boards and make the connections with the wire-wrapping tool. You can apply wrapping wire directly to leads of transistors, resistors and capacitors and then solder them in place as shown in Fig. A-4.

There are a few other types of semiconductor devices you will encounter and with these, too, one needs to observe all operating instructions and restrictions to the letter.

Diodes are one way streets and contain an electronic traffic cop that stops any electric current that trys to flow the wrong way. This one-way current flow idea is referred to as forward bias. Diodes are used to rectify alternating current (ac) and make direct current (dc) out of it. The diode allows the ac current to flow in one direction but blocks it when it reverses, thus ac becomes dc.

Zener diodes are special kinds of diodes used to regulate a voltage supply—like a traffic cop that allows only just so much traffic to flow through a one-way street and no more. The cop in this diode ground, all electrons, except those needed to keep an exact and constant voltage in the circuit. Zener diodes are designated by little extensions on the line of their symbol that indicates the blocking action. Figure A-5 shows a Zener diode in a typical circuit for regulating voltage.

Light-emitting diodes (LEDs) are another special kind of diode—the kind that "glows in the dark" when forward biased. LEDs emit green, yellow, or red light in the visible spectrum and infrared invisible light. Infrared LEDs are much more powerful than visible LEDs but of course you can't see the light. They make excellent object detectors and communications devices, and in the area of parapsychology other uses that may have implications for the future. (See especially Chapter 4.) The important thing to keep in mind about LEDs is to never exceed the limits of the current that the LED is manufactured to conduct. A resistor is usually used in series with an LED to limit the current to a safe value.

Transistors are sometimes used as simple amplifiers but most often they are used as electronic switches. They are often used to switch LEDs on and off, as a matter of fact. In general, you can substitute any general-purpose switching transistor for any other general-purpose switching transistor. Always substitute NPN type transistors for other NPNs and PNPs for PNPs.

Capacitors block the flow of direct current both ways, while allowing alternating current to pass through. Intelligent and discriminating traffic cops, when it comes to

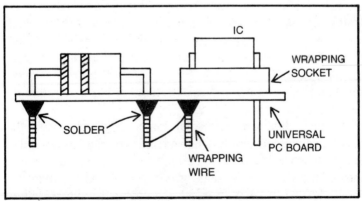

Fig. A-4. Use of wrapping wire for IC projects.

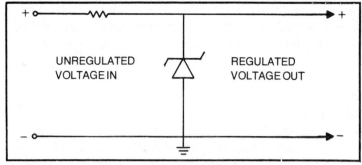

Fig. A-5. Typical circuit using a zener diode.

separating out the ac from the dc, they also serve as a storage depots for electrical energy; in fact, this quality makes big capacitors quite dangerous since they can store a large amount of electrical energy for a considerable time after the power has been disconnected. The voltage may be low, but the current can be quite high, and it is the current, not the voltage (which, after all is only the *potential* of a circuit for carrying current) which is dangerous. I have had a large electrolytic capacitor melt the tip of a screwdriver when I discharged it. That cured me of using screwdrivers for discharging capacitors! Don't ever do it. Discharge capacitors of their lethal charges by *carefully* placing a screwdriver across the leads of the capacitor and to ground. Use only one hand while doing this. I find it wise when poking around where strange currents might be lurking to keep one hand in my pocket, working as if I had only one hand.

The storage capacity of capacitors is always noted in units called farads after Michael Faraday, the 19th century chemist and physicist who discovered the laws obeyed by capacitors. A farad, however, is a bigger than life measure seldom encountered so that most capacitors you will deal with have capacities measured in microfarads (μF) and picofarads (pF). One μF is 0.0000001 of a farad and 1 μF = 1,000,000 pF, just to give you an idea of the order of these electrical storage capacity terms.

The value of a capacitor is usually printed right on it, but be forewarned that the powers that print the numbers do not always tell you if it is μF or pF. As a rule of thumb, small

301

capacitors with printed numbers between 1 and 1000 are almost always rated in pF and large capacitors marked between 0.001 and 1000 are rated in μF. You can substitute one value of capacitor for another within narrow limits without affecting the operation of a circuit. For example never worry about the difference between 0.22 and 0.25. Changing or substituting values of capacitors by as much as 100 percent will usually not cause a malfunction. However, changes in excess of about 10% of the value specified by the circuit designer are likely to alter the operation of the circuit. Changing the capacitor values in a filter circuit will change the frequencies being filtered, for example, and changing them in a timing circuit will change the timing periods.

What you really need to be careful about where capacitors are concerned (other than not to get "bitten" by the electricity lurking within one) is to use the proper voltage rating, printed on the capacitor itself, usually right under the capacity marking. *The voltage rating of any capacitor you use must be higher than the highest voltage present in the circuit in which it is used.* To be on the safe side, all your capacitors should be voltage rated higher than the power supply voltage for the device you are building.

The leads of certain types of capacitors (electrolytic) are marked + and − (polarized) and these leads must be connected into your circuit in the proper direction. See Fig. A-6. The proper polarization is indicated in the schematic diagram if it is important.

Capacitors have many important applications. Because of their ability to store and release electrical currents in an even rhythm they are used to smooth out rectified ac voltage into steady dc current and to remove sudden surges of voltage called spikes which would trigger ICs falsely. Capacitors are used to block direct current signals while passing alternating current signals on through, or to bypass an ac signal around a circuit (or to ground it) and to filter out unwanted portions of a fluctuating signal. Other uses include integration or differentation of a fluctuating signal, performing timing functions, storing electrical charges to keep tran-

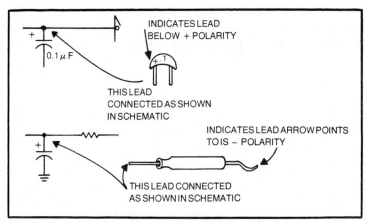

Fig. A-6. Polarity markings on capacitors.

sistors turned off or on, and storing charges to be later dumped through an LED or flashtube.

Resistors are frequent companions to capacitors and perform only one function, but it is a vital one. Resistors resist or limit the flow of electrical current. This resistance is measured in ohms, in honor of Georg Simon Ohm. Ohm's Law states that the electrical potential difference (voltage) across a conductor is proportional to the current flowing through it. This idea is expressed in a simple formula $E=IR$, or E (the voltage) is equal to I (the current) multiplied by R (the resistance). The other variations of the formula are $R=E$, and $I=E/R$. It is a handy thing to memorize these three statements about Ohm's law for handy reference.

Resistors are used to limit the flow of current to devices that must have just a certain amount, such as LEDs,

Fig. A-7. A potentiometer gives a variable voltage.

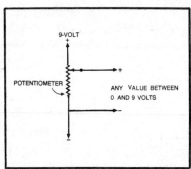

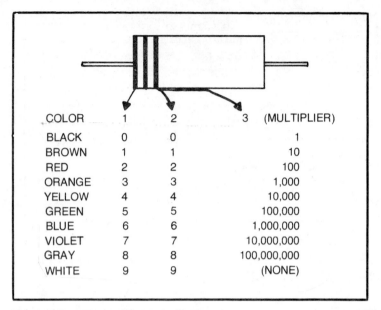

COLOR	1	2	3 (MULTIPLIER)
BLACK	0	0	1
BROWN	1	1	10
RED	2	2	100
ORANGE	3	3	1,000
YELLOW	4	4	10,000
GREEN	5	5	100,000
BLUE	6	6	1,000,000
VIOLET	7	7	10,000,000
GRAY	8	8	100,000,000
WHITE	9	9	(NONE)

Fig. A-8. Resistors are known by the colors they show.

transistors, and speakers. Resistors can also divide voltages and provide a convenient source of variable voltage through a potentiometer, which is simply a variable resistance (Fig. A-7).

By limiting voltages, resistors also perform the very valuable function of controlling the charging time of capacitors, which is why the two are so often found hanging around together. You will have to learn to identify resistors by a color code consisting of three colored bands around the resistor as shown in Fig. A-8. If the resistor carries a fourth color band that will indicate the tolerance of the resistor; i.e., how close it really comes to being the resistance it claims to be. A gold-colored fourth band indicates that the resistance will be true within a tolerance of 5 percent. Silver indicates ± 10 percent and no band at all means the tolerance is no better than ± 20 percent. This is okay since resistance values are not all that critical usually. You can get away with a good deal of substitution of resistors as long as you stay within about 10 to 20 percent of what is being specified. Do, however, stay within the power rating of a resistor or you are likely to burn it up. If no power rating is specified it usually means you can get by with a ¼- or ½-watt unit.

And that, in just a few pages is all you need to know to get started on the projects in this book. If you are a beginner start with some of the simple projects and work up to the more advanced ones after you have developed confidence in yourself. And keep in mind that with these parapsychology projects *you* will always be the most important element in your project. Lots of luck!

Index